THE SHADOW
OF THE WALL

EDITED BY JEREMY SLACK,
DANIEL E. MARTÍNEZ, AND SCOTT WHITEFORD

Foreword by Josiah Heyman
Photographs by Murphy Woodhouse

THE SHADOW

OF THE WALL

Violence and Migration on the U.S.–Mexico Border

THE UNIVERSITY OF
ARIZONA PRESS

TUCSON

The University of Arizona Press
www.uapress.arizona.edu

ISBN-13: 978-0-8165-3559-0 (paper)

Cover design by Sara Thaxton
Cover photo by Murphy Woodhouse

Publication of this book is made possible in part by funding from the Ford Foundation.

Library of Congress Cataloging-in-Publication Data are available at the Library of Congress.

Printed in the United States of America
♾ This paper meets the requirements of ANSI/NISO Z39.48-1992 (Permanence of Paper).

CONTENTS

FOREWORD

JOSIAH HEYMAN

LEARNING FROM DEPORTED people is of the highest importance to morality, public policy, and social analysis. This book uses rigorous methods to tell a story that is little known and that matters greatly: the contemporary experience of deportation from the United States to Mexico. It merits careful attention.

The U.S. border regulatory system is complex and dense. Vast flows of goods and money cross with easy approval and minimal scrutiny, though important capitalist flows are illegalized, such as some drugs and profits from them. Similarly, millions of people cross U.S. borders, including the Mexican border, on a daily basis, with legal approval though often pointed scrutiny. Indeed, the inverse story to this book is the privileged movement of finance, commodities, and elites and professionals back and forth across the border. There is extensive permanent legal immigration, usually involving more people than unauthorized migration. Borders are also key sites in the realization of fundamental human rights, asylum from persecution, and government evasion of such moral obligations. Dominant discourses of both left and right tend to neglect these points in favor of associating the border and the immigration system with deportable and deported migrants.

Deportation encompasses a vast range of people, policing activities, and enforcement sites ranging from near-border arrests of recent entrants to removal of deeply rooted settlers, some of them legal permanent residents. Indeed, the Migrant Border Crossing Study (MBCS I and II) also includes people who were not formally deported but accepted voluntary departure without deportation process. This research has transcended the limitations of previous studies. While Mexican researchers have repeatedly but briefly surveyed people coming and going from the country at its northern border, activist groups in shelters have assembled complaints concerning U.S. treatment after deportation, and scholars using qualitative methods have reported stories from the field, the MBCS provides a comprehensive synthesis of systematic surveys, probing interviews, and rich ethnographic observations about deportees and deportation processes from the Mexican side of the border. The work here is unsurpassed in its relevance and quality.

Importantly, we learn about the *perverse* consequences of U.S. border and deportation processes and Mexican governance. *Perverse* is a harsh term, one I use deliberately to point to harmful intentional and accidental consequences of policies that on the surface claim to seek the public good. Some of these perversities are deliberate and others are unintentional by-products (see Heyman 2012), but all are harmful and merit documentation, analysis, and change. The backdrop is the crimogenic and violence-inducing "war on drugs" in the United States and Mexico. While drug policies are not directly the subject of this book (see Campbell 2009; Payan, Staudt, and Kruszewski 2013), their side effects are critical to the material it presents. United States policies that perversely raise the price of and the profit from illegal drugs through border interdiction have induced an extensive, dangerous web of criminal organizations on both sides of the border but that are overtly active in Mexico. Mexico's legacy of corrupt arrangements with violent regional warlords and hidden income streams, in turn, promotes these nefarious power centers (Bailey and Godson 2000; Astorga Almanza 2005; Flores Pérez 2013). The United States, of course, is pleased to have a deferential, authoritarian neighbor. Indeed, this political economy is best described not as drug smuggling alone but as a triangular set of exchanges: deadly guns and munitions to Mexico, harmful drugs to the United States (also sold within Mexico), and unaccountable money orchestrating it all (Heyman 2011). Labor migrants and refugees typically were and are unconnected to these activities, but this book shows increasing capture of migration processes by criminal organizations, a perverse rearrangement with terrible human consequences.

The extent of this capture remains incompletely known, but the research presented here sheds light on these disturbing developments. Issues addressed include the control of spaces of passage; the de facto taxation of movement up to and across the border; the hierarchies of smuggling businesses (from human migration facilitation to large-scale shipment of guns and money); the role of kidnapping and the use of fear to obtain labor, information, and silence; and above all the widespread miasma of violence. This is exacerbated by the places where and the times when people are deported, including removals to Mexican cities that are dominated by criminal organization recruiters; this occurs in part through official U.S. policy, the Alien Transfer Exit Program (ATEP). An important contribution of this book, then, is revealing how U.S. policy inexcusably pushes previously peaceful migratory flows into criminal worlds reinforced by the impunity and terror of Mexican governance.

The MBCS research occurred during a period shaped by what legal scholar Juliet Stumpf (2006) has called "crimmigration." It is part of the broad increase in the United States in the use of criminal charges, convictions, and imprisonment (Alexander 2010)—and then in this case expulsion from the country to Mexico, where the MBCS team did the interviews. Crimmigration includes the conversion of immigration violations—previously largely treated as noncriminal administrative charges—into criminal law violations, such as illegal entry. Such crimes, as the authors point out, are often tried in mass trials near the border under the Orwellian-named Consequence Delivery System (previously Operation Streamline). The criminal convictions remain as a lifetime stigma on aspiring workers and refugees. Similarly, reentry to the United States after deportations and denials of admission has been criminalized, not just on paper but in real practice. Significantly, the MBCS shows the reasons why some migrants take this legal risk to return to the United States. Crimmigration interacts with new policies of so-called expedited removal and reinstatement of removal that enable Department of Homeland Security (DHS) officers, without due process, to deport people from the United States; formal deportation thus increasingly replaces voluntary departure, which leaves no record. Deportation itself is not criminal but rather administrative, but it is enduring, and reentry from deportation entails either a difficult legal and social process (Gomberg-Muñoz 2015) or a criminal reentry violation.

Many of the deported people studied by the MBCS were arrested near the border, subject to expedited removal, and permanently stigmatized with deportation. A substantial portion of the others was removed from U.S. jails and prisons near the border and in the national interior. The Secure Communities Program ranks people to be turned over from local jails and state prisons, often before actual trial and conviction, to Immigration and Customs Enforcement to be deported. Despite the language of "secure communities," implying these are terrible criminals, most such people are identified because of recent entry or previous deportability. The offense involved often is trivial, such as driving without a license (unobtainable for unauthorized immigrants in many states); while minor crimes have low enforcement priorities, previous removal, for example, catches them instead. Finally, a smaller number but notable set of deportations take place under the Criminal Alien Program, removing convicted criminals once they have served their sentences—given U.S. legal biases, often for drug crimes. U.S. removal policies have promoted a cycle of criminals (a minority of all deportees) being deported, connecting to criminal organizations in home countries, and sometimes returning to the United States (Santamaría 2013; Lawrence 2016). The work in this book extends our knowledge of these processes to Mexico-U.S. cycles. This is not to say that most migrants are ex- or future criminals but rather to point out a perverse process of criminal formation or reinforcement by means of immigration policy despite the actual low rate of criminality among unauthorized immigrants and immigrants in general (Ewing, Martínez, and Rumbaut 2015).

An important accomplishment of this book is teasing out the different ties that deported and departing people have in the United States. Examining the presence of ties of personal sentiment, relationships, cultural and linguistic knowledge, a sense of home, and other feelings and habits—what the authors call "place attachment"—helps explain why the border web of risks, barriers, and punishment has incomplete capability to deter returning migrants. A memorable summary of the findings found in the book's introduction is that "most deportees are in fact highly connected to the United States, and despite increased enforcement, they still largely intend to cross again." Some cluster in Mexican northern border cities while others try and try again to return. We come away from this book with increased respect for the limitations of top-down policies at borders.

But this limitation of intentional border sorting comes at a cost. Again, as the authors memorably write, "despite failing to break people's resolve to return to the United States, these practices put migrants directly in harm's way." People who feel American (to use north-of-the-border language), who speak English, who know the streets, and who love children, spouses, parents, siblings, and friends will then subject themselves to migrant facilitators, criminal entrepreneurs, kidnappers, and other inadvertently perverse ways of returning home. The point is not to blame the victims, who personally are good, bad, or indifferent as we all are, but to take notice of the outcomes that a xenophobic, racist, hypocritical, and inadequate immigration and asylum policy unnecessarily imposes on migrants—and on us all (Heyman 1998; Hing 2006).

Global immigration changes remarkably quickly, including at the U.S.-Mexico border. Since the second wave of the MBCS was completed, net migration (entries minus exits) from Mexico has gone to zero and in some years below zero. This does not mean that there is no authorized and unauthorized migration to the United States from Mexico—the phenomena described here continue—but the level of such entrances is much lower than it had been in the middle of the decade of the 2000s. Deportations remain elevated, if slightly declining, because people are being snatched out of lives in the interior of the country—the core reason we are discussing comprehensive immigration reform—and because most unauthorized entrants arrested near the border are legally branded with deportation rather than being allowed to depart with no record. And, in recent years the trickle of Central Americans (Guatemalans, Salvadorans, and Hondurans) arriving at the U.S.-Mexico border has grown substantially, many of them openly surrendering to U.S. authorities, being arrested (misleadingly inflating unauthorized entrant apprehension statistics), and requesting asylum from ferocious violence and persecution in their home countries. The MBCS was conducted among Mexicans, in Mexican sites, while Central Americans are returned directly to their home countries. Hence, the studies reported here do not directly address this increasingly important migratory flow. But they do provide considerable insight on the current situation. They identify the web of criminality, violence, and exploitation in Mexico through which Central Americans shockingly must pass. They also examine the processes and conduct of the United States enforcement and removal machine. Scholars and activists will certainly build on these studies to diagnose the new situation.

The Shadow of the Wall: Violence and Migration on the U.S.-Mexico Border is a bold and successful effort to reclaim the conversation about border and immigration policy. It confronts the vitriol streaming from certain politicians and media outlets with carefully researched, convincing evidence. But to imaginary threats of border invasions (Chavez 2001), it is not enough to say that migration is down and the border is largely secure. Indeed, it is secure for legal residents of the United States but not for deportable migrants and their families. We must speak honestly and unsparingly about the actual activities and effects of U.S. migration, drugs, and weapons policies as well as wider issues of tolerated authoritarianism and underdevelopment in Mexico and Central America. Readers need to learn about unheard-of levels of violence, death, and mass incarceration. And readers also will encounter a more complex understanding of contemporary border migrants, one that breaks with both the pro- and anti-immigrant caricatures portrayed in the media. Rigorous quantitative and qualitative research designs matter in rendering these results reliable and persuasive. Writing results for public policy think tanks and the media as well as for demanding scholarly audiences matter as multiple paths of communication. Getting out of the university, getting into the shelters night after night, utilizing high-quality methods and tools of analysis, reporting back to readers honestly and unsparingly—all these qualities make this a work of public scholarship of the highest order.

REFERENCES

Alexander, Michelle. 2010. *The New Jim Crow: Mass Incarceration in the Age of Colorblindness*. New York: New Press.

Astorga Almanza, Luis Alejandro. 2005. *El siglo de las drogas: El narcotráfico, del Porfiriato al nuevo milenio*. Mexico City: Plaza y Janés.

Bailey, John J., and Roy Godson, eds. 2000. *Organized Crime and Democratic Governability: Mexico and the U.S.-Mexican Borderlands*. Pittsburgh, Pa.: University of Pittsburgh Press.

Campbell, Howard. 2009. *Drug War Zone: Frontline Dispatches from the Streets of El Paso and Juárez*. Austin: University of Texas Press.

Chavez, Leo R. 2001. *Covering Immigration: Popular Images and the Politics of the Nation*. Berkeley: University of California Press.

Ewing, Walter, Daniel E. Martínez, and Rubén G. Rumbaut. 2015. *The Criminalization of Immigration in the United States*. https://www.americanimmigrationcouncil.org /research/criminalization-immigration-united-states.

Flores Pérez, Carlos Antonio. 2013. *Historias de polvo y sangre: Génesis y evolución del tráfico de drogas en el estado de Tamaulipas*. Mexico City: Centro de Investigaciones y Estudios Superiores en Antropología Social.

Gomberg-Muñoz, Ruth. 2015. "The Punishment/El Castigo: Undocumented Latinos and U.S. Immigration Processing." *Journal of Ethnic and Migration Studies* 41 (14): 2235–52.

Heyman, Josiah McC. 1998. *Finding a Moral Heart for U.S. Immigration Policy: An Anthropological Perspective*. Washington, D.C.: American Anthropological Association.

———. 2011. *Guns, Drugs, and Money: Tackling the Real Threats to Border Security*. Washington, D.C.: American Immigration Council. https://www.americanimmigrationcouncil .org/research/guns-drugs-and-money-tackling-real-threats-border-security.

———. 2012. "Capitalism and US policy at the Mexican border." *Dialectical Anthropology* 36 (3/4): 263–77.

Hing, Bill Ong. 2006. *Deporting Our Souls: Values, Morality, and Immigration Policy*. New York: Cambridge University Press.

Lawrence, Michael. 2016. *Law Enforcement and Perverse Effects: The Evolution of the Central American Maras*. Security Sector Reform Governance Center, February 29. http://www.ssrresourcecentre.org/2016/02/29/law-enforcement-and-perverse-effects -the-evolution-of-the-central-american-maras/.

Payan, Tony, Kathleen A. Staudt, and Z. Anthony Kruszewski, eds. 2013. *A War That Can't Be Won: Binational Perspectives on the War on Drugs*. Tucson: University of Arizona Press.

Santamaría, Gema. 2013. "La difusión y contención del crimen organizado en la sub-región México-Centroamérica." In *La diáspora criminal: La difusión transnacional del crimen organizado y cómo contener su expansion*, edited by Juan Carlos Garzón and Eric L. Olson, 58–99. Washington, D.C.: Woodrow Wilson International Center for Scholars. http://www.wilsoncenter.org/sites/default/files/LA_DIASPORA _CRIMINAL_0.pdf.

Stumpf, Juliet P. 2006. "The Crimmigration Crisis: Immigrants, Crime, and Sovereign Power." *American University Law Review* 56 (2): 367–419.

PREFACE

The Migrant Border Crossing Study:
Combining Activism, Advocacy, and Research

THIS BOOK IS AN anthology about the first two waves of the Migrant Border Crossing Study (MBCS), which is a mixed-methods, binational research project that has been carried out since 2007. The goal of the MBCS is to produce socially relevant, rigorous social science data about migration, immigration enforcement, and violence on the border. The research presented in this volume is meant to give an overview of the breadth of scholarly work produced through the postdeportation surveys, interviews, and ethnography that make up this research project. By closely collaborating with activists and advocates, our approach has been to highlight issues that need answers or quantitative exploration/validation. We call for scholars to orient themselves not simply to the study of advocates as political actors but to work for them, exploring those questions that have not been answered and can aid in efforts to effect social change. This process is not a simple one, and there will be conflicts along the way, but this engagement has a direct impact on the relevance and importance of research both inside and outside of academia.

Daniel E. Martínez began the MBCS after two years of conducting research on border-crosser deaths in southern Arizona at the Pima County Office of the Medical Examiner in Tucson, Arizona, an area of research in which he continues to be engaged. Southern Arizona experienced an exponential increase in migrant deaths in the early 2000s stemming directly from increased border enforcement efforts along the U.S.-Mexico border in the 1990s, which effectively funneled migration into the region (Rubio-Goldsmith et al. 2006). This region experienced relatively little unauthorized migration when compared with other traditional crossing points, such as San Diego, California, and El Paso, Texas. As such, relatively little scholarship existed focusing primarily on unauthorized migration in southern Arizona (for an exception, see O'Leary 2009), which at the time was the single most traversed area along the border (Customs and Border Protection 2015b). What do migrants experience when crossing through this harsh desert region? How do these experiences compare with other regions along the border? Why do some people perish in southern Arizona and others survive? Why do specific death types appear to be patterned temporally and according to age, biological sex, and region of origin? These questions became the starting point for a desire to produce high-quality, generalizable quantitative data about the crossing that could be used to better understand what migrants experience during their undocumented crossing attempts, including their interactions with U.S. authorities. While documentation of abuse of migrants by U.S. authorities had previously been conducted by groups such as No More Deaths (No More Deaths 2008), this was frequently dismissed as "anecdotal" or "biased." We wanted to go one step further by employing a rigorous methodology to overcome these criticisms while studying not only the frequency of abuse but also how and why this mistreatment occurs.[1]

From October of 2007 to July of 2009, in what would constitute the first wave of the MBCS, a group of ten graduate student volunteers conducted survey interviews in a migrant shelter in Nogales, Sonora. This involved approximately 115 trips to Nogales. Once or twice a week, four members of our team would leave the University of Arizona at 5:00 p.m. and return between 12:00 and 2:00 a.m., depending on the line to reenter into the United States. We would be lucky if we completed two surveys per person. With over three hundred questions, these surveys took more than an hour to complete, and we were careful not to interfere with the operations of the shelter, ensuring that people were informed of the rules by shelter staff, were allowed to shower, and were able to eat and reserve a bed. The shelter would often exceed its bed capacity, with people sleeping on the floor and on mats. We collected a total of 415 surveys with people who had crossed the border through the Tucson sector, had been apprehended by U.S. authorities, and had been repatriated to Nogales, Sonora, all within six months before being surveyed.

As we began to wrap up data collection on the first wave (i.e., MBCS I), we spoke to the Ford Foundation, which was interested in the potential impact of the project. Together, Scott Whiteford, Jeremy Slack, and Daniel E. Martínez wrote a proposal first to research potential field sites and then to complete surveys and conduct ethnographic work that would eventually constitute the second wave of the MBCS (i.e., MBCS II). Housed at the University of Arizona, the second wave was carried out in Tijuana and Mexicali, Baja California; Nogales, Sonora; Ciudad Juárez, Chihuahua, and Nuevo Laredo, Tamaulipas, as well as in Mexico City with people who were aerially repatriated. In order to establish the logistical framework for the second wave, Jeremy Slack and Scott Whiteford made visits to each city in 2009 and 2010 to investigate local sites, confirm potential academic collaborators, and present the results of the first wave. This occurred at a particular moment in time that both helped and hindered collaboration: the uptick in border violence generally referred to as President Calderón's drug war.

Many U.S. universities began to sever ties to Mexico and impose travel bans in the late 2000s. Violence in Ciudad Juárez, which at one point was one of the most dangerous cities in the world, had reached unprecedented levels by 2010, and attacks against members of the U.S. embassy, as well as the death of a former student at the University of Texas at El Paso, raised alarms. As a result, many Mexican academics, especially those who had grown accustomed to collaboration, were abandoned. This was particularly problematic for some areas where freedom of speech was significantly threatened stemming from the murders of dozens of Mexican journalists. Our colleagues in Tamaulipas had been threatened and did not want to lead research projects about violence. Nevertheless, as foreign academics, we had an opportunity to document and speak about issues that could not be discussed locally. However, on the U.S side of the border, the project generated concern about the risks to researchers as well as the population we studied; thus, we carefully considered what questions to ask and how to ask them.

To accomplish this, we convened academics from Mexico and the United States as well as members of the local activist and advocate community at the University of Arizona in January of 2010. We presented the data gathered through the first wave of the MBCS and discussed how to better focus the project on the questions that would have the most relevance to policy makers and nongovernmental organizations and that could ultimately affect policy. We added survey modules about the U.S.-citizen children of migrants, customer satisfaction with coyotes, kidnapping, and labor exploitation, to name a few. The survey consisted of 250 questions, and because of the diversity of the cities in which surveys were administered, it touched on a range of border-crossing experiences and strategies encompassing the complex local geographies of migration (i.e., the inherent difference between migrating through the desert vs. through an official port of entry with false documents, across a river, or by sea along the coast). By examining these nuanced differences across the border, this workshop significantly improved the final survey instrument, especially because it helped guide our research to provide answers to questions with which nongovernmental organizations and advocacy groups had been grappling in their respective local areas. In all, we completed 1,109 surveys during the second wave of the MBCS between 2009 and 2012.

When studying such pressing social issues, it is important to go beyond pure "research for research's sake" and challenge the traditions of top-down expertise of ivory-tower academics. As scholars, we have been deeply influenced by activist and participatory methodologies (Fals-Borda and Rahman 1991; Masuda et al. 2011; van Olphen et al. 2015; Minkler and Wallerstein 2003; Austin 2003, 2004, 2010; Hale 2006, 2008; Pulido 2006). This literature emphasizes close collaboration, input from community members, and the equitable dissemination of research results. However, there is often a lack of specificity, as Laura Pulido (2008) has stressed that organizations generally crave positivistic, technical knowledge rather than the in-depth, critical theory that most activist scholars produce. Many scholars simply discuss their own experiences participating as activists, rarely acknowledging the inherent conflicts of interest, unequal power relations, and the privileged position from which these activities take place (e.g., formal credentials, academic salaries, high mobility both professionally and geographically). This project is an attempt to use research in the service of those fighting for change.

While not all projects are suitable to follow the precise frameworks of Community Based Participatory Research (CBPR) or Participatory Action Research (PAR), research that provides support to groups in struggle can have a far greater impact than research questions driven by canonical or theoretical questions that may be divorced from conflicts on the ground. This requires flexibility and adaptability to the changing terrain around us. In our case, the uptick in violence significantly altered our research questions and even our methodological approach. The MBCS represents a large-scale attempt to use research in support of activists, advocates, NGOs, and think tanks. This required not only community involvement before data collection but collaboration afterward to make results available to a wide audience.

In 2013, during debates about Senate Bill 744 (i.e., "comprehensive immigration reform"), we released a preliminary report consisting of accessible tables and figures as well as rigorously collected, methodologically sound data about politically contested issues relating to migration and deportation (Slack et al. 2013). We traveled to Washington, D.C., to discuss findings from this preliminary report with representatives from the Washington Office on Latin America, Women's Refugee Commission, Latin American Working Group, American Immigration Council, and members of Congress, among others. While they were excited about our research, these stakeholders stressed refinement. In our minds, we had produced a concise report, shorter than even our survey instrument, but we were encouraged to reduce our findings to the infamous Washington, D.C., "one-pager" or even into one sentence. After much work, we settled on the following: "Most deportees are in fact highly connected to the United States, and despite increased enforcement, they still largely intend to cross the border again." Armed with this new pithy conclusion, we reached out to the media, worked with messaging groups in Washington, D.C., and held a press conference where our report was cited in over 140 news stories. We presented our research findings to local border organizations and at several academic conferences, conducted dozens of interviews with the media, and spoke to congressional staffers on the Hill in Washington, D.C. Daniel E. Martínez testified at an ad hoc congressional hearing chaired by Rep. Raúl Grijalva (D-AZ), and Sen. Chris Koons (D-DE) presented a list of amendments to Senate Bill 744 on the Senate floor, citing our report as a means to reform removal protocols.

We wrote additional reports about the abuse of migrants by U.S. authorities and the systematic removal of people's possessions, concluding that people who are processed through multiple agencies reported losing possessions at much higher rates, especially among migrants who were sent to prison or processed through Operation Streamline (Martínez and Slack 2013). After years of lobbying, the U.S. Border Patrol agreed to rewrite their repatriation agreements to include guarantees that repatriated immigrants will receive their possessions (Breisblatt 2016). While we do not know whether U.S. authorities will accomplish the monumental task of ensuring that people do not lose their possessions in the labyrinthine system of prisons, processing centers, and detention facilities, it is nonetheless a step in the right direction.

With all marginal steps toward progress come sudden and unexpected challenges. Namely, in 2014, public attention was captivated by the influx of Central American families and children fleeing their homes. It is important to note that official statistics on apprehensions present a problem for estimating the increase in Central American migration. Namely, as people became aware of the possibility of gaining asylum, Central American border crossers began to actively seek out U.S. authorities, either once they cross into the United States in remote areas or at ports of entry, rather than avoid them. However, the U.S. Border Patrol records these encounters as apprehensions even though the recent influx of Central American border crossers is the result of unique "push" and "pull" factors when compared with contemporary unauthorized Mexican migration or migration from Central America in prior decades. Despite scholars' and agents' best efforts, knowing the true number of people attempting border crossings has always been guesswork at best. Scholars have routinely used apprehension statistics as a proxy for migration flows (Espenshade 1995). Nevertheless, once these metrics are no longer counting undocumented migrants but asylum seekers directly approaching agents as opposed to people trying to avoid detection, the number of apprehensions skyrockets.

The media largely neglected this nuance. Instead of discussing the increase in asylum seekers, the focus was shifted to the "flood" or "wave" of "'illegal' immigrants pouring across the border." This drastically altered perspectives on immigration and Border Patrol reform. The hurricane of news reports, aid organizations, and anti-immigrant militias completely altered the conversations about comprehensive immigration reform that had begun emerging in 2013. Most importantly, this misguided discourse reenergized anemic anti-immigrant mobilization efforts.

While widespread popularity and media coverage of anti-immigrant groups such as American Border Patrol, the Minutemen Civil Defense Corps, and the Minutemen Project began in 2005, the activities of these groups on the ground quickly dissipated (Ward and Martínez 2015). Also, the coverage of these groups was never proportional to their actual active membership, with generally very few people actually participating but a plethora of stories about them in the media. However, after the murders committed by Shawna Forde, the leader of a Minutemen splinter group (Neiwert 2012); the murder/suicide of U.S. Border Guard founder J. T. Ready (Muskal 2012); and the conviction of Minutemen Project founder and longtime anti-immigrant activist Chris Simcox for child molestation (Hauser 2016), it quickly called into question the legitimacy of these groups. Nevertheless, the rise of the Tea Party and more recently Donald Trump's successful 2016 presidential campaign offered a new, legitimized space and outlet for people harboring anti-immigrant sentiments.

This resurgence in anti-immigrant mobilization efforts escalated after the Border Patrol leaked photos of children locked inside their processing centers (Darby 2014). The narrative characterized the Border Patrol as overwhelmed by the "tidal wave" of immigrants and in need of more support in the form of agents and financial resources. However, with undocumented migration falling to levels not seen in decades during FY 2014, agents in the El Paso sector apprehend a mere 4.7 migrants per agent per year (Customs and Border Protection 2015a). Moreover, reports that Central Americans, particularly unaccompanied minors, were being granted asylum stoked fears regarding an influx of transnational gangs and human trafficking. While never explicitly articulated, driving the antichild refugee backlash was the fear of an increase in the nonwhite, future voting, foreign-born population in the United States. Nevertheless, seeking asylum is in fact an international human right, and characterizations by the media of asylum seekers as "illegal immigrants" neglects this reality.

Moreover, woefully little discussion about the security situation in the northern triangle countries, particularly gang-controlled El Salvador and coup-addled Honduras, has leaked into mainstream consciousness. Also absent is the United States' role in creating these crises, either through its neoliberal policies and support of corrupt, unethical governments (Phillips 2015) or through the various processes of deportation (Zilberg 2011). The mass removal of people from U.S. prisons has led to a complex, often intertwined geography of the relationships between prison gangs in the United States and street gangs throughout Latin America (Zilberg 2011).

This book is an attempt to reclaim the conversation. By using methodologically rigorous, grounded, empirical research all along the U.S.-Mexico border, we aim to provide a tool to fight against the imaginary threats of the border. Our research challenges the fact-free, racially driven fear tactics that currently dominate the political field.

NOTE

1.   It should be noted that many criticisms are ready made regardless of methodology, research, or even facts.

REFERENCES

Austin, Diane E. 2003. "Community-Based Collaborative Team Ethnography: A Community-University-Agency Partnership." *Human Organization: Journal of the Society for Applied Anthropology* 62 (2): 143.
———. 2004. "Partnerships, Not Projects! Improving the Environment Through Collaborative Research and Action." *Human Organization: Journal of the Society for Applied Anthropology* 63 (4): 419.

————. 2010. "Confronting Environmental Challenges on the US-Mexico Border: Long-Term Community-Based Research and Community Service Learning in a Binational Partnership." *Journal of Community Practice* 18 (2/3): 361–95.

Breisblatt, Joshua. 2016. "New U.S.-Mexico Repatriation Agreements to Seek to Protect Returning Migrants." In *Immigration Impact*. Washington, D.C.: American Immigration Council.

Customs and Border Protection. 2015a. *United States Border Patrol: Sector Profile—Fiscal Year 2014*. Washington, D.C.: Customs and Border Protection.

————. 2015b. *United States Border Patrol: Southwest Border Patrol—Total Illegal Alien Apprehensions by Fiscal Year*. Washington, D.C.: Customs and Border Protection.

Darby, Brandon. 2014. "Leaked Images Reveal Children Warehoused in Crowded U.S. Cells, Border Patrol Overwhelmed." *Breitbart News*, June 5. http://www.breitbart.com/texas/2014/06/05/leaked-images-reveal-children-warehoused-in-crowded-us-cells-border-patrol-overwhelmed/.

Espenshade, Thomas J. 1995. "Unauthorized Immigration to the United States." *Annual Review of Sociology* 21:195–216.

Fals-Borda, Orlando, and Muhammad Anisur Rahman. 1991. *Action and Knowledge: Breaking the Monopoly with Participatory Action Research*. New York: Apex Press.

Hale, Charles R. 2006. "Activist Research v. Cultural Critique: Indigenous Land Rights and the Contradictions of Politically Engaged Anthropology." *Cultural Anthropology* 21 (1): 96–120.

————. 2008. *Engaging Contradictions: Theory, Politics, and Methods of Activist Scholarship*. Berkeley: University of California Press.

Hauser, Christine. 2016. "Founder of a Minuteman Border Group Is Convicted of Child Molestation." *New York Times*, June 9. http://www.nytimes.com/2016/06/10/us/founder-of-a-minuteman-border-group-is-convicted-of-child-molestation.html?_r=0.

Martínez, Daniel, and Jeremy Slack. 2013. "What Part of 'Illegal' Don't You Understand? The Social Consequences of Criminalizing Unauthorized Mexican Migrants in the United States." *Social and Legal Studies* 22 (4): 535–51.

Masuda, Jeffrey, Genevieve Creighton, Sean Nixon, and James Frankish. 2011. "Building Capacity for Community-Based Participatory Research for Health Disparities in Canada: The Case of 'Partnerships in Community Health Research.'" *Health Promotion Practice* 12 (2): 280–92.

Minkler, Meredith, and Nina Wallerstein. 2003. *Community-Based Participatory Research for Health*. San Francisco: Jossey-Bass.

Muskal, Michael. 2012. "Border Guard Founder J. T. Ready Blamed in Murder-Suicide." *Los Angeles Times*, May 3. http://articles.latimes.com/2012/may/03/nation/la-na-nn-arizona-shooting-20120503.

Neiwert, David. 2012. "How the Brutal Murders of a Little Girl and Her Father Doomed the Xenophobic Minuteman Movement." *Alternet*, July 23. http://www.alternet.org/story/156128/how_the_brutal_murders_of_a_little_girl_and_her_father_doomed_the_xenophobic_minuteman_movement.

No More Deaths. 2008. *Crossing the Line: Human Rights Abuses of Migrants in Short-Term Custody on the Arizona/Sonora Border*. Tucson, Ariz.: No More Deaths. http://forms.nomoredeaths.org/wp-content/uploads/2014/10/CrossingTheLine-full.compressed.pdf.

O'Leary, Anna Ochoa. 2009. "Mujeres en el cruce: Remapping Border Security Through Migrant Mobility." *Journal of the Southwest* 51 (4): 523–42.

Phillips, James J. 2015. *Honduras in Dangerous Times: Resistance and Resilience*. Lanham, Md.: Lexington Books.

Pulido, Laura. 2006. *Black, Brown, Yellow, and Left: Radical Activism in Los Angeles*. Berkeley: University of California Press.

———. 2008. "FAQs: Frequently (Un)Asked Questions About Being a Scholar Activist." In *Engaging Contradictions: Theory, Politics, and Methods of Activist Scholarship*, edited by Charles R. Hale, 341–66. Berkeley: University of California Press.

Rubio-Goldsmith, Raquel, Melissa McCormick, Daniel Martínez, and Inez Magdalena Duarte. 2006. *The "Funnel Effect" and Recovered Bodies of Unauthorized Migrants Processed by the Pima County Office of the Medical Examiner, 1990–2005*. Tucson, Ariz.: Binational Migration Institute, University of Arizona.

Slack, Jeremy, Daniel Martínez, Scott Whiteford, and Emily Peiffer. 2013. "In the Shadow of the Wall: Family Separation, Immigration Enforcement and Security." Report, Center for Latin American Studies, University of Arizona. https://las.arizona.edu/sites/las.arizona.edu/files/UA_Immigration_Report2013web.pdf.

van Olphen, Juliana, Nina Wallerstein, Jill Evans, Rhonda McClinton Brown, Jessica Tokunaga, and Miranda Worthen. 2015. "A San Francisco Bay Area CBPR Training Institute: Experiences, Curriculum, and Lessons Learned." *Pedagogy in Health Promotion* 1 (4): 203–12.

Ward, Matthew, and Daniel E Martínez. 2015. "Know Your Enemy: How Repatriated Unauthorized Migrants Learn About and Perceive Anti-immigrant Mobilization in the United States." *Migration Letters* 12 (2): 137.

Zilberg, Elana. 2011. *Space of Detention: The Making of a Transnational Gang Crisis Between Los Angeles and San Salvador*. Durham, N.C.: Duke University Press.

ACKNOWLEDGMENTS

THIS PROJECT WOULD NOT have been possible without the generous support of the Ford Foundation, Mexico and Central America Office. We must thank not only their financial support but logistical support connecting our project with others working diligently on issues of migration and drug violence in Mexico. This network has proved invaluable for increasing the impact of our work by getting it into the hands of people who can use it to complement their own efforts. Of particular importance is the work of Kimberley Krasevac and her support but also her critiques, which helped push this research into new areas and answer important, relevant questions that expand beyond the boundaries of academia.

We have also received financial support from the Programa de Investigación de Migración y Salud (PIMSA), Health Initiative of the Americas, at the University of California, Berkeley, for Wave I. We thank the National Institutes of Health BUILDing Scholars program for summer sabbatical funding to write up this book and Dr. Luis Zayas for his comments and suggestions on early drafts.

We would also like to thank the Drugs Security and Democracy Fellowship funded by the Social Science Research Council and the Open Society Foundation for their support of Jeremy Slack and his complementary ethnographic research. This funding, as well as the network of scholars, has been invaluable to the improvement and development of this project.

The Center for Latin American Studies, the Department of Mexican American Studies, the School of Sociology, the School of Geography and

Development, and the College of Social and Behavioral Studies at the University of Arizona also provided support and funding throughout this research. The supportive atmosphere of the University of Arizona made it possible to conduct this unique work and blend the academic and policy aspects, making its impact far greater than it otherwise would have been.

We owe a particular debt of gratitude to all of the people who conducted surveys throughout the U.S.-Mexico border region. This project would not have been possible without their commitment and hard work in sensitive and often uncomfortable environments.

Thanks to *Migration Letters* for permission to reprint M. Ward and D. E. Martínez, "Know Your Enemy: How Repatriated Unauthorized Migrants Learn About and Perceive Anti-immigrant Mobilization in the United States," *Migration Letters* 12, no. 2 (2015): 137–51 (http://www.tplondon.com/journal /index.php/ml/article/view/398).

WAVE I

Kraig Beyerlein

Prescott Vandervoet

Kristin Klingman

Paola Molina

Shiras Manning

Melissa Burham

Kylie Walzak

Kristen Valencia

Lorenzo Gamboa

WAVE II

Tijuana: Ramona Pérez, Alaina Gallegos (San Diego State University [SDSU])

Mexicali: Alfonso Cortez-Lara (Colegio de la Frontera Norte, Mexicali [COLEF, Mexicali)

Nogales: Jeremy Slack (University of Arizona [UA])

Ciudad Juárez: Sonia Bass Zavala (Universidad Autónoma de Ciudad Juárez [UACJ]), Tony Payan (University of Texas at El Paso), Consuelo Pequeño (UACJ), Martha Estela Pérez (UACJ), Raúl Holguín (UACJ)

Nuevo Laredo: Blanca Vázquez (Colegio de la Frontera, Nuevo Laredo [COLEF, Nuevo Laredo]), Soledad Tolentino (COLEF, Nuevo Laredo)

Ciudad de México: Paola Velasco (Universidad Nacional Autónoma de México [UNAM])

INTERVIEWERS

Patricia Hohl (UA)

Murphy Woodhouse (UA)

Richard Casillas (UA)

Ana Julieta González (UA)

Cynthia Rodríguez (SDSU)

Karla Elisa Méndez Delgado (COLEF, Mexicali)

Diana Correa (COLEF, Mexicali)

Cecilia Martínez (UACJ), Adrian Valenzuela (UACJ)

Alejandra Payán (UACJ)

Luis Isaac Rocha (UACJ)

Jorge Leyva (UACJ)

Yadira Cortés (UACJ)

Mayra González (UACJ)

Yaneth Cossio (UACJ)

Armando Taunton Rodríguez (COLEF, Nuevo Laredo)

Carlos Gerardo Cruz Jacobo (COLEF, Nuevo Laredo)

Jose Ignacio Aguinaga Medina (COLEF, Nuevo Laredo)

Adriana Guillermina Wagner Perales (COLEF, Nuevo Laredo)

Armando Orta Pérez (COLEF, Nuevo Laredo)

Naomi Ramírez (SDSU)

Sean Tengco (SDSU)

Charles Whitney (SDSU)

Jose Huizar (SDSU)

Oscar Hernández (UNAM)

Andrea Bautista (UNAM)

Uriel Melchor (UNAM)

Janett Vallejo (UNAM)

Monserrat Luna (UNAM)

Sandra Albicker (Colegio de la Frontera Norte, Tijuana [COLEF, Tijuana])

Diana Peláez (COLEF, Tijuana)

Gabriel Pérez Duperou (COLEF, Tijuana)

Adriana Acle (COLEF, Tijuana)

We also owe special thanks to Francisco Loureiro Herrera and Gilda Irene de Loureiro from the San Juan Bosco shelter, Raquel Rubio-Goldsmith, Josiah Heyman, Kraig Beyerlein, Prescott Vandervoet, Kathryn Rodríguez, Celeste González de Bustamante, Jessica Hamar Martínez, Anna Ochoa O'Leary, Margaret Bellini, Mario Vásquez-León, Ricardo Martínez-Schuldt, Lindsay Rojas, Michael Bonilla, Alyssa Borrego, Lawrence Gipe, Jeffrey Baninster, Guillermo Yrizar Barbosa, Celestino Fernandez, Kelsey Gonzalez, and Christine Scheer. Also, thanks to hosts at COLEF, Matamoros, Cirila Quintero and Oscar Misael Hernández, and hosts at COLEF, Tijuana, Laura Velasco, Dolores Paris Pomba, Rafael Alarcón, and Alonso Meneses.

Of particular importance to this research is the hard work being conducted at the shelters along the U.S.-Mexico border, which feed and provide shelter for thousands of people every day. They are the front lines of mass removal from the United States and deal with grueling hours as people are dropped off at all hours of the night, often overflowing into the kitchens and dining rooms. While we have interacted with far too many volunteers and employees to thank, we must thank Polo, Fernando, Erik, and José from the San Juan Bosco shelter in Nogales; and Constantino Velásquez, Izolda, Lupita, and Manuel uno and Manuel dos from the Scallibrini migrant shelter in Nuevo Laredo, Tamaulipas.

We would also be remiss if we did not acknowledge the gratitude we feel to the thousands of migrants who shared their lives and stories with us over the years. The tenacity of people struggling to improve their lives or return to family in the United States despite the dangers of the desert and penalties they face if they are caught is always awe inspiring. To talk to people day after day who risk their lives for the chance at a full life demonstrates the cruelty and misguided nature of our current approach to immigration and border enforcement.

THE SHADOW
OF THE WALL

INTRODUCTION

JEREMY SLACK, DANIEL E. MARTÍNEZ,
AND SCOTT WHITEFORD

ROBERTO'S JOURNEY (APRIL 29, 2011): NOGALES, SONORA

Roberto was thirty-one and had crossed eleven times. Originally from Guerrero, Mexico, he had been in the United States off and on since 1996. He crossed through Naco, a small border town in eastern Sonora. It was a short trip. Within thirty minutes, the Border Patrol caught him. Because of his desperation to return to his family in California, he ran. They yelled, "Don't run cabrones *[assholes]!" and he stopped immediately. With his plans of working in Napa Valley, California, dashed, he was again removed to Nogales, Sonora. This was his first failed crossing attempt since his removal from the United States, where he was living and working with his family.*

One day Roberto was leaving the park where he had taken his children to play. Suddenly, his car was struck by another vehicle while passing through an intersection. The driver, an American who spoke no Spanish, called the police, and even though Roberto had insurance, he had no driver's license. He admitted that he was undocumented but pleaded with the police officer not to take his children and to let him call someone to pick them up. The officer acquiesced, and Roberto called his brother-in-law. After a few minutes the officer got anxious and started pressuring Roberto. "How long until he gets here? We need to go now!" Roberto got desperate with the growing pressure from the officer. He asked a woman who had been helping him translate to watch

his children and the police took him away. "I had no other option but to trust her,"
Roberto said, still in shock that he had to leave his children with a stranger. Luckily,
his brother-in-law arrived shortly thereafter. Because Roberto's wife is undocumented,
she could not come get them either, leaving these U.S.-citizen children in an extremely
precarious position.

After failing to return home to his family, he was processed through the mass trial
system known as Operation Streamline. Along with forty other migrants, he was
shackled at the feet, waist, and wrists for three hours before being paraded in front of
a federal judge in Tucson, Arizona. He pled guilty to illegal reentry and was sentenced
to forty days in jail. When asked why he pled guilty, he simply stated, "Why would
anyone want to fight when they (the lawyers) tell you that you cannot win."

When asked what he will do next, he said that he plans on working in agriculture
near Hermosillo, Sonora, until he saves up enough money to cross again. He faces
an escalated sentence if caught again, but his resolve to return home is unwavering.

Stories like Roberto's are commonplace. The complicated processes of apprehension, processing, detention, deportation, and criminalization as well as extensive ties to family in the United States and a deep resolve to return despite the involved costs, hardship, and pain typify the contemporary migrant experience. In the second wave of the MBCS, we found that the typical migrant was from west-central (35%) or southern (26%) Mexico, had a mean of 8.1 years of formal education and earned roughly $350 a month before their most recent crossing attempt.[1] They lived in a household with four other family members, two of whom were children under the age of eighteen. On average, 57 percent were the head of their household, and 42 percent were the sole income provider for their family. Forty-nine percent had at least one U.S.-citizen family member, and 19 percent had U.S.-citizen children under the age of eighteen. On average, they had crossed the border without authorization 6.5 times and had been apprehended 3.3 times. Seventy-one percent used the services of a guide or coyote and paid an average of $2,300 to cross. The border-crossing experience is often a perilous one. During their most recent border-crossing attempt, the typical migrant walked through the desert for 2.2 days, with 40 percent running out of water and 31 percent running out of food. Thirteen percent encountered *bajadores* ("stickup crews"), with over 60 percent of those who encountered them being robbed. Among those who traveled in groups, which included all but 9 percent of our sample, 13 percent were abandoned while crossing, and 14 percent witnessed fellow group members left behind.

Despite the dangers of the crossing, some realized short-term success. Thirty-nine percent successfully arrived at their desired U.S. destination but were later apprehended by police or other officials through interior immigration enforcement measures and deported. The apprehension process presented a series of additional risks for many of our respondents, including routine mistreatment and criminalization. For example, 12 percent reported physical abuse by U.S. authorities, and 20 percent reported verbal abuse. Excluding food and water, 27 percent had their possessions taken and not returned while in U.S. custody, including identifying documents and money. Like Roberto, approximately 26 percent were processed through Operation Streamline, which is a federal immigration trial en masse that prosecutes border crossers for "illegal entry" or "illegal reentry," both of which carry criminal charges. Finally, just over 13 percent were processed through the Alien Transfer and Exit Program (i.e., laterally repatriated), and 20 percent were returned to Mexico between the hours of 10:00 p.m. and 5:00 a.m.

Throughout the life span of this project and the years that have followed, we have been shocked time and again by the vitriol streaming from certain politicians and media outlets regarding undocumented immigration and border security. This discourse has, yet again, taken center stage in local and national political debates. The most obvious example is Donald Trump's assertion on June 16, 2015, that unauthorized Mexican immigrants are "bringing drugs," "bringing crime," and are "rapists" (Ye Hee Lee 2015). Other examples include Arizona governor Jan Brewer's claim that headless bodies are frequently found in the Arizona desert as well as characterizations of lawlessness, danger, and hordes of immigrants "swarming" into the United States to take advantage of public services (Jacobson 2012; Farley 2010). Although the immigration-crime link has largely been empirically disproven (Mears 2001; Cantor, Noferi, and Martínez 2015; Orrenius and Coronado 2005; Martínez, Stowell, and Lee 2010; Ousey and Kubrin 2018), and despite experiencing the lowest levels of unauthorized migration in decades (Gonzalez-Barrera 2016), these tropes about the dangers of an open border continue to sway voters (Chavez 2013). This racial anxiety may be one of the key factors that drove white voters to turn out in large numbers for Trump.

Requests for $30 billion in additional border and immigration enforcement spending under the Hoeven-Corker amendment to Senate Bill 744 of 2013, Donald Trump's absurd call for a "wall" along the nearly two-thousand-mile southwestern border, and an additional fifteen thousand immigration agents are mainstays of today's political debates. However, because the United States already spends more than $18 billion per year on border and immigration enforcement (Associated Press 2013), it is important to examine more closely what this spending entails. Calls for more enforcement are rarely, if ever, followed by a critical understanding of what is actually being spent and what it does to the border. Because of this, a more progressive response—one that asserts the border is already secure—is almost as problematic in that it gives carte blanche to continue the activities currently occurring in the name of border enforcement as if they are successful. As we argue in this volume, the very policies and practices taking place along the border have produced unheard-of levels of violence, higher death rates, and a mass incarceration machine that has been criminalizing migrants and locking up asylum seekers in for-profit prisons that lobby for increased enforcement and harsher penalties.

This book is an examination of the consequences of the current approach to border and immigration enforcement. While scholars have written extensively about the "prevention through deterrence" strategy that began in the mid-1990s (Dunn 1996, 2009; Nevins and Aizeki 2008; Nevins 2002), we argue that this framework is no longer appropriate to understand the immense, complex apparatus of enforcement. Rather, the implementation of the Consequence Delivery System (CDS) in 2011, a program designed to guide agents into delivering punishment based on the level of offenses committed by migrants, is a more appropriate lens through which to view contemporary border and immigration enforcement. The CDS generates escalating punishments for those with more apprehensions in the hopes that they will not return. While it is important to note that the dangers of the physical geography of the border are certainly still an important part of the strategic plan, the CDS is a significant shift in policy. The strategy has changed. The "Gatekeeper Era," characterized by the "prevention through deterrence" strategy in the 1990s and early 2000s, was predicated on a general deterrence strategy. Instead of relying solely on physical barriers, the extreme temperatures, long walks, and other natural hazards of the desert and river to deter migrants, the U.S. Border Patrol (USBP) now wields the full force of the carceral state against migrants.

It is hard to assert that the main goal of the CDS is the prevention of would-be migrants in Mexico who may be contemplating a journey. Rather, the focus on an individual punishment, designated by special rubrics given to agents, makes it obvious that the goal is preventing *repeat* migration. Thus, the CDS is in many ways an actuarial approach to immigration enforcement; it cites the prevention of future "crimes" (i.e., unauthorized migration) as rationale for increasingly severe punishments for a select subpopulation—those with strong social ties and place attachment to the United States who are the most likely to be repeat border crossers. This has significant implications for people who have put down roots in the United States. As interior enforcement has ramped up significantly since the establishment of the U.S. Department of Homeland Security (DHS) in 2002, a greater number of people have been removed despite having spent years living in the United States and now have few options other than to return to their families in the United States. While some scholars have noted negative migration flows in Mexican sending regions for the first time and have begun to discuss the end of mass labor migration to the United States (Durand 2013), we argue that many deportees do not return to their cities of origin. Rather, many stay near the border and attempt to return to their lives and families in the United States. In many ways, interior immigration enforcement and deportation have themselves become the new drivers of unauthorized Mexican migration to the United States.

Through postdeportation surveys, interviews, and ethnographic work along the U.S.-Mexico border, this book chronicles the lived experiences of people who have gone through this escalated, punishment-focused immigration enforcement apparatus. We examine the specific components of border enforcement and their effects on people who no longer call Mexico their home, concluding that those with extensive ties to the United States are highly determined to return. We have produced novel data about what it is like to cross the border in the post-Gatekeeper, DHS era of enforcement. The CDS approach is predicated on an increasingly punitive approach to immigration enforcement that has also played a part in fomenting violence in Mexico. The border zones where almost half a million Mexicans are deported each year have experienced tremendous violence. Migrants often interact and witness this violence on another level, as they frequently cross the border side by side with drug traffickers and are often the victims of kidnapping, robbery, or extortion during their journeys and upon return to Mexico. This book explores how the relationships between organized crime and the state exacerbate the violence migrants experience on both sides of the border during migration, deportation, and the subsequent trauma of separation from one's family.

IMPLICATIONS OF THE
CONSEQUENCE DELIVERY SYSTEM

Our fine-grained approach to researching the intricate practices and processes of enforcement not only helps us move past the "prevention through deterrence" narrative that has continued to dominate research about migration but also helps policy makers understand the nuances of current border policing practices. Not all deportations are created equally. Disentangling these differences is essential for engaging with current debates in policy and advocacy. We must dispel notions that border enforcement is simply the product of agents patrolling select areas of the border zone. When we discuss the immense costs of enforcement, it includes the various types of immigration checkpoints, mass trial programs such as Operation Streamline, arrangements with local and state law enforcement, incarceration in immigration detention as well as federal prison, and the myriad private agencies tasked with transporting, detaining, and processing migrants. Immigration and Customs Enforcement (ICE) has a separate mandate from Customs and Border Protections (CBP), which is further broken down into the Office of Field Operations (OFO), who work at ports of entry (POE), and the U.S. Border Patrol (USBP), who generally work between POEs. This has only become more complicated and convoluted since the creation of the DHS in 2002. Whereas before DHS, USBP, and CBP were part of the institution tasked with providing immigration services (the Immigration and Naturalization Service [INS]), now they are located squarely within the logic of the "war on terror." What was once the INS is now known as the U.S. Citizenship and Immigration Services (USCIS) and is a parallel organization to CBP and ICE. The significance of this rearrangement must be carefully examined. While INS was never the paragon of service (Heyman 2001), the events of September 11th significantly increased the power and ability of those tasked with preventing another terrorist attack to operate without oversight. Until recently, CBP's mission statement discussed terrorism but mentioned nothing about immigration (Customs and Border Protections 2015).

While scholars have noted that the USBP has still largely based its day-to-day operations on the mass apprehension of border crossers (Heyman and Ackleson 2009), there are new ad hoc layers to enforcement that have been seriously neglected by immigration and border scholars. This includes the mass trials known as Operation Streamline, which convicts upward of thirty thousand people per year with "illegal entry" (8 USC § 1325) and "illegal re-entry" (8 USC

§ 1326); the lateral deportation of individuals who cross in one USBP sector to another area of the border (Alien Transfer and Exit Program [ATEP]); and the Operation Against Smuggling, Initiative on Safety and Security (OASISS), which has been used to sentence accused human smugglers to prison in Mexico based on statements collected in the United States. Programs such as the Criminal Alien Program, which encompasses the Secure Communities and 287(g) programs, and other arrangements that either deport noncitizens from prisons or aid in the arrest and removal of undocumented people living in the interior of the United States also contribute to the concentration of individuals along the border where they are easily incorporated into the CDS. The migration experience has changed drastically with these two tiers—removal from the interior and punishment at the border. The "border," broadly conceptualized, acts as a multiplier for the 1996 Illegal Immigration Reform and Immigration Responsibility Act (IIRIRA), which increased the penalties for noncitizens by expanding the list of deportable offenses and violations deemed "aggravated felonies" (Coleman and Kocher 2011; Coleman 2007; Kanstroom 2012). The "aggravated felony," which includes offenses that are neither "aggravated" nor "felonious," can include a combination of misdemeanors that will result in removal for noncitizens, including legal permanent residents. The ever-expanding list of deportable offenses has made it increasingly easy for people to lose status. Because Mexicans have made up the largest group of immigrants for several decades, they have been targeted at higher rates, as shown by the racial bias in immigration-related stops as well as the removal of Mexicans through the Criminal Alien Program for less severe offenses when compared with other national origin groups (Coleman and Kocher 2011; Coleman and Stuesse 2015; Dowling and Inda 2013; Cantor, Noferi, and Martínez 2015). However, if and when people who have been formally removed from the United States decide to cross again, they are charged with reentry regardless of the severity of their infractions and face an escalating prison sentence for each attempt. These generally start at three months and can reach up to twenty years, although this length of sentence is rarely, if ever, given.

While still not the norm, the increase in people deported after prison sentences as a result of interior enforcement programs has caused significant challenges. The stigma of being a "deportee" has permeated border life, creating a bifurcated image of the "good migrant" and the "bad deportee." As discussed in chapter 8, the processes of criminalization have a social dimension, causing significant and lasting problems for those incarcerated even after they are deported.

Many of the shelters where we work have experienced violent incidents, often needing police intervention. The shelters also place strict limits on what migrants can and cannot do during their stays (e.g., restricted use of cell phones; a ban on knives, nail clippers, or razors; no reentry after leaving; limited contact between migrants of the opposite sex; scrutinizing migrants perceived to be coyotes; and so forth). These strategies, while often harsh to an outside observer, are generally necessary to maintain control and order within and around shelters. Some shelters that allow for more relaxed atmospheres may have problems with drugs or become the territory of one particular human smuggler (coyote). This, as well as incursions by armed groups of men and threats by drug cartels, has created a previously unheard-of level of tension for those dedicated to providing services to migrants.

When we began the MBCS project in 2007, we did not anticipate the increase in drug trafficking–related violence in northern Mexico, nor did we expect the changes in border and immigration enforcement that would occur in the following years. What began as a group of graduate students traveling to Nogales, Sonora, one hour south of the University of Arizona where we were studying, quickly morphed into a border-wide study involving six different research sites, thirteen institutions, and more than sixty researchers. Combined with ethnographic work conducted during and after surveying, we have produced a unique data set that speaks to challenging topics such as kidnapping, drug trafficking, and cartel recruitment. The MBCS is not only a new methodological approach for interrogating migration and deportation but also a firm commitment to working closely with advocates and activists both in terms of the development of our questions and our efforts to disseminate, publicize, and push for real policy change. We have chosen to focus on the dimensions of violence that migrants experience from U.S. authorities as well as the crossing experience and the criminal actors who have proliferated along the U.S.-Mexico border.

VIOLENCE ON THE BORDER

We explore the role of violence in shaping migratory experiences by drawing from diverse conceptions of violence ranging from the structural inequalities that lead to a loss of life (Farmer 1996, 2003; Galtung 1969) to its symbolic dimensions manifested in the acceptance of mistreatment because of a migrant's irregular immigration status (Bourdieu and Wacquant 1992; Bourdieu 2001; Slack and Whiteford 2011b; Holmes 2013). In chapter 2 we examine the dimensions of what we call "poststructural violence." Rather than referring to commonly held definitions of poststructural theory (see Dixon and Jones 1998), we use this term to refer to the various ways people negotiate violent contexts, moving from one (usually oppressive) social structure to another (generally also oppressive but qualitatively different) structure. What choices do they make to change roles within the context of the border? With each move (from peasant worker, to migrant, to drug smuggler, to hit man, and so forth) new forms of violence become part of their structural reality (Slack and Whiteford 2011a, 2011b; Izcara Palacios 2012, 2016). While some roles may offer additional forms of protection, others expose them to new vulnerabilities and potential violence. Poststructural violence helps us understand the choices people make as they negotiate their vulnerable state, thereby shaping each individual migrant's experience.

Violence became the focal point of our work especially with the unique context of heightened drug-related violence on the border as well as the shocking events of August 2010, when seventy-two migrants were massacred in Tamaulipas. It was clear that the deportees we interviewed had a front-row seat to this violence as they travel through the clandestine spaces of the border. In chapter 8, Slack and Campbell explore how drug trafficking has led to "illicit regimes" along the border. The most powerful criminal organizations (i.e., drug cartels) dictate rules and regulations for clandestine border spaces, controlling all illegal activity through violent coercion and extortion and creating a mimetic form of state control (Slack and Campbell 2016). In chapter 6, we explore the consequences of exposure to gang culture in federal prisons and detention facilities (Martínez and Slack 2013) and the increase of migrant kidnapping in Mexico in the ninth chapter (Slack 2015).

However, we must also acknowledge that violence is not the only driving force in migration. For people to engage in such a difficult and dangerous activity, there must also be benefits, such as the reunification of families and successfully pulling oneself out of poverty. Our methodological approach, concentrating on people's stories immediately after removal, leads us to focus on the extremely negative aspects of migration, which are much more apparent during this extremely stressful experience. Migration is a complex social phenomenon, too complex to fully explore in just one volume. Moreover, despite the focus on some of the more shocking aspects of violence, we must not neglect the often more banal violence of being forced to walk for days, paying thousands of dollars to human smugglers, and being separated from loved ones, simply in search of work. Scholars are often attracted to the extreme examples, the stories that affect us most deeply during our research and keep us up at night. Unfortunately, this can desensitize us to the commonplace tragedies of migration. Namely, even in the face of horrific drug violence, we must not ignore the devastation of families separated by our broken immigration system and the removal of people who are socially and culturally American, with little to no knowledge of their country of origin. In order to create an inclusive understanding of these issues, we must create a more complex understanding of the people engaging in migration, one that may break with both the pro- and anti-immigrant caricatures commonly portrayed in the media.

Proimmigrant discourse is often dominated by tropes of heteronormative, hard-working family "men" in an attempt to create the most sympathetic figure possible. The campaign to pass the Development, Relief, and Education for Alien Minors (DREAM) Act constantly paraded valedictorians, genius-level undocumented students, or those with shockingly pristine military and community-service records. While this is an important discursive tool to convince the public of the value of immigrants, it also simultaneously creates an impossible standard. What about the rest? The average students, teenagers who have had run-ins with the law, and even those with more serious infractions should not be erased from our discussions of the impacts of current immigration policies and the need for reforms that do not leave people behind. This book is an attempt to bring everyone in, to understand the big picture of who is being removed from the United States and what this is causing, not only for the individuals themselves but also for their families in the United States and Mexico.

BOOK OUTLINE

This book is a compilation of selected works produced through the first two waves of the MBCS. The three editors of this volume, along with other collaborators, are authors of all chapters in a variety of configurations. As the principal investigators of the MBCS, we have been closely involved with the fieldwork, data management, analyses, and publications that have resulted from this project.

This compilation is an interdisciplinary reader for people interested in the United States' current approach to immigration control, especially in light of resurgent anti-immigrant sentiments. We hope that the chapters encompassed in this volume will provide scholars the opportunity to move beyond "prevention through deterrence" narratives and begin to take a more detailed look at the machinery of immigration and border enforcement. This book is also meant to be a tool for policy makers interested in empirical data about migration, border enforcement, and the impacts of drug violence in Mexico.

Section one addresses the context, research methodology, and our theoretical understandings of violence. Through qualitative, ethnographic research conducted during both phases of the MBCS, we explore dimensions of how violence has affected both migrants and research process. Chapter 1—by Martínez, Slack, and Martínez-Schuldt—is an in-depth methodological overview of the MBCS. This chapter is generally aimed at academics and other professionals interested in specific nuanced understandings of the production of social science data. For readers whose interests lie in migration or other conceptual issues, we suggest proceeding directly to chapter 2. The methods chapter examines the two waves of the MBCS, the first taking place in Nogales, Sonora, and the second, expanded version that was conducted along the entire border. We compare the two waves with previous quantitative studies, such as the Mexican Migration Project (Massey, Durand, and Malone 2002; Durand and Massey 2004), the work of Wayne Cornelius (Cornelius 2005; Cornelius and Lewis 2007), and the Colegio de la Frontera's flagship project, the Encuesta de Migración en la Frontera (EMIF; Santibáñez et al. 1997; Bustamante 2000). In turn we argue that this methodology helps to unify the qualitative and quantitative divide in migration studies, addressing concerns about human rights, violence, and drug trafficking in a mixed-methods study. In chapter 2, Jeremy Slack and Scott Whiteford discuss the different forms of violence that shape the migrant experience and how the recent expansion of drug-related violence along the border has caused new rifts among migrants. In the third chapter, Slack, Martínez, and Vandervoet explore how the rise in violence caused us to question both our own exposure to violence as researchers, the impact this has on research participants, and how institutional stances banning research cause unforeseen challenges in fieldwork.

The second section takes an in-depth look at enforcement procedures and practices. These chapters explore the many dimensions of the Consequence Delivery System by examining the experiences of those who have been through it. The survey data allow us to get a better understanding of who is processed through these programs, why, what impacts the programs have on deportees, and how these practices vary along the border. In chapter 4, Slack, Martínez,

Whiteford, and Peiffer demonstrate how these programs fail to deter people from future migration but centralize the punishment of migrants as the key aspect of enforcement. Despite failing to break people's resolve to return to the United States, these practices put migrants directly in harm's way. In chapter 5, Slack, Martínez, Lee, and Whiteford explore the spatial dimensions of enforcement, noting that levels of mistreatment and the application of the CDS vary significantly along the border. Moreover, this lack of formal rigidity also leads us to question the role of abuse in the border enforcement strategy. With such widespread and consistent documentation of abuse, how does this fit into the overall strategy of punishment adopted by USBP? In chapter 6, Martínez and Slack examine the social processes of criminalization that occur as people are sent to federal prisons or detention facilities and are exposed to gang culture, drug smugglers, and human smugglers after being branded as criminals for migration violations. The zero-tolerance policies toward unauthorized immigration have led not only to the criminalization of immigration law but to the incorporation of economic and family migrants into the vicious industrial incarceration complex.

For the final section of this book, we explore the unintended consequences of border and immigration enforcement. This involves examining the changes among extralegal actors involved with the clandestine movement of people and goods across the border. In chapter 7, Daniel Martínez discusses the ways human smuggling has adapted to this new era of heightened enforcement, noting that more migrants find their guides along the border than in home communities, which suggests greater organization and sophistication. In chapter 8, Slack and Campbell explore how the clandestine spaces of the border are governed and controlled through the hierarchical power of drug cartels that have influenced the border crossing in numerous ways. Rather than focus on binary, yes-no questions about whether or not coyotes are involved with drug trafficking, we examine how these relationships have shaped the experiences of migrants. Chapter 9 focuses on the rise in organized crime along the border and the proliferation of mass kidnapping. In that chapter, Slack concludes that kidnapping is not simply about ransom but rather about the control of bodies and extracting labor through brutal forms of recruitment into organized crime. In chapter 10, Matthew Ward and Daniel Martínez discuss how migrants receive information about and perceive of anti-immigrant groups such as the minutemen. We conclude with a discussion about the way forward. How can we use research to create an impact on the lives of those we study? How can we create a new methodological standard for migration research that will lead to academic insights and concrete empirical findings useful in the policy and advocacy world?

NOTE

1.   Throughout, dollar amounts refer to U.S. currency unless otherwise specified.

REFERENCES

Associated Press. 2013. "Obama Administration Spent 18B on Immigration Enforcement." *USA Today*, January 7. http://www.usatoday.com/story/news/nation/2013/01/07/obama-immigration-enforcement/1815667/.

Bourdieu, Pierre. 2001. *Male Domination*. Vol. 1. Oxford: Blackwell.

Bourdieu, Pierre, and Loïc Wacquant. 1992. *An Invitation to Reflexive Sociology*. Chicago: University of Chicago Press.

Bustamante, Jorge A. 2000. "Migración irregular de México a Estados Unidos: 10 años de investigación del Proyecto Cañón Zapata." *Frontera Norte* 12 (23). http://www.redalyc.org/articulo.oa?id=13602301.

Cantor, Guillermo, Mark Noferi, and Daniel. E. Martínez. 2015. "Enforcement Overdrive: A Comprehensive Assessment of ICE's Criminal Alien Program." American Immigration Council, November 1. https://www.americanimmigrationcouncil.org/research/enforcement-overdrive-comprehensive-assessment-ice%E2%80%99s-criminal-alien-program.

Chavez, Leo. 2013. *The Latino Threat: Constructing Immigrants, Citizens, and the Nation*. Stanford, Calif.: Stanford University Press.

Coleman, Mat, and Angela Stuesse. 2015. "The Disappearing State and the Quasi-Event of Immigration Control." *Antipode* 48: 524–43. doi:10.1111/anti.12209.

Coleman, Mathew. 2007. "Immigration Geopolitics Beyond the Mexico-US Border." *Antipode* 39 (1): 54–76. doi:10.1111/j.1467-8330.2007.00506.x.

Coleman, Mathew, and Austin Kocher. 2011. "Detention, Deportation, Devolution and Immigrant Incapacitation in the US, Post 9/11." *Geographical Journal* 177 (3): 228–37. doi:10.1111/j.1475-4959.2011.00424.x.

Cornelius, Wayne. 2005. "Controlling 'Unwanted' Immigration: Lessons from the United States, 1993–2004." *Journal of Ethnic and Migration Studies* 31 (4): 775–94.

Cornelius, Wayne A., and Jessa M. Lewis. 2007. *Impacts of Border Enforcement on Mexican Migration: The View from Sending Communities*. La Jolla, Calif.: Center for Comparative Immigration Studies.

Customs and Border Protection. 2015. "About CBP." http://www.cbp.gov/about.

Dixon, Deborah P., and John Paul Jones. 1998. "My Dinner with Derrida; or, Spatial Analysis and Poststructuralism Do Lunch." *Environment and Planning A* 30 (2): 247–60.

Dowling, Julie, and Jonathan Inda. 2013. *Governing Immigration Through Crime: A Reader*. Stanford, Calif.: Stanford University Press.

Dunn, Timothy J. 1996. *The Militarization of the U.S.-Mexico Border, 1978–1992: Low-Intensity Conflict Doctrine Comes Home.* Austin: CMAS Books, University of Texas at Austin.

———. 2009. *Blockading the Border and Human Rights: The El Paso Operation that Remade Immigration Enforcement.* Austin: University of Texas Press.

Durand, Jorge. 2013. "Nueva fase migratoria." *Papeles de población* 19 (77): 83–113.

Durand, Jorge, and Dougals S. Massey, eds. 2004. *Crossing the Border: Research from the Mexican Migration Project.* New York: Russell Sage Foundation.

Farley, Robert. 2010. "Gov. Jan Brewer Talks of Beheadings in the Arizona Desert." *Politifact.* http://www.politifact.com/truth-o-meter/statements/2010/sep/08/jan-brewer/gov-jan-brewer-talks-beheadings-th-arizona-desert/.

Farmer, Paul. 1996. "On Suffering and Structural Violence: A View from Below." *Daedalus* 125 (1): 261–83.

———. 2003. *Pathologies of Power: Health, Human Rights, and the New War on the Poor.* Berkeley: University of California Press.

Galtung, Johan. 1969. "Violence, Peace, and Peace Research." *Journal of Peace Research* 6 (3): 167–91.

Gonzalez-Barrera, Ana. 2016. "Apprehensions of Mexican Migrants at U.S. Borders Reach Near-Historic Low." *Fact Tank*, April 14. http://www.pewresearch.org/fact-tank/2016/04/14/mexico-us-border-apprehensions/.

Heyman, Josiah McC. 2001. "Class and Classification at the US-Mexico Border." *Human Organization* 60 (2): 128–140.

Heyman, Josiah McC., and Jason Ackleson. 2009. "United States Border Security after September 11." In *Border Security in the Al-Qaeda Era*, edited by John Winterdyck and Kelly Sundberg, 37–74. Boca Raton, Fla.: CRC Press.

Holmes, Seth. 2013. *Fresh Fruit, Broken Bodies: Migrant Farmworkers in the United States.* Berkeley: University of California Press.

Izcara Palacios, Simón Pedro. 2012. "Coyotaje y grupos delictivos en Tamaulipas." *Latin American Research Review* 47 (3): 41–61.

———. 2016. "Post-Structural Violence: Central American Migrants and Drug Cartels in Mexico." *Revista de Estudios Sociales* 56: 12–25.

Jacobson, Louis. 2012. "Illegal Alien Facts vs. the Truth-O-Meter." *Politifact*, June 20. http://www.politifact.com/truth-o-meter/article/2012/jun/20/ten-illegal-alien-facts-truth-o-meter/.

Kanstroom, Daniel. 2012. *Aftermath: Deportation Law and the New American Diaspora.* New York: Oxford University Press.

Martínez, Daniel, and Jeremy Slack. 2013. "What Part of 'Illegal' Don't You Understand? The Social Consequences of Criminalizing Unauthorized Mexican Migrants in the United States." *Social and Legal Studies* 22 (4): 535–51.

Martínez, Ramiro, Jacob I. Stowell, and Matthew T. Lee. 2010. "Immigration and Crime in an Era of Transformation: A Longitudinal Analysis of Homicides in San Diego Neighborhoods, 1980–2000." *Criminology* 48 (3): 797–829.

Massey, Douglas S., Jorge Durand, and Nolan J. Malone. 2002. *Beyond Smoke and Mirrors: Mexican Immigration in an Era of Economic Integration*. New York: Russell Sage Foundation.

Mears, Daniel P. 2001. "The Immigration-Crime Nexus: Toward an Analytic Framework for Assessing and Guiding Theory, Research, and Policy." *Sociological Perspectives* 44 (1): 1–19.

Nevins, Joseph. 2002. *Operation Gatekeeper: The Rise of the "Illegal Alien" and the Making of the U.S.-Mexico Boundary*. New York: Routledge.

Nevins, Joseph, and Mizue Aizeki. 2008. *Dying to Live: A Story of U.S. Immigration in an Age of Global Apartheid*. San Francisco: Open Media / City Lights.

Orrenius, Pia M., and Roberto Coronado. 2005. *The Effect of Illegal Immigration and Border Enforcement on Crime Rates Along the US-Mexico Border*. La Jolla: Center for Comparative Immigration Studies, University of California, San Diego.

Ousey, Graham C., and Charis E. Kubrin. 2018. "Immigration and Crime: Assessing a Contentious Issue." *Annual Review of Criminology* 1 (1). doi:10.1146/annurev-criminol-032317-092026.

Santibáñez, Jorge, J. Bustamante, D. Delaunay, and J. Santibañez. 1997. "Metodología de la encuesta sobre migración en la Frontera Norte de México." In *Taller de medición de la migración internacional*. Edited by J. Bustamante, D. Delaunay, and J. Santibañez, 206–229. Tijuana, Baja California: Colegio de la Frontera Norte.

Slack, Jeremy. 2015. "Captive Bodies: Migrant Kidnapping and Deportation in Mexico." *Area* 48 (3): 271–77. doi:10.1111/area.12151.

Slack, Jeremy, and Howard Campbell. 2016. "On Narco-Coyotaje: Illicit Regimes and Their Impacts on the US–Mexico Border." *Antipode* 48 (5): 1380–99. doi:10.1111/anti.12242.

Slack, Jeremy, Daniel Martínez, Scott Whiteford, and Emily Peiffer. 2013. "In the Shadow of the Wall: Family Separation, Immigration Enforcement and Security." Report, Center for Latin American Studies, Tucson: University of Arizona. https://las.arizona.edu/sites/las.arizona.edu/files/UA_Immigration_Report2013web.pdf.

Slack, Jeremy, and Scott Whiteford. 2011a. "Viajes Violentos: La transformación de la migración clandestina hacia Sonora y Arizona." *Norteamérica* 2 (2): 79–107.

———. 2011b. "Violence and Migration on the Arizona-Sonora Border." *Human Organization* 70 (1): 11–21.

Ye Hee Lee, Michelle. 2015. "Donald Trump's False Comments on Mexican Immigrants and Crime." *Washington Post*, July 8. https://www.washingtonpost.com/news/fact-checker/wp/2015/07/08/donald-trumps-false-comments-connecting-mexican-immigrants-and-crime/.

1

RESEARCH METHODS

DANIEL E. MARTÍNEZ, JEREMY SLACK,
AND RICARDO MARTÍNEZ-SCHULDT

INTRODUCTION

THE AIM OF this chapter is threefold. First, we detail the strengths of a post-deportation methodology and contend that scholars should consider adopting this methodological approach in their migration research. We demonstrate that a postdeportation methodology allows for a closer examination of several underexplored topics related to immigration and deportation that require more attention from scholars, particularly given the rise in formal removals (i.e., deportations) since the early 2000s. Instead of interrogating deportation as a hypothetical consequence as many of the studies related to "deportability" have done (De Genova and Peutz 2010; De Genova 2002; Núñez and Heyman 2007), we focus on its material consequences (for an exception, see Golash-Boza 2015). Second, we describe how the Migrant Border Crossing Study (MBCS) complements and expands on existing quantitative studies of unauthorized Mexican migration. Third, we discuss the ways in which our methodological approach bridges the qualitative-quantitative divide in migration studies by incorporating and testing theoretical contributions of qualitative researchers through rigorous random-sample surveys. This, combined with in-depth interviews and ethnographic participant observation along the border, has led to a unique strategy with findings that can advance the scholarly understanding of undocumented migration, border and immigration enforcement, violence along the border, and the effects of deportation.

In what follows, we describe the quantitative and qualitative methodologies that drive the MBCS. The complementary nature of these approaches demonstrates the power of combining emotionally powerful narratives with rigorous and generalizable data. Rather than simply utilizing qualitative data as a scoping or supportive activity, which some scholars have described as the typical mixed-methods trap (Denzin and Lincoln 2005), our qualitative and quantitative strategies work in a symbiotic manner, with quantitative data providing a broader context and generalizability for qualitative data. For instance, this approach allows us to overcome the potential limitations of the documentation of various abuses migrants experience during their journeys, which are frequently critiqued or dismissed as being based on "isolated incidents," egregious cases, or anecdotal evidence. Presenting qualitative accounts of migrant abuse alongside systematically collected quantitative data capturing the frequency of these events in a generalizable manner strengthens the argument that migrant mistreatment is routine, which is especially important when attempting to convince policy makers of needed reforms.

Because the chapters making up this volume represent a number of diverse articles based on the first two waves of the MBCS, a detailed discussion of the different phases of the projects will prove useful to the reader. For instance, chapter 2 was written based on qualitative scoping research. Chapters 7 and 10 drew on data gathered through wave one of the MBCS, which was collected exclusively in Nogales, Sonora. And chapters 4, 5, and 9 were based on data collected in the most recent wave of the MBCS carried out in five border cities and in Mexico City. Collectively, these articles illustrate that (1) the postdeportation methodology is ideal for gaining greater insight into the *contemporary* dynamics of the migration and deportation experience, (2) the MBCS's unique methodology overcomes many of the limitations of existing quantitative studies of unauthorized Mexican migration, and (3) it is possible to integrate qualitative *and* quantitative methods into a research project in a manner in which they complement one another and extend the scholarly understanding of unauthorized Mexican migration.

EXISTING STUDIES ON UNAUTHORIZED MEXICAN MIGRATION AND DEPORTATION

There is a vast qualitative and quantitative literature on the border-crossing experiences of unauthorized Mexican migrants. Qualitative studies of border crossers have offered rich, detailed accounts of people's perilous treks through Mexico and across the border as well as their attempts to avoid detection while also providing systematic social scientific analyses of the journey (Samora 1971; Hagan 2008; Hagan and Ebaugh 2003; O'Leary 2008, 2009; Gomberg-Muñoz 2011). These studies describe how people prepare spiritually (Hagan 2008; Hagan and Ebaugh 2003) and logistically (Spener 2009; O'Leary 2009) for the journey and describe the physical struggles and conditions people endure in an effort to avoid detection (O'Leary 2008). However, qualitative studies of the border-crossing experience are limited in that they do not utilize large random samples that can be used to make generalizations about the unauthorized migration experience (for a debate, see Small 2009; Katz 2001, 2002). In the mid-2000s, during the peak of unauthorized migration from Mexico, several thousand people crossed the U.S.-Mexico border without documentation every day, making it extremely difficult to generalize to the broad range of experiences and practices along the two-thousand-mile border, particularly when using a qualitative approach.

The scholarly understanding of unauthorized Mexican migration has also been advanced considerably by three major ongoing studies: the Mexican Migration Project (MMP), the Mexican Migration Field Research Program (MMFRP), and the Encuesta sobre Migración en la Frontera Norte de Mexico (EMIF-Norte). The MMP has perhaps been the single most important study contributing to the sociological understanding of migration from Mexico to the United States; hundreds of books, monographs, articles, book chapters, and doctoral dissertations have been published using these data.[1] The MMP, which was established in 1982 and is now housed at Princeton University, has collected data on 8,557 migrant and nonmigrant heads of household in 161 migrant-sending communities across 24 Mexican states as of 2017. The MMP relies on an ethnosurvey, which is a dynamic method that allows researchers the flexibility to collect quantitative and qualitative information on people's lifetime migration trips to the United States (Massey 1987; Massey and Zenteno 2000). The project has also conducted in-depth interviews using a snowball sample in receiving communities among people who have established their homes in the United States.[2] The MMFRP, housed at the University of California, San Diego, has also been an important source of quantitative and qualitative data on Mexican migration from sending communities in the states of Jalisco, Zacatecas, Yucatán, and Oaxaca as well as several receiving communities across the United States, each of which is studied every three years. As of 2016, the MMFRP had interviewed 14,985 migrants and potential migrants across these communities using quasi-longitudinal, in-depth, random-sample surveys and ethnographic approaches. The project has resulted in rich case studies and survey data of these communities that have allowed researchers to examine the reasons people migrate, both legally and in an unauthorized manner, as well as how the migration from each community has been affected by increased border enforcement and the 2007–2009 Great Recession (Cornelius and Lewis 2007; Cornelius et al. 2010). Since its inception, the MMFRP has produced fourteen books and special journal issues.

The Colegio de la Frontera del Norte (COLEF)—in conjunction with multiple Mexican governmental agencies, including Instituto Nacional de Migración (INM) and Consejo Nacional de Población (CONAPO)—has conducted the Encuesta sobre Migración en las Fronteras in northern Mexico (EMIF-Norte) since 1993. Building on Jorge Bustamante's seminal Proyecto Cañon Zapata and using a probabilistic random sample in high-migrant-traffic areas near Mexico's northern border (Colegio de la Frontera Norte 2017; Passel, Cohn, and Gonzalez-Barrera 2012), the EMIF-Norte has examined the relationships between community, household, and individual-level economic conditions and migratory flows within Mexico and between the United States and Mexico. EMIF-Norte data on returned Mexicans are weighted on location of repatriation using statistics from Mexico's Instituto Nacional de Migracion and therefore are representative of the population.[3] Yet this data source has been largely underutilized by scholars in the United States probably because of its novel yet unorthodox methodology.

The MMP, MMFRP, and EMIF-Norte have each contributed significantly to the scholarly understanding of unauthorized Mexican migration to the United States. However, these studies are not without limitations. For example, the majority of data gathered through the MMP were collected from migrants whose most recent crossing attempt occurred *before* increased border enforcement measures and the blurring of immigration and criminal law, both of which began in the mid-1990s. Thus, the MMP has surveyed relatively few *recent* border crossers. For instance, only twenty respondents in MMP's 2016 MIGFILE, which consists of ethnosurveys with 8,252 heads of households, had attempted an unauthorized border crossing through southern Arizona during the study period of the first wave of the MBCS (2007–2009). Southern Arizona has been the single most important crossing corridor for unauthorized Mexican migrants during the past decade. As a comparison, the first wave of the MBCS surveyed 415 migrants who had recently attempted to cross the Sonora-Arizona border between 2007 and 2009. In a similar vein, among the 1,109 migrants surveyed in the second wave of the MBCS, 947 had most recently attempted a border crossing between 2009 and 2012, while just 36 MMP respondents had attempted a border crossing during the same time period. Therefore, MMP data may not be generalizable to the contemporary border crossing and deportation experience.

The MMP and MMFRP are also limited in that they may suffer from retrospective bias, as many participants in these studies were surveyed a considerable amount of time after their most recent border-crossing attempt in their communities of origin. In the case of the MMFRP, data are collected on the border-crossing experiences of their most recent cohorts of migrants—generally in the year immediately preceding the fieldwork, which may limit issues stemming from retrospective bias and memory recall. However, the MMFRP is generalizable only to the communities in the four Mexican states where data were collected. On the other hand, because both waves of the MBCS were carried out near the border postdeportation, not only is retrospective bias limited but migrants from nearly all of Mexico's states are represented in the surveys. Finally, while the EMIF-Norte does provide valuable insights on recent migration between Mexico and the United States as well as the demographic profiles of those engaged in the migration process, there are a limited number of questions regarding the conditions of people's border-crossing experiences, firsthand experience with border and immigration enforcement, and human rights violations.

Waves one and two of the MBCS are uniquely positioned to speak to contemporary unauthorized Mexican migrants' border-crossing and deportation experiences when compared to other data sources. We contend that if scholars truly want to understand what unauthorized migrants experience when crossing the border and upon deportation, they should be surveyed near the border while in transit, not in sending communities years after their most recent migration trip. Furthermore, the MBCS is able to complement existing data sources by widening the scope of questions related to the conditions of migrants' recent crossing attempts, encounters with U.S. authorities, and deportation experience.

Although expanding rapidly, the extant literature on deportation is less established than the robust literature on unauthorized Mexican migration. Nevertheless, researchers working in this area have made important theoretical contributions to the scholarly understanding of deportation. For example, Daniel Kanstroom (2007) traces the legal history of deportation and argues that it constitutes an important form of postentry racialized social control insofar that noncitizens are routinely removed from the United States, often for minor criminal infractions. Nicholas De Genova has also contributed to this expanding body of literature. In his seminal article, De Genova (2002) focuses extensively on "illegality" and "deportability," arguing that the constant threat of deportation "has rendered undocumented migrant labor a distinctly disposable commodity" (438). In other words, deportability creates a complicit and cheap labor force vital in the maintenance and perpetuation of capitalism. In her recent book, Golash-Boza (2015) contributes to these lines of inquiry by drawing on 147 in-depth interviews with Guatemalan, Dominican, Jamaican, and Brazilian deportees and argues that mass deportation is simultaneously a consequence and perpetuator of global capitalism, racialized social control, and the neoliberal cycle. But there has been less attention paid to the deportation of Mexicans from the United States, which make up the largest share of deportees (Transactional Records Access Clearinghouse 2014). However, the MBCS's postdeportation methodology enables us to provide empirical evidence regarding the material consequences of recent Mexican deportations.

Our aim with the MBCS has been to bridge the qualitative-quantitative divide in the scholarship on unauthorized Mexican migration. We have also attempted to contribute to the growing body of literature on deportation by providing reliable and generalizable data on people's lived experiences with immigration enforcement processes. In what follows, we provide a comprehensive overview of our postdeportation methodology, which has served as the basis for the collection of chapters throughout this book.

MAJOR COMPONENTS OF THE MBCS

There are three essential components of the ongoing MBCS research project: (1) Wave 1 (i.e., MBCS I), which was carried out in Nogales, Sonora, between October 2007 and July 2009; (2) Wave 2 (MBCS II), which was executed in Tijuana and Mexicali, Baja California; Nogales, Sonora; Ciudad Juárez, Chihuahua; Nuevo Laredo, Tamaulipas; and Mexico City between July 2009 and June 2012; and (3) complementary ethnographic research and more than two hundred in-depth interviews across the five field sites during our study period. We anticipate carrying out a third wave of the MBCS in the years to come. In addition to continuing to collect data along Mexico's northern border, we also plan to expand the MBCS into Guatemala, Honduras, and El Salvador.

MBCS I: THE NOGALES PROJECT

By FY 2002, approximately 36 percent of all U.S. Border Patrol apprehensions and 42 percent of known border-crosser deaths along the United States' southwestern border were occurring in southern Arizona (i.e., the Tucson sector), a pattern that would continue for nearly the next decade. But unauthorized Mexican migrants had not always crossed and died in high numbers in this region; increased border enforcement efforts beginning in the mid-1990s effectively funneled unauthorized migration away from traditional urban crossing points in areas such as Tijuana–San Diego and Juárez–El Paso into southern Arizona (Dunn 1996; Andreas 2000; Cornelius 2001; Rubio-Goldsmith et al. 2006). Nevertheless, relatively little scholarship focused exclusively on unauthorized migration in southern Arizona (for an exception, see O'Leary 2008, 2009), and to the best of our knowledge, no quantitative studies had surveyed migrants in a systematic manner about their border-crossing, apprehension, and deportation experiences in the region. This was a major impetus that inspired our research team to carry out the first wave of the MBCS. During the summer of 2007, Daniel E. Martínez and Kristin Klingman began traveling to Nogales, Sonora, to informally speak with recently repatriated Mexican migrants in a migrant shelter to learn more about their experiences crossing the Sonora-Arizona border. These conversations played a vital role in helping inform the contents of our survey questionnaire.

Between October 2007 and July 2009, a research team of eleven graduate students from the University of Arizona in the academic disciplines of sociology, Mexican American studies, Latin American studies, and geography made over one hundred trips from Tucson, Arizona, to Nogales, Sonora, and completed 415 in-depth surveys consisting of 350 questions each. The project was approved by the University of Arizona's Institutional Review Board. The MBCS I consisted of several survey modules that focused on the conditions and circumstances of migrants' most recent crossing, apprehension, processing, and deportation experiences; migrants' knowledge and exposure to humanitarian aid organizations and anti-immigrant mobilization efforts in the Sonora-Arizona region (i.e., the Minutemen); the role of religion in migrants' decisions to migrate; and demographic characteristics.

THE RESEARCH SITE

All surveys in Wave I were completed at a migrant shelter in Nogales, Sonora. The shelter, which was privately owned and operated, was an ideal site in which to carry out our postdeportation survey for several reasons. First, the shelter, which operates on a daily basis from 7 p.m. to 7 a.m., was the only one in Nogales at the time that provided lodging for up to three nights to both men and women. Second, repatriated migrants were systematically brought to the shelter several times throughout the evening by Mexican federal agents from Grupos Beta and Repatriación Humana directly from the ports of entry as they were returned to Mexico by U.S. officials. Finally, because Nogales, Sonora, was beginning to experience unprecedented levels of drug trafficking–related violence and because we were sensitive to the vulnerable states in which many migrants found themselves after being repatriated, the shelter provided a safe space for researchers and study participants in which to interact (see Slack, Martínez, and Vandervoet 2011; Martínez, Slack, and Vandervoet 2013; and Slack, Martínez, and Vandervoet, chap. 3 of this volume).

SELECTION CRITERIA

In order to be eligible to participate in the first wave of the MBCS, potential participants must have been at least eighteen years old and speak Spanish well enough to complete the survey. Only two potential participants were unable to complete the survey because they only spoke an indigenous language. In addition to the age and language requirements, potential participants must have also attempted a border crossing into Arizona, been apprehended by U.S. authorities, and been repatriated to Mexico, all within six months of being surveyed. Despite this six-month cutoff, the overwhelming majority of MBCS I respondents were surveyed a week after their most recent crossing attempt. We established these selection criteria in order to (1) reduce potential retrospective bias and (2) be able to make reasonable comparisons between migrants who had crossed in a similar time and geographic location.

SAMPLING

The shelter maintained a daily bed list, which tracked each guest's name, age, sex, and state of origin in Mexico. But we opted not to randomly sample potential participants using the shelter's bed list in order to preserve our respondents' anonymity. Instead, we utilized a spatial-sampling technique that consisted of randomly selecting every kth person, where k equals a randomly generated number from one to nine in five previously defined areas of the shelter, such as in a commons space, sleeping quarters, near the water cooler, and in a hallway as

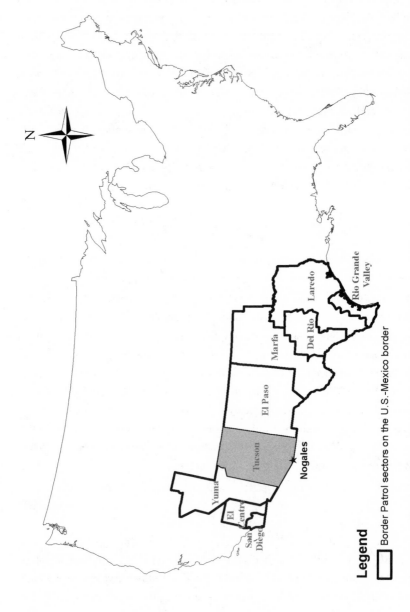

Legend

☐ Border Patrol sectors on the U.S.-Mexico border

FIGURE 1.1 Border patrol sectors on the U.S.-Mexico border. Source: Rolando Díaz Caravantes, El Colegio de Sonora.

shelter guests returned from eating. Each randomly selected potential participant was approached discreetly by one of our research team members, screened for eligibility, and invited to participate in the survey if they met the eligibility criteria. In all, we screened 688 people, 429 of whom were eligible to participate in the study. Those who were not eligible had (a) never crossed the border and were on their way up to do so or (b) had last crossed over six months before being screened. Among the 429 migrants eligible to participate, only fourteen refused to participate, resulting in a 96.7 percent response rate.

WEIGHTING THE DATA AND COMPARABLE DATA SOURCES ON REPATRIATED MEXICAN MIGRANTS

One potential limitation of the first wave of the MBCS is that we sampled exclusively among migrants who relied on the services of the shelter. In other words, "shelter goers" may be qualitatively distinct from "non–shelter goers." With the exception of migrants with local contacts, or in rare cases in which migrants from higher socioeconomic backgrounds were able to afford to stay in a hotel after being repatriated, we are confident that the majority of migrants repatriated to Nogales, Sonora, were transported to the shelter by Mexican federal agents. However, we attempted to increase the representativeness of our sample and reduce any potential discrepancies between "shelter goers" and "non–shelter goers" by applying poststratification probability weights constructed using data on sex, age, and Mexican region of origin from monthly U.S. Border Patrol apprehension statistics in the Tucson sector during our study period (2007–2009). Because *apprehensions* may be somewhat different from *repatriations* due to various factors (e.g., lateral repatriations, transfers between detention facilities across the southwestern United States, etc.), we would have ideally constructed our weights using repatriation data collected by Mexico's Instituto Nacional de Migración (INM). However, INM did not begin systematically collecting data on Mexican state of origin until 2010; therefore, we relied on Border Patrol apprehension statistics to construct the probability weights.

Table 1.1 (below) provides descriptive statistics for sex, age, region of origin, and the top six Mexican states represented in MBCS for our unweighted and weighted MBCS samples. The table also provides information for these characteristics based on monthly U.S. Border Patrol apprehensions in the Tucson sector between 2007 and 2009. As noted, the representativeness of our

TABLE 1.1 Descriptive statistics for sex, age, and place of origin for MBCS I and U.S. Border Patrol data

CHARACTERISTICS	MBCS I (UNWEIGHTED), OCTOBER 2007–JULY 2009 (N = 415)	U.S. BORDER PATROL APPREHENSIONS, TUCSON SECTOR, FY 2007–FY 2009[a] (N = 937,735 FOR WHICH SEX WAS RECORDED; N = 901,770 FOR WHICH REGION/STATE WAS RECORDED[b])	MBCS I (WEIGHT 1), OCTOBER 2007–JULY 2009 (N = 415)	MBCS I (WEIGHT 2), OCTOBER 2007–JULY 2009 (N = 415)
Male	88%	83%	86%	87%
Female	12%	16%	14%	13%
Age (mean)	30.5	27.0	32.2	30.4
Region of birth in Mexico				
North	9%	14%	15%	14%
Traditional	20%	23%	24%	23%
Central	21%	31%	31%	31%
South	50%	31%	30%	33%
Top six Mexican states in MBCS I				
Chiapas	17%	7%	11%	12%
Guerrero	11%	7%	6%	6%
Oaxaca	10%	9%	6%	6%
Veracruz	10%	7%	7%	7%
Puebla	6%	10%	7%	7%
Michoacán	6%	8%	5%	5%

Note: Sample size may vary slightly by characteristic because of missing data. Percentages may not sum to 100 because of rounding.

[a] Data were used to construct probability weights.

[b] Data are for migrants eighteen years of age and older.

sample increases once the probabilities weights are applied (see Martínez et al. 2017 for an extensive overview of MBCS I's methodology and a thorough discussion of the representativeness of the sample relative to known population characteristics).

MBCS II: VIOLENCE AND (IN)SECURITY

After completing data collection for the first wave of the MBCS, Jeremy Slack, Daniel E. Martínez, and Scott Whiteford received funding support from the Ford Foundation Mexico to execute a second wave of the project across the U.S.-Mexico border. The aim of the second wave was to not only continue to collect generalizable data on migrants' border crossing, apprehension, and deportation experiences but also to focus on the various forms of violence migrants encounter during their migration trajectories. After scouting potential field sites, data collection for the second wave began in July of 2009 and continued until September of 2012.

THE RESEARCH SITES

Throughout the second wave of the MBCS, we continued to collect data in Nogales, Sonora, but also expanded data-collection efforts into Tijuana and Mexicali, Baja California; Ciudad Juárez, Chihuahua; Nuevo Laredo, Tamaulipas; and Mexico City. Doing so allowed us to focus on important geographic variations in migrants' experiences across the border. The Mexican cities of Tijuana, Mexicali, Nogales, and Nuevo Laredo received the highest numbers of repatriations/deportations in the lead up to the second wave of the project, making them ideal sites in which to survey repatriated migrants. We chose Ciudad Juárez despite a relatively low number of repatriations to the city because Juárez was experiencing unprecedented levels of drug trafficking–related violence in 2009, and we were interested in understanding how this violence affected migrants' experiences postdeportation. We also completed surveys in Mexico City to examine how the Mexican Interior Repatriation Program (MIRP) operated, which was a program that sent migrants apprehended in the Tucson sector to Mexico City during the summer months. This program has since been expanded. In total, our sample cities accounted for 66 percent of all repatriations to Mexico in 2011 (Instituto Nacional de Migración 2011).

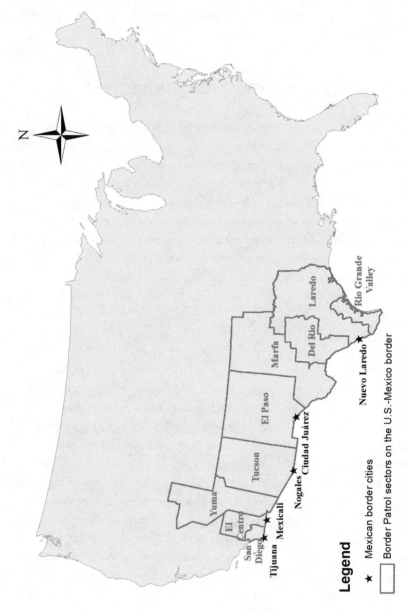

FIGURE 1.2 Mexican border cities along the U.S.–Mexico border. Source: Rolando Díaz Caravantes, El Colegio de Sonora.

Legend

★ Mexican border cities

☐ Border Patrol sectors on the U.S.-Mexico border

We conducted surveys and interviews in migrant shelters and at ports of entry as migrants were repatriated to Mexico. Generally, shelters were the preferred setting, as our surveys were quite lengthy and we wanted to have a relatively safe, low-pressure atmosphere where we could speak one-on-one with our study participants. Shelters generally do not allow for multiple entrances and exits on a given day, meaning that once migrants enter a shelter, they typically do not depart until the following morning. Few shelters had televisions, radios, or computers, and cell phones were often not allowed, which ultimately allowed researchers to speak with respondents with few distractions.

While none of the shelters in which we worked were officially operated by the government, we generally conducted fieldwork in shelters that had formal relationships with the Mexican government. This ensured that the shelters would have a large number of deportees brought directly there by Grupos Beta, the Instituto Nacional de Migración, or a state agency such as the Instituto Tamaulipeco. This helped increased the representativeness of the samples drawn in these shelters.

SELECTION CRITERIA

In order to be eligible to participate in Wave II of the MBCS, a potential participant had to have attempted their most recent border crossing sometime after September 11, 2001, have been apprehended by any U.S. authority (either while crossing the border or in the interior United States), and have been deported to Mexico within a month before being surveyed. These selection criteria are somewhat expanded when compared with the selection criteria used in the first wave of the MBCS. We established these criteria in order to capture a larger sample of migrants who had been residing within the United States for a longer period of time. This allowed us to compare and contrast the experiences of migrants who had been caught while crossing the border and those who had been apprehended in the interior United States.

SAMPLING

When collecting data, we would generally arrive slightly before or at the time that each shelter opened, which was usually between 5 p.m. and 7 p.m. Once a sizable group had arrived, we would present the members of the research team and the aims of the project. For instance, in Nogales, Sonora, deportees would wait in a chapel at the shelter to be checked into the shelter for the night. This was an ideal setting for us to introduce ourselves, identify for whom we worked, and describe what we would be doing at the shelter that evening. Once people were then checked in, read the rules of the shelter, and assigned a bunk, we would engage in a spatial-sampling technique, selecting every kth person in a previously defined area of the shelter.

When completing surveys at ports of entry, we again randomly selected every kth person after they entered into Mexico and were registered with the Instituto Nacional de Migración. In both the shelters and at the ports of entry, researchers randomly selected potential participants, screened them for eligibility, and invited them to participate in the survey. In all, we completed 1,109 surveys with eligible respondents and achieved a 94 percent response rate. Although we collected data between 2009 and 2012, 90 percent of the surveys were completed in 2011.

WEIGHTING THE DATA AND COMPARABLE DATA
SOURCES ON REPATRIATED MEXICAN MIGRANTS

As with the first wave, we constructed and applied poststratification probability weights to increase the representativeness of our sample and reduce potential bias stemming from surveying migrant shelters and official ports of entry, but only in a limited number of locations. We followed a similar procedure for the construction of weights for MBCS II as we did in the first wave. The MBCS II weights adjust sample percentages of sex, region of origin, and area of repatriation to match the known population or alternative population estimates of these percentages. The repatriated Mexican migrant population information for the year 2011 comes from Instituto Nacional de Migración data on sex and area of repatriation and EMIF-Norte's data on region of origin.

The primary goal of weighting on these characteristics is to correct for the sampling design's oversampling of migrants from southern Mexico and the undersampling of migrants from northern Mexico. In addition, MBCS II had a larger proportion of females (17.6%) than represented in INM data (9.8%). Unlike the first wave of the MBCS, we constructed a single sampling weight by employing an iterative proportional fitting, or raking, method for MBCS II (Deming and Stephan 1940). We employ this weighting method for two reasons: (1) we were interested in weighting on multiple migrant characteristics and (2) because the marginal totals for the characteristics in the 2011 population are known (e.g., 90.2% were male or 2.4% were repatriated to Mexico City) across all three characteristics, but joint distributions (e.g., the percentage of those repatriated to Mexico City who were also male, etc.) in the population are unknown (Deming and Stephan 1940). To avoid the construction of weights with values greater than ten, we were forced to omit respondents repatriated to Coahuila (N = 6). Unfortunately, about 11 percent of the population was repatriated through Coahuila, but neither of the cities that received repatriated migrants was included in the sample frame, narrowing the generalizability of the results to all adults over the age of eighteen repatriated through the remaining states. Table 1.2 compares the unweighted and weighted MBCS estimates to the EMIF and INM data. The representativeness of the sample increases once the weights are applied.

LIMITATIONS OF WAVES I AND II

MBCS data are not without limitations. First, because of safety concerns, we relied notably on migrant shelters as field sites, particularly in the first wave of the MBCS. However, during the years we conducted our fieldwork, it became standard practice for the Mexican government (e.g., federal, state, or local officials) to transport people directly to the shelters to keep them off the streets. The construction and application of probability weights, however, helps overcome some of the potential discrepancies between those who relied on the services of a shelter and those who did not (see Martínez et al. 2017). Second, given our eligibility criteria in both waves, our data are representative only of migrants who were apprehended, either while crossing the border or by local law enforcement after successfully arriving at their U.S. destination, and repatriated/deported to Mexico. While it is possible that some people engage in undocumented migration and never interact with U.S. authorities, with the increase in border enforcement as well as interior enforcement of immigration laws, it is becoming increasingly rare to find such individuals. The MBCS is not intended to replace existing research projects focusing on unauthorized Mexican migration but rather aims to complement those studies by providing an in-depth look at the crossing/deportation experience.

A third limitation of the MBCS is that the data are cross-sectional in nature and therefore only represent a snapshot of one's most recent border-crossing attempt and repatriation/deportation. Some respondents had never successfully

TABLE 1.2 Descriptive statistics of sex, age, and place of origin for MBCS II across weighted and unweighted data sets

CHARACTERISTICS	MBCS II (UNWEIGHTED, N = 1,109)	MBCS II (WEIGHTED,[a] N = 1,103)	EMIF (WEIGHTED, N = 7,227)	INM (N = 349,806)
Male	82%	90%	87%	90%
Female	18%	10%	13%	10%
Age (mean)	31.9	32.1	31.1	–
18–23	21%	19%	22%	–
24–28	18%	18%	23%	–
29–33	19%	21%	20%	–
34–39	22%	24%	17%	–
40+	20%	19%	18%	–
Region of origin				
North	13%	20%	20%	–
Traditional	34%	35%	35%	–
Central	21%	19%	19%	–
South	32%	26%	26%	–
Top six Mexican states in MBCS II				
Oaxaca	10%	8%	7%	–
Michoacán	9%	9%	9%	–
Guerrero	8%	7%	6%	–
Jalisco	6%	6%	5%	–
Veracruz	6%	6%	7%	–
Puebla	6%	5%	5%	–

Note: Sample size may vary slightly by characteristic because of missing data. Percentages may not sum to 100 because of rounding. Data set used for weighting (EMIF) includes only persons eighteen years of age or older who were interviewed by EMIF researchers in 2011, excluding non-Mexicans.
[a]Weighted by sex, region of origin, and region of repatriation.

arrived at their desired destination in the United States, while others had crossed successfully dozens of times. Despite gathering baseline information on a migrant's number of lifetime crossing attempts and apprehensions, we only documented details regarding people's most recent border-crossing and repatriation/deportation experience to be able to make reasonable comparisons between cases. As such, this approach did not allow us to consider respondents' experiences during trips that had taken place before their most recent crossing attempt.

A COMPARISON OF THE WAVE I
AND WAVE II SAMPLES

We surveyed migrants through two different waves of the MBCS: MBCS I, which was carried out exclusively in Nogales, Sonora, between October 2007 and July 2009, and MBCS II, which was executed between July 2009 and September 2012 in Tijuana and Mexicali, Baja California; Nogales, Sonora; Ciudad Juárez, Chihuahua; Nuevo Laredo, Tamaulipas; and Mexico City. Table 1.3 (below) provides a side-by-side comparison of several selected characteristics from both waves of the MBCS.

Although the two waves vary in terms of the time periods and geographic locations in which the data were collected, the eligibility requirements, and the data used in the construction of the weights to increase the representativeness of the samples (e.g., monthly U.S. Border Patrol apprehension statistics in MBCS I vs. INM repatriations and EMIF-Norte data in MBCS II), there are striking similarities between the two samples in terms of respondents' demographic characteristics and border-crossing experiences. For example, the two samples line up quite well in terms of age, sex, educational attainment, lifetime crossing attempts, lifetime apprehensions, coyote use, days spent crossing the border during one's most recent attempt, physical abuse by U.S. authorities when apprehended, and family currently living in the United States. Collectively, these descriptive findings point to high levels of reliability and validity between the two weighted samples and suggest that our data are generalizable to apprehended and repatriated/deported Mexican migrants.

The two samples, however, do vary in some respects. For instance, there are notable differences in Mexican region of origin, indigenous-language speakers, coyote fees, encounters with *bajadores* ("stickup crews"), lived U.S. experience, and detention after apprehension. These differences can be explained by several factors. First, the expanded selection criteria between the two projects (e.g., having attempted a border crossing since 9/11 in MBCS II rather than in the past six months in MBCS I) resulted in more respondents with greater lived experience in the United States being surveyed in MBCS II when compared with MBCS I. Second, the inclusion of other field sites beyond Nogales, Sonora, led a more representative cross section of respondents from diverse sending communities that rely on other important crossing points along the border (e.g., Southern California and South Texas) in MBCS II. And third, notable changes in border and immigration enforcement—such as the recent focus on interior

TABLE 1.3 Comparisons of MBCS Wave I and Wave II by selected characteristics

CHARACTERISTICS	MBCS I (WEIGHTED), NOGALES (2007–2009)	MBCS II (WEIGHTED), TIJUANA, MEXICALI, NOGALES, JUÁREZ, N. LAREDO, AND MEXICO CITY (2009–2012)
Demographics		
Age (mean)	32 years	32 years
Male	86%	90%
Female	14%	10%
Years of education	7.1 years	8.1 years
Indigenous-language speaker	20%	8%
Region of origin		
North	15%	20%
Traditional	24%	35%
Central	31%	19%
South	30%	26%
Crossing experience		
Lifetime crossings (median)	3 attempts	3 attempts
Lifetime apprehensions (median)	2 times	3 times
Used a coyote or guide	71%	71%
Coyote fee (among coyote users)	$1,621	$2,314
Days spent traveling during last crossing	2.4 days	2.2 days
Encountered *bajadores*	31%	14%
Successfully arrived at U.S. destination on most recent attempt?	n/a	39%
Social ties to the United States		
Have lived or worked in United States	68%	75%
How long (in years)?	7.5 years	8.8 years
Current home in United States	16%	30%
Family currently living in United States	77%	81%
U.S.-citizen family members	n/a	49%
U.S.-citizen children	n/a	20%
Immigration Enforcement		
Physical abuse by U.S. authorities	12%	12%
Verbal abuse by U.S. authorities	34%	20%
Detained after processing	24%	38%
Operation Streamline	n/a	24%
Secure Communities	n/a	25%
Future crossing intentions (cross again in future?)[a]		
Yes	41%	55%
No	49%	23%
Don't know	10%	22%
Sample size	N = 415	N = 1,109

Note: Sample size may vary slightly by characteristic because of missing data.

[a]MBCS I asked "Do you plan on crossing the border again, or not?"; MBCS II asked "Is it possible that you will cross again sometime in the future, or not?"

removals, increased formal deportations, and the adoption of "zero-tolerance" policies such as Operation Streamline, which is aimed at reducing unauthorized entry and reentry—help explain why the cost of hiring coyotes and the likelihood of detention increased between MBCS I and MBCS II.

Drawing on our insights gained during MBCS I, we were able to include several questions in MBCS II that were not asked of respondents in the first wave. For instance, in MBCS I we did not inquire as to whether someone had successfully arrived at their U.S. destination after their most recent crossing attempt. We asked this question in MBCS II and found that 39 percent had managed to avoid detection near the border and arrived at their destination. In a similar vein, in the first wave we did not systematically gather information on migrants' experience with Operation Streamline, which was implemented in the Tucson sector in 2008, after the data collection had already begun. And given the selection criteria used in the first wave, we did not have a sizable subsample of people who were apprehended in the interior of the United States through Secure Communities. Nevertheless, we were able to make adjustments in MBCS II to ensure we captured migrants' experiences with these enforcement programs. As noted in table 1.3, 24 percent and 25 percent of MBCS II respondents were processed through Operation Streamline or caught as a consequence of Secure Communities, respectively. Furthermore, we neglected to capture information regarding migrants' ties to U.S.-citizen family members in the first wave, which is something that has become increasingly important to examine empirically as formal deportations and interior removals, leading to family separation and dissolution, have increased. These are just a few of the examples in which the MBCS II has built on and expanded the scope of our project.

ETHNOGRAPHIC FIELDWORK AND IN-DEPTH INTERVIEWS

Jeremy Slack collected the majority of the qualitative data during the scoping phase of research (2008–2010), during data collection (2010–2012), and in a follow-up year funded by the Social Science Research Council and the Open Society Foundation's Drugs, Security, and Democracy fellowship. There were two primary goals of this ethnographic research: first, to provide rich human accounts of how the violence of the border affects people, and second, to explore topics that we deemed too risky to include in the survey. Risky topics included questions about drug trafficking, drug-trafficking organizations, and other illicit activities along the border.

In general, in-depth interviews were conducted alongside surveys. Slack kept a separate set of notes, which included quotes and narratives of previous deportations or instances of abuse that would not appear in our quantitative survey instrument. These accounts were recorded by hand, connected to the corresponding survey using a unique identifier, and typed a few hours after the interview. This approach allowed us to make comparisons between data recorded in the survey instrument and information gathered in the in-depth interviews. It also gave us the ability to pair demographic information captured in the survey with the qualitative field notes. We often include these complementary vignettes alongside our quantitative data to better understand the broader context of these accounts.

With two exceptions—migrants' experiences with kidnapping and witnessing violence against women—all qualitatively collected data pertained to migrants' *most recent* crossing, apprehension, and deportation experiences. Kidnapping and witnessing violence against women were relatively rare events that could occur at a number of different points during the journey or after deportation. Thus, in order to capture as much information on these topics as possible, it was necessary to expand the temporal selection criteria regarding these specific experiences (e.g., "Have you ever experienced . . ." versus "Thinking about your most recent crossing attempt, did you experience . . .").

Because of the time involved, qualitative research rarely follows a random design; rather, details regarding certain topics and experiences are actively sought. However, the addition of in-depth stories about kidnapping, violence against women, and the dynamics of abuse by U.S. Border Patrol and law enforcement officials can provide vivid details about why these events occur. Thus, we were able to record vital information that would otherwise be overlooked in a quantitative research design by complementing the random nature and exclusive selection criteria of survey research with a qualitative approach.

On the other hand, ethnography is the most appropriate tool for researching the criminal, hidden, and violent world of the border. Staying at the shelters at night and spending the day walking with migrants as they search for work, try to get money for a ride home, or arrange another trip across the border offers greater insight into the complex interactions between migrants and the obstacles they must navigate to stay safe. For instance, this exposes processes such as the recruitment of deportees and migrants into drug-trafficking organizations as well as the deceptive techniques criminals use to kidnap and extort migrants. The intersection of drug-related violence and migration is an important, under-explored topic addressed in this volume. By researching kidnappings in chapter 9, Slack explores the hidden uses of kidnapping that are far more complex than simple ransom narratives that dominate media and popular conceptions. In chapter 8, Slack and Campbell also explore how drug cartels have created sets of rules for human smugglers to follow, mimicking the state's prohibitions, taxation, and regulation for the clandestine world.

We view these as complementary research activities. Because we hope to continue the MBCS with future waves of research, the qualitative component of our research will not only address unanswered questions from the survey but will also potentially generate new avenues of inquiry to be included in subsequent quantitative survey instruments. We hope that our postdeportation methodology—which includes a survey component, in-depth interviews, and ethnography—will prove beneficial not only to the advancement of migration-deportation studies but for mixed-methods research in general as well.

CONCLUSION

With the drastic changes in border and immigration enforcement over the past decade, it is important for scholars to explore new and innovative methodological approaches. While the impact and contribution of the MMP, MMFRP, and EMIF cannot be overstated, the addition of other quantitative approaches to the migration canon could develop the literature into new and unexplored territory, especially as patterns within migration systems shift as a result of global economic, social, political, and environment forces. Namely, the MBCS's focus on human rights, violence, the crossing experience, and specific immigration enforcement programs complements the extant literature. In this chapter we have given a thorough overview of the methodological approaches to data collection and the general aims of the MBCS. We stress that this research provides generalizable data for long-held questions related to border enforcement practices. Moreover, by complementing this quantitative data with qualitative ethnographic work, it expands on methodological approaches to mixed-methods research.

This volume outlines the various findings and theoretical contributions of the MBCS, highlighting the different areas where our postdeportation methodology has the potential to contribute to the broader field of migration and deportation studies as a whole. We urge scholars to take up seriously the challenges of empirical research on deportation as the number of formal removals (often combined with a criminal charge such as illegal entry or illegal reentry) has quickly surpassed the number of returns (an administrative process), resulting in greater criminalization of noncitizens. This highlights the fact that not all deportations are created equally. Careful research is required to understand the different mechanisms of removal that make up the deportation regime (De Genova and Peutz 2010). The MBCS attempts to disentangle these different processes, highlighting the specific mechanisms of criminalization and violence that underlie our immigration enforcement apparatus.

NOTES

1. For a complete list of publications, see http://mmp.opr.princeton.edu/research /publications-en.aspx.
2. For a detailed overview of the MMP's methodology, see http://mmp.opr.princeton .edu/research/studydesign-en.aspx.
3. For a description of EMIF-Norte's methodology, see http://www.colef.mx/emif /eng/bases_metodologicas.php.

REFERENCES

Andreas, Peter. 2000. *Border Games: Policing the U.S.-Mexico Divide.* Ithaca, N.Y.: Cornell University Press.

Colegio de la Frontera Norte. 2017. "Bases Metodológicas." https://www.colef.mx/emif /bases_metodologicas.php#.

Cornelius, Wayne A. 2001. "Death at the Border: Efficacy and Unintended Consequences of US Immigration Control Policy." *Population and Development Review* 27 (4): 661–85.

Cornelius, Wayne A., David Fitzgerald, Pedro Lewin Fischer, and L. Muse-Orlinoff. 2010. *Mexican Migration and the U.S. Economic Crisis: A Transnational Perspective.* San Diego, Calif.: Center for Comparative Immigration Studies.

Cornelius, Wayne A., and Jessa M. Lewis. 2007. *Impacts of Border Enforcement on Mexican Migration: The View from Sending Communities.* San Diego, Calif.: Center for Comparative Immigration Studies.

De Genova, Nicholas. 2002. "Migrant 'Illegality' and Deportability in Everyday Life." *Annual Review of Anthropology* 31: 419–47.

De Genova, Nicholas, and Nathalie Mae Peutz. 2010. *The Deportation Regime: Sovereignty, Space, and the Freedom of Movement.* Durham, N.C.: Duke University Press.

Deming, W. E., and F. F. Stephan. 1940. "On a Least Squares Adjustment of a Sampled Frequency Table When the Expected Marginal Totals Are Known." *Annals of Mathematical Statistics* 11 (4): 427–44.

Denzin, Norman K., and Yvonna S. Lincoln. 2005. *The Sage Handbook of Qualitative Research*: Thousand Oaks, Calif.: Sage.

Dunn, Timothy. 1996. *The Militarization of the US-Mexico Border 1978–1992: Low-Intensity Conflict Doctrine Comes Home*. Austin: CMAS Books, University of Texas at Austin.

Golash-Boza, Tanya Maria. 2015. *Deported: Immigrant Policing, Disposable Labor, and Global Capitalism*. New York: New York University Press.

Gomberg-Muñoz, Ruth. 2011. *Labor and Legality: An Ethnography of a Mexican Immigrant Network*. New York: Oxford University Press.

Hagan, Jacqueline M. 2008. *Migration Miracle: Faith, Hope, and Meaning on the Undocumented Journey*. Cambridge, Mass.: Harvard University Press.

Hagan, J. M., and H. R. Ebaugh. 2003. "Calling upon the Sacred: Migrants' Use of Religion in the Migration Process." *International Migration Review* 37 (4): 1145–62.

Instituto Nacional de Migración. 2011. "Boletín mensual de estadísticas migratorias 2011." Secretaria de Gobernación. Mexico City: Instituto Nacional de Migración. http://www.politicamigratoria.gob.mx/work/models/SEGOB/CEM/PDF/Estadisticas/Boletines_Estadisticos/2011/BoletinEst2011.pdf.

Kanstroom, Daniel. 2007. *Deportation Nation: Outsiders in American History*. Cambridge, Mass.: Harvard University Press.

Katz, Jack. 2001. "From How to Why: On Luminous Description and Causal Inference in Ethnography (Part 1)." *Ethnography* 2 (4): 443–73.

———. 2002. "From How to Why: On Luminous Description and Causal Inference in Ethnography (Part 2)." *Ethnography* 3 (1): 63–90.

Martínez, Daniel E., Jeremy Slack, Kraig Beyerlein, Prescott Vandervoet, Kristin Klingman, Paola Molina, Shiras Manning, Melissa Burham, Kylie Walzak, Kristen Valencia, and Lorenzo Gamboa. 2017. "The Migrant Border Crossing Study: A Methodological Overview of Research Along the Sonora-Arizona Border." *Population Studies* 71 (2): 249–64. doi:10.1080/00324728.2017.1306093.

Martínez, Daniel E., Jeremy Slack, and Prescott Vandervoet. 2013. "Methodological Challenges and Ethical Concerns of Researching Marginalized and Vulnerable Populations." In *Uncharted Terrains: New Directions in Border Research Methodology, Ethics, and Practice*. Edited by Anna Ochoa O'Leary, Colin M. Deeds, and Scott Whiteford, 101–20. Tucson: University of Arizona Press.

Massey, Douglas S. 1987. "Understanding Mexican Migration to the United States." *American Journal of Sociology* 92 (6): 1372–1403.

Massey, Douglas S., and Rene Zenteno. 2000. "A Validation of the Ethnosurvey: The Case of Mexico-US Migration." *International Migration Review* 34 (3): 766–93.

Núñez, Guillermina Gina, and Josiah McC. Heyman. 2007. "Entrapment Processes and Immigrant Communities in a Time of Heightened Border Vigilance." *Human Organization* 66 (4): 354–65.

O'Leary, Anna Ochoa. 2008. "Close Encounters of the Deadly Kind: Gender, Migration, and Border (In)Security." *Migration Letters* 5 (2): 111–21.

———. 2009. "The ABCs of Migration Costs: Assembling, Bajadores, and Coyotes." *Migration Letters* 6 (1): 27–35.

Passel, J., D. Cohn, and A. Gonzalez-Barrera. 2012. *Net Migration from Mexico Falls to Zero—and Perhaps Less.* Washington, D.C.: Pew Hispanic Center.

Rubio-Goldsmith, Raquel, M. Melissa McCormick, Daniel Martínez, and Inez Magdalena Duarte. 2006. *The "Funnel Effect" and Recovered Bodies of Unauthorized Migrants Processed by the Pima County Office of the Medical Examiner, 1990–2005.* Tucson: Binational Migration Institute, Mexican American Studies and Research Center, University of Arizona.

Samora, Julian. 1971. *Los Mojados: The Wetback Story.* Notre Dame, Ind.: University of Notre Dame Press.

Slack, J., D. Martínez, and P. Vandervoet. 2011. "Methods of Violence: Researcher Safety and Adaptability in Times of Conflict." *Practicing Anthropology* 33 (1): 33–37.

Small, Mario. 2009. "'How Many Cases Do I Need?': On Science and the Logic of Case Selection in Field-Based Research." *Ethnography* 10 (1): 5–38.

Spener, David. 2009. *Clandestine Crossings: Migrants and Coyotes on the Texas-Mexico Border.* Ithaca, N.Y.: Cornell University Press.

Transactional Records Access Clearinghouse. 2014. "ICE Deportations: Gender, Age, and Country of Citizenship." http://trac.syr.edu/immigration/reports/350/.

2

VIOLENCE AND MIGRATION ON THE ARIZONA-SONORA BORDER

JEREMY SLACK AND SCOTT WHITEFORD

INTRODUCTION

ALEJANDRO'S EYES WERE VACANT, blood red, and darting randomly about the room.[1] He was scratching vigorously at his arms and shifting constantly in his seat. It was obvious that he was high, but he informed me, "No soy migrante. Soy burrero" (I am not a migrant. I am a drug mule).[2] I was taken aback by his honesty. I had spoken to other *burreros* (drug mules) before, but never while they were attempting to blend into the general population of economic migrants. At the shelter where we have been working for the previous two years, it is understood that in order to stay here, one must pretend to be a migrant. Because of this, it is rare that people admit to being professionally involved with drug trafficking, human smuggling, or robbing migrants in the desert. However, the connections between migrants and "border professionals" who engage in the clandestine border economy as a vocation represent a complicated web of structural factors and individual agency that results from the desperation and violence that envelop undocumented migration.

The year this chapter was originally written, 2010, was a particularly shocking year with regard to immigration and the border. We saw a rise in scapegoating of so-called illegals culminating in Arizona law SB 1070 to criminally prosecute undocumented migrants and require police to check immigration status. The seventy-two hopeful migrants who were shot dead at a ranch along the Texas border in Tamaulipas, allegedly by members of Los Zetas, a criminal syndicate in Mexico, represent a startling example of the escalation of violence along the border. The year ended with a record-breaking 222 bodies recovered in the Arizona desert (Soto and Martínez, 2018). These tragic events shaped the context of the research and writing of this article. Migrant deaths have since decreased in southern Arizona, but so have the number of unauthorized immigrants crossing through the region. As such, the migrant death rate in southern Arizona was a record high of 220 deaths per 100,000 apprehensions in FY 2016 (Soto and Martínez 2018).

The forces generating these types of events for Central American and Mexican migrants have been described as "structural violence" by many scholars (Nevins 2005, 2008; Spener 2009). The concept of structural violence, first developed by Johan Galtung (1969), explicitly focuses the analysis on inequality and social, political, and economic mechanisms used to create or enforce inequality and continued marginalization. "Violence is present when human beings are being influenced so that their actual somatic and mental realizations are below their potential realizations" (Galtung 1969, 168). The forces that limit people's ability to realize their full life potential also compel people to migrate or, in many cases, lose their lives. As Paul Farmer (2004, 307) wrote, "The concept of structural violence is intended to inform the study of the social machinery of oppression. Oppression is a result of many conditions, not the least of which resides in consciousness." In this article, we will discuss violence as it relates to the undocumented border-crossing experience and question the explanatory power of structural violence when it fails to take into account the heterogeneity of actions and reactions of each individual.

This article is based on qualitative research conducted in Nogales, Sonora, Mexico, which was the center for deportations in the most active border patrol sector during our fieldwork. We randomly sampled participants at a shelter for people who have been deported or repatriated from the United States to Mexico. Of the seventy-one in-depth interviews,[3] twenty-eight relayed experiences of being incarcerated in the United States, sixteen had encounters with border bandits and were robbed, nine reported contact with the drug trade during their migratory experience, seven were kidnapped, and four reported witnessing rapes of female migrants.

These numbers are indicative of the dangers that make up the invisible landscapes of history, politics, and domination present on the border (Whiteford and Whiteford 2005). Moreover, contemporary border enforcement practices—such as apprehensions, complicated processing practices by United States authorities, and criminal proceedings—separate families and groups, breaking down the social networks used by individuals to lessen the dangers of crossing. How individuals and families react and manage the vulnerability caused by structural forces represents a significant driver of violence along the border.

STRUCTURAL VIOLENCE AND BEYOND

Violence is often far more insidious than anticipated and, indeed, it is often invisible on first inspection (Bourgois 2009; Fassin 2009). It is necessary to understand how people attempting to cross the border act and react in attempts to subvert border enforcement and how these actions influence the procedures and issues that arise for the security regime. Through our firsthand experiences we have seen that this can include but is not limited to (1) different crossing patterns and strategies, (2) engaging in the drug trade, (3) human smuggling, (4) robbery, or (5) participation in the sex industry. These strategies (unless directly coerced) are attempts to defray the costs of undocumented crossing and recuperate losses that need to be repaid to moneylenders at home. It is clear that while structural factors greatly limit people's actions and motivations, individual agency is involved with the different choices people make to limit the vulnerability imposed by situations out of their control.

The concept of structural violence explicitly focuses the analysis on inequality and the social, political, and economic mechanisms used to either create or enforce the inequality and continued marginalization of a group of people. This expanded definition is useful in that it exposes the forms of violence that are not immediately visible but that lie underneath the surface, causing incredible amounts of pain and death without firing a single bullet or landing a single blow (Farmer 2003).

In the case of migration, the various U.S. organizations that are in charge of immigration and the border—Customs and Border Protection (CBP), U.S. Border Patrol (USBP), Department of Homeland Security (DHS), Immigration and Customs Enforcement (ICE), and others—control and/or punish undocumented migrants while providing little formal support for migrants' basic legal and human rights (Nevins 2005, 2008; Spener 2009). In Mexico and Central America, economic policies have led to the end of rural subsistence farming, encouraging people to migrate to urban centers or to the United States to find work (Schneider and Wolfson 2005). This leads to a system where migrants provide cheap labor and support consumption in the United States while simultaneously enduring extreme risks to their physical and emotional well-being, which threatens their survival and decreases their life expectancy. There are, however, other economic activities that can be far deadlier than migration even though they tend to follow a similar logic of desperation and necessity.

The more than 150,000 deaths associated with the drug war in Mexico between 2006 and 2014 are tied to structural violence, direct violence, and state-sanctioned violence. The lack of economic opportunity, the unquenchable appetite for drugs in the United States, and the (temporary) power associated with being a *narco* (drug kingpin) are all part of a larger structure that leads to these countless deaths.

The concept of structural violence, however, can be all encompassing when it comes to defining social ills. We seek to add specificity in the case of migration by highlighting how people act and react within these structures, especially at times and places of upheaval, change, and unfamiliarity for those involved. Structural violence frameworks can have the unfortunate tendency to neglect the way people react to marginalization and repression, in turn influencing the structures of power that ultimately create violence.

In Paul Farmer's (1996) seminal article "On Suffering and Structural Violence: A View from Below," he lays out how endemic poverty and oppressive regimes lead to a form of violence. He focuses on a man named Chouchou from Haiti and the story of his fatal beating for supposed political insurgency that amounted to little more than an offhand comment overheard by plainclothes military officers. While Farmer proceeds to analyze the position of Chouchou and others with respect to their societies, noting that their mortality rates are much higher as a result of the inequality and lack of access to goods and services, he does not discuss motivation. For our analysis, we would like to put the murderous soldiers alongside Chouchou in order to compare how and why each came to experience the structures of violence in a different manner.

In order to do this, we need to question the convoluted pathways that lead to these manifestations of violence. Chouchou and his murderers probably had much in common: ethnicity, education, poverty, etc. However, there was some point when the murderers decided to join with a more powerful force to limit their own vulnerability vis-á-vis society as a whole. Obviously, the same options are not available to everyone, but by questioning the decision to stay a nail or become a hammer, we blur the lines of victimhood and expand the continuum of violence (Bourgois 2009). However, as is the case with joining a drug cartel in Mexico, this decision can ultimately have the reverse effect, as there is far greater mortality for someone who joins the bloody conflict to control the sale of drugs to the United States than for a migrant worker. That is why we see this decision-making process as a form of violence in and of itself.

We suggest the term *poststructural violence* to describe the way people react within the confines of a situation precipitated by structural violence. While it is slightly problematic to use the word *poststructural*, as it could be interpreted that the conditions of structural violence have ended (or refer to the large body of poststructural theory, which we are deliberately avoiding), we intend *poststructural* to imply the actions undertaken to mitigate the effects of a particular individual's precarious situation. It represents passing from one set of structural concerns to another. We also do not see poststructural violence as separate from structural violence; rather, it is an overlapping situation that can be used to expand and specify the multiple layers that make up the continuum of violence. This continuum may need to be revisited in that it denotes a linear relationship that is probably not the case, as multiple forms can and do exist simultaneously, and it is this overlap that creates the landscape of violence.

Moreover, even Galtung's (1969) original discussion of structural violence questions the distinction between structural and what he calls "personal violence"—one individual acting against another. "It may be argued that the distinction is not clear at all: it disregards slights of the structural element in personal violence and the personal element in structural violence" (Galtung 1969, 177). Galtung continues by discussing the socialization process that limits personal freedoms and leads people to react violently. For instance, "a bully would be seen as the inevitable product of socialization into a violent structure: he is the rebel, systematically untrained in other ways of coping with his conflicts and frustrations because the structure leaves him with no alternatives" (Galtung 1969, 178).

As individuals arrive at the border region, they inevitably get involved with actors such as their guides, bandits, or drug traffickers who have very different agendas from the would-be crossers. This exposes people to conditions of extreme vulnerability without social or economic safeguards from either their own country or the country of destination. Not only are people newly exposed to the border, and for a brief period of time at that, but also the very area constantly undergoes changes. The ways people access the United States, both legally and illegally, constantly shift: new visa categories, different threats, new crossing areas, different modes of crossing—bikes, horses, vehicles, or walking. How people react within these structures of violence is an important and complex reality of border crossing. This is the crux of our supposition that there is a poststructural element that occurs for individuals within these contexts. It requires people to navigate a series of difficult decisions and, by attempting to move beyond the structures of violence (i.e., their vulnerability), they are taking roles that increase their chances of death while decreasing their vulnerability to structural violence.

Primo Levi's (1988) use of the "gray zone" describes the multitude of ways people react to marginalization and violence. Levi, a holocaust survivor, writes about the difficulty in distinguishing who is the victim and who is the victimizer as people within the labor camps vie for any sort of advantage that will increase the likelihood of their survival. As Philippe Bourgois and Jeff Schonberg (2009, 20) write, "Levi (1988) and other survivors assert that we do not have the right to judge the actions of inmates in the concentration camps because the gray zone was omnipotent (Steinberg 2000). He implicitly contradicts himself, however, by devoting much of his writing to eloquently dissecting the moral dilemmas of human agency at Auschwitz through detailed descriptions of individual behaviors, decisions, and interpersonal betrayals."

This is an important contribution not only to the complexity of the gray zone but also to how structural violence is malleable in the hands of the individual. Bourgois (2009) notes that there is complexity to violence that is not often acknowledged. The poststructural arena highlights the complexity of human agency while avoiding the mechanistic and paternalistic explanations and blanket victimization that may be assumed from structural violence. The following vignette is a counterpoint to the opening anecdote from Alejandro in that we see a similar set of opportunities and the difficulty involved in resisting entering into the drug trade.[4]

Luis had recently been deported from the United States back to Nogales, Mexico.[5] He had been working as a nurse in California for six years before being deported to Nogales. It was 3:00 a.m. when he arrived, so he decided to go to the bus station. While he was waiting there for the sun to rise, he was approached by four men who told him they were from a shelter and could offer him a place to sleep and eat. He started to go with the men but began to feel uneasy and tried to leave, at which point they drew guns and instructed him to get into the van. The men were armed with *cuernos de chivo*,[6] or AK-47s, and gathered a group of repatriated migrants to cross the border. Luis said that he was told to cross as a distraction so that the drug runners could see border patrol approaching and evade capture. While he was not forced to carry drugs, it is entirely plausible that he or others have been made to traffic drugs. He was told that they would kill him if he failed.

Upon arrival in Phoenix, he was held in a "safe house" and instructed to pay $3,000 or else they would not let him go. His other option was to go and kill someone to prove his loyalty. He was able to get a family member to wire transfer $2,700 but was later apprehended by ICE agents and deported to Mexico (February 18, 2009).

While it is difficult to ascertain how frequent instances like this occur, the fact that we have seen several similar instances firsthand speaks to a general worsening of the situation in the Arizona-Sonora borderlands. What is particularly interesting is the difference between the opening story about being a drug trafficker and Luis's resistance to this lifestyle. Why such variation? Moreover, Luis's decision seems far more levelheaded when compared to Alejandro's. Alejandro is far more likely to die as a result of his vocation than he would otherwise. And yet people continue to engage with drug trafficking. If Luis did not have the money to pay the ransom, perhaps he would have been more likely to take the other option, but who knows? In light of the massacre of seventy-two would-be migrants in August 2010, we must question this decision-making process yet again.

Everyone interacting with the clandestine border is attempting to navigate its perils for monetary gain, whether as an economic migrant looking for work in the United States or as a coyote (a human smuggler), *burrero* (drug mule), or *bajador* (a thief/bandit known to rob people crossing through the desert) more actively engaging with how to circumvent U.S. prohibitions of labor and commodities. The following outlines in general terms the process of crossing the border into the Arizona desert.

OVERVIEW OF UNDOCUMENTED CROSSING: THE TUCSON SECTOR

The decision to migrate is largely driven by structural forces such as international intervention, global trade, and institutions forcing millions of vulnerable people with no option other than to leave their community in search of a new livelihood (Nevins 2005; Spener 2009).

The growing militarization of the border, including the border wall, presents new risks, including the border patrol, vigilante groups, a brutal desert to cross, and ultimately unscrupulous employers. Women, children, and monolingual indigenous migrants are particularly vulnerable. Once they cross into the United States, many are apprehended in the desert, picked up at a work raid, arrested for a minor legal infraction, or have their legal permanent resident (LPR) status removed because of criminal convictions. Most are repatriated to Mexican border towns with no money for food, shelter, or transportation home.

The trip to the border for many people, especially Central Americans desperate to find work, is an expensive obstacle course that often includes dealing with abusive Mexican authorities, encountering drug gangs, the danger of being robbed or injured while riding the trains to the border, or being arrested and deported from Mexico. Mexico's Human Rights commission reported 9,758 kidnappings of immigrants from September of 2008 to February of 2009 in Mexico.[7] Nine out of 10 reported that their lives were threatened (Comisión Nacional de los Derechos Humanos 2009; for a detailed description of Central American crossing experiences, see Hagan 2008).

There are many distinct regions of the U.S.-Mexico border. The research on which this article is based was done in the Tucson sector,[8] centered by the border cities of Ambos Nogales. During our fieldwork, it was estimated that more than three-thousand people crossed the border every day in this region, while Nogales, Sonora, received a huge portion of the nearly five hundred thousand[9] deportees returned to Mexico per year (Instituto Nacional de Migración 2005). The repatriation of about one hundred thousand individuals in just one year to Nogales, Sonora (Secretaria de Relaciones Exteriores 2006), with an official population of less than two hundred thousand people (Instituto Nacional de Estadisticas y Geografia 2005), had a profound impact on the city and region.

As one of the most active sectors for USBP apprehensions, the Tucson sector has developed a sophisticated business of human smuggling and trafficking. The criminalization of unauthorized migrants and militarization of the border has led to an overlap of drug cartels that are using this area to smuggle marijuana, cocaine, heroin, and amphetamines and of coyotes smuggling people through the desert. Migrants can be used as decoys, as the case of Luis demonstrates, allowing others to escape apprehension and successfully transport drugs into the United States but also as a way to recuperate the costs of failed crossing attempts or to recruit new labor.

The ultimate form of violence against migrants passing through the border-lands is death. The National Commission for Human Rights (Comisión Nacional de los Derechos Humanos 2007) of Mexico estimates that one migrant dies every day since Operation Gatekeeper,[10] which started in San Diego in 1994 as an expansion of Operation Blockade/Hold the Line, initiated in 1993 in El Paso, Texas (Dunn 2009; Nevins 2008). Before FY 2010, the deadliest year was 2005, with estimates for the number of deaths in Arizona around 238 and 516 border wide.[11] The number of reported deaths in 1995 and 1996 was sixty-one and fifty-nine, respectively (Cornelius 2005; Nevins 2008). From 2000 to 2004, the average rose to 410 reported deaths per year (Cornelius 2005).

PROFESSIONALS ON THE BORDER: COYOTES, *BAJADORES*, AND *BURERROS*

Undocumented crossing is a dynamic and rapidly changing system that reacts to United States enforcement and to the whims of powerful transnational drug cartels. In this section, we will describe just how the different actors interact, creating a system that increases the vulnerability of migrants and shows some unintended consequences of U.S. security policies. Massey, Durand, and Malone (2002) have documented a massive increase in the percentage of undocumented migrants employing coyotes to assist them in crossing as well as a huge increase in the cost of these services. The average price to cross was over $1,600 in the mid-2000s (Comisión Nacional de los Derechos Humanos 2007), and it is clear that there have been drastic changes in the level of profitability and organization of clandestine border crossings.

Municipal police officers interviewed in Nogales, Sonora, Mexico, agreed that there had been a consolidation of migration and drug networks. Many migrants also reflected a great deal of concern about this issue. We were told of one woman's experience crossing where she suspected that the guides were really only concerned with trafficking drugs. They were a group of forty-four in all. Suddenly, the guides shouted that the *perrera* (a border patrol truck that resembles a dog catcher, hence the name) was coming. Everyone bolted, and the guides disappeared. "Why would they just leave us there if they didn't have something else more valuable?" she asked.[12] The process of locating a guide in the Sonora-Arizona region also seems to be quite different from previous research that suggests people rely mostly on guides from their hometowns (Cornelius and Lewis 2007; Lopez Castro 1998, also see Martínez, chap. 7 in this volume). As one migrant succinctly stated, "Están por todos lados. Encuentras uno que parece más o menos de confianza y te vas con el" (They are everywhere. You find one [guide/coyote][13] that seems more or less trustworthy, and off you go with him).[14] Moreover, some coyotes do collaborate with the bandits, known locally as *bajadores*, which rob migrants. One in five migrants we interviewed reported being robbed during their previous crossing attempt (based on seventy-one sem-istructured interviews).[15] A twenty-five-year-old man from Zacatecas recounted that his group was once confronted by a group of armed men with bandanas covering their faces who ordered them to hand over everything. "If you hide money, we are going to shoot you in the foot and leave you here to die."[16] Of the sixteen migrants that were robbed by *bajadores*, six explicitly accused the coyote of being involved either because the migrants were robbed and the guide was not or because other people that had used the same guide were robbed in the same fashion before. David Spener (2009) also discounts robbery as a frequent aspect of *coyotaje*. He classifies it as false *coyotaje*, an aberrant form.[17]

Complicated links between the different clandestine groups that operate in the limited space of the border-crossing corridors represent a little-understood phenomenon. The three major illicit activities in this region, run by *bajadores*, coyotes, and *narcos* through the use of drug mules known as *burreros*, make up the clandestine geography of illicit border activity. Each group maintains autonomy in some sense, but collaboration and consolidation is increasingly common. When migrants are kidnapped or held at "safe houses," usually in Phoenix, Arizona, we can clearly see how human smuggling and drug trafficking has merged.

Coyotes frequently take advantage of the well-known likelihood of robbery and convince their clients to entrust all of their money to the guide in case they encounter *bajadores*. A nineteen-year-old from Oaxaca who had attempted to cross through Agua Prieta, Sonora, Mexico, had entrusted five thousand pesos ($400 at the time) to his guide, which he lost when the coyote abandoned them in the desert. His uncle and his pregnant wife also gave their cash to the coyote for safekeeping.

On the other hand, two people reported being caught by *bajadores* but the coyote was able to reason with them and prevented the bandits from robbing the group. Another stark contrast is in the treatment of women. Four people reported seeing women being raped by *bajadores*; four others witnessed other forms of sexual abuse, such as forcing women to undress. One woman reported that *bajadores* raped a different woman in her group. Two men had tried to intervene, and they were shot and killed.[18] An older woman named Priscila said that *bajadores* raped a *muchacha* (young girl) in her group.[19] The men held a pistol to her boyfriend's head and told him that if he moves, he is going to die right now. After they had gone, the young girl that had been raped said she wished they had killed her.[20]

However, two other migrants reported that the women in their group were separated and left alone while only the men were robbed. If anything is clear from these scenarios, it is that the complicated set of rules and standards that govern the relationships between the different border actors is constantly shifting and being reevaluated. Since profit seeking does not end with robbery or payment for crossing, people are also frequently held in so-called safe houses, to be ransomed for several thousand dollars. In the seven interviews with migrants who were kidnapped, in order to be let free from the safe houses, they have been told to pay between $1,800 and $3,500 in addition to the arranged price for crossing. More work needs to be done to fully understand kidnappings, especially since the information in this paper is based on the stories of people who were apprehended by ICE or USBP during or shortly after the kidnapping, which most likely represents only a fraction of total victims.

The drug war has had an impact on the profitability of drug trafficking and has caused the cartels to diversify their income-generating activities with robberies and kidnappings (Stratfor 2008). These events have also had an impact on our research. We have seen a large decline in robberies since several *bajadores* were murdered by *narcos* in Nogales, Sonora, Mexico.[21]

Because of the vulnerability created during the migration process, individuals become more likely to accept $1,800 to cross through the desert with a backpack full of marijuana rather than attempt to find a way to come up with $1,600 to pay for a guide.[22] This choice is the aftermath of structural violence, representing something new, whereupon the individual's limited choices within a structurally controlled atmosphere lead him or her to engage with a violent system. People are dealing with the results of structural forces and deciding how best to mitigate their vulnerability and marginalization, a key example of "poststructural violence." This is obviously a difficult choice, but the drug cartels have dedicated resources to attracting as many people as possible to work in their profitable and dangerous business.

While Tony Payan (2006) has deemed non–"point of entry" (POE) drug smuggling, meaning traffic through the deserts on foot, to be an insignificant and rare phenomenon, our research, carried out in another border region, suggests a different pattern. It is definitely the case that the majority of drugs are smuggled in large trucks, and valuable drugs, such as heroin and cocaine, are probably never taken in backpacks through the desert but smuggled in dummy compartments in cars or in truck cargo. However, migrants have reported seeing over thirty *burreros* during a single attempt to cross. The following story shows both how coordinated professional drug mules have become as well as how easy it is to get stuck in the drug trade.

JOSÉ'S STORY

José, a short man with baggy clothes and a shaved head, was originally from Veracruz but had been living in Ciudad Juárez, the epicenter of the drug violence in recent years. Despite having originally crossed as a migrant to work in Los Angeles ten years ago, he had crossed the border several times with backpacks filled with marijuana. His first trip was through Magdalena, Sonora, Mexico, a town about forty miles south of the border.

Burdened by the weight of fifty pounds of marijuana and the supplies for the journey, they could only walk for short stretches. José explained that there were ten people carrying the drugs as well as a guide and the *encargado* (boss); both were armed.

José informed me that the *encargado* knows top cartel members personally. Only his word will save you if you lose a shipment of drugs. The *encargado* has to tell them that it was the *migra* (border patrol) or soldiers or *bajadores* that took the drugs. This is to ensure that no one runs off with the drugs.

They walked for three days and nights, hiding and sleeping in the day, walking at night. They diverged from the traditional migrant paths after the first day and went really high up in the "sierra," where the *migra* rarely goes. Soon they arrived at a series of ranches that helped them transport the drugs by signaling when the coast was clear and providing shelter.

Upon arrival in Tucson, Arizona, they were driven to the Tufesa bus station and sent back to Mexico. He said that they were supposed to pay him $1,300 there, but they didn't. José said he was going to go back to see them in Mexico and collect his money. He shrugged and said, "No me pagaron. Esta vez, no me pagaron" (They didn't pay me. This time they didn't pay me).[23]

José probably will be tasked with another journey through the desert in order to collect his pay. This starts a cycle that frequently ends in death or jail. People have been exposed to a form of violence and a criminal lifestyle as a direct result of the vulnerability and marginalization created by securitization of the border, United States immigration policies, the demand for drugs, and the lack of work opportunities at home. Because there is individual agency involved in the decision to participate in the drug industry, it is important to acknowledge that this violence has a social and economic utility. In David Riches's (1986) discussion of violence, he addresses the need for perpetrators to legitimize violence: the most acceptable way to do this is to establish it as a form of tactical "preemption." In the case of drug trafficking or engaging in human smuggling, migrants are preempting their vulnerable state after failing to enter the United States. Rather than meet with the possible fate of being unable to enter the United States and return home with greater debt than before, they are acting in a way that will limit the possibilities of monetary failure by gambling their lives.

POSTSTRUCTURAL VIOLENCE: CRIMINALIZATION AND SYMBOLIC DIMENSIONS

In an attempt to continue the policies of deterrence as a strategy to control undocumented migration, Operation Streamline was started in the Tucson sector during FY 2008. United States officials are selecting migrants to be prosecuted criminally for entering the United States unlawfully. Operation Streamline usually involved about seventy people being tried and almost invariably convicted en masse five days a week for entering the United States without authorization (see Green 2008). People with a criminal record in the United States or who were formally deported are sentenced anywhere from thirty days to twenty years in prison, depending on prior offenses.[24] First-time deportees are given a formal deportation as long as they plead guilty. This deportation means that the migrants now have a criminal record in the United States and would be sentenced to jail time if they return. The migrants are shackled at their feet, hands, and waist during the trial and then sent immediately to the processing center where they will be formally deported. "¡Te mata psicologicamente!" (It kills you psychologically!) said a young man sick with worry after being unable to find his wife who was not sent to the same streamline trial.[25]

The threat of a long period of incarceration is intended to deter individuals from attempting to cross again, but it also increases their vulnerability. People detained in prisons for long periods of time will be in greater need of immediate income, and the drug business can offer a tempting solution. The current tendency to prosecute immigration violations criminally, frequently detaining migrants alongside the mainstream prison population, has serious consequences for the safety and well-being of people attempting to look for work in the United States or reunite with loved ones and is yet another example of how policies generate a more criminal and dangerous situation for migrants and the border in general. A thirty-four-year-old woman from Durango explained that the prison is a very violent place, where drug use is common. She witnessed a stabbing right before she left. "I am not a bad person! I am not a bad mother! I only need to get back to my children."[26]

There are always forces at work creating vulnerability and marginalization, but as the dominant structures are controlled, in this case by the United States' efforts to criminalize a process that was once overlooked, individual reactions to repression create a different type of violence. Whether people actively decide to participate in criminal enterprises such as the drug trade or are coerced into compliance, the root causes of this action can be traced directly to the marginalization caused by structural violence. However, the agency of individuals must not be ignored. Since violence can be used as an attempt to take back power, it is important to note that people may also be engaging in illegal activities as a response to their lack of power (Arendt 1970; Riches 1986). In the case of poststructural violence, it is not simply the act of engaging in violent and dangerous activities as a result of marginalization but being directly or indirectly subversive to state-supported structures such as United States security operations on the border.

CONCLUSIONS

Moving across Mexico and through the U.S.-Mexico border is a daunting task. For those who have already made the journey once or twice before, the surprise of an increasingly militarized border comes as a shock. The increase of the number of border patrol agents on the United States side and a growing number of the military troops on the Mexican side have added to dangers for migrants crossing the border by an overall escalation of violence.

More research is needed to fully understand these processes. The border crossing is a highly dynamic situation, changing quickly in reaction to border securitization. It is a dynamic relationship between smugglers and enforcers, constantly shifting as one adapts to the other's actions and reactions. This makes an already difficult research topic even more elusive because not only are the people constantly on the move but also the experience can differ drastically from one month to the next, resulting in a lack of standardization or consistency in data.

The concept of poststructural violence highlights the role of both the United States and Mexico in exposing people to multiple forms of danger and creating a dynamic whereupon individuals are put in direct conflict with the state. When Galtung (1969) first introduced the idea of structural violence, he left the discussion open as to how personal violence and structural violence relate to one another. The articulation of physical violence between individuals is increased where structural violence affects people more once they are separated from their communities and social networks (Bourdieu 2000; Bourdieu and Wacquant 1992; Bourgois 2001; Scheper-Huges 1992; Wolseth 2008). The conditions of poststructural violence that arise on the U.S.-Mexico border intensify the risk and vulnerability created by multiple actors and forces with varied motives and goals. With little understanding or support of border legal systems or the rules of cartels and gangs, migrants run the risk of losing everything.

Exploring the depths of insecurity, crime, violence, and migration is fundamental in the struggle to influence immigration reform. As academic researchers, it is necessary to produce work that is highly relevant and does justice to the stories and people willing to share their lives with us. Moreover, it is important to reevaluate crime as the near exclusive realm of the criminologist and bring a new perspective that focuses on the inherent violence hidden behind the choices of those involved. In the case of today's dangerous and violent border-crossing dynamics, it is imperative to deepen understandings of violence and the unintended consequences of immigration policy.

NOTES

Originally published as J. Slack and S. Whiteford, "Violence and Migration on the Arizona-Sonora Border," *Human Organization* 70, no. 1 (2011): 11–21. Adapted and reprinted by permission.

1.   This and all subsequent names are pseudonyms.
2.   Personal communication, April 22, 2009.

3. Sixty-five of these interviewees are male. The shelter where we work is starkly divided by gender, and while the larger team has been working on collecting survey data from female migrants, we have not yet fully incorporated the qualitative approach into a larger research team.

4. It is important to note that we do not know exactly how or why Alejandro got involved with drug trafficking. All we know is that he had at one point entered the United States for work but returned to northern Mexico. This is undoubtedly a complicated initiation process that is not well understood.

5. This vignette appears courtesy of our colleague Paola Molina.

6. Literally, goats' horns, based on the shape of the guns.

7. The National Commission for Human Rights collected accounts from people who had been kidnapped and who had approached authorities. Four hundred ninety-one people were interviewed about their experiences in this time period. From these interviews, they estimated the number of people being held simultaneously and then arrived at the overall figure.

8. There are nine sectors along the U.S.-Mexico border. From east to west they are McAllen, Laredo, Del Rio, Marfa, El Paso, Tucson, Yuma, El Centro, and San Diego.

9. The 2006 USBP statistics represent a high of 600,000 in 2000 and 450,000 in the most recent figure available at this time. However, these statistics represent events, not people. So each individual may have two or three apprehensions. Other USBP statistics report about 100,000 individuals being repatriated to Nogales, Sonora, Mexico, in the previous year (2007).

10. Operation Gatekeeper was started in 1994. The basic strategy was to fortify urban areas so that people would be less successful in their attempts to cross there, forcing them to attempt to cross in more dangerous rural areas in the hope that this would deter people from crossing.

11. No More Deaths cites 238, while the Secretaria de Relaciones al Exterior (Mexican State Department) reports 516. *La Jornada*, August 14, 2010, http://www.jornada .unam.mx/2007/04/26/index.php?section=politica&article=007n1pol.

12. Personal communication, March 2, 2010.

13. We have found that while these terms are often interchangeable, if there are multiple people involved in the smuggling experience, the guide is the one who physically accompanies migrants through the desert, and the coyote is the one who makes the arrangements, like a manager.

14. Personal communication, June 12, 2010.

15. For another discussion of the dangers of *bajadores*, see O'Leary 2009.

16. Personal communication, April 8, 2010.

17. However, he also makes an inaccurate historical reference to *bajadores* as similar to "man snatchers" from the bracero program that steals workers from different recruiters and that has evolved into kidnapping (Spener 2009, 306n9). This would be closer to *enganchadores* (people that look for potential migrants, sometimes trying to coax them away from other coyotes) in our experience. The cooperation

between guides and bandits may take the form of a security tax to allow the coyotes to keep operating in the area, or it may be an arrangement where the guide takes a percentage of the stolen goods. However, more research is needed to fully explore these relationships.

18.   Personal communication, May 13, 2010.

19.   Because of the sensitivity of this line of questioning, for the purposes of our structured interviews, we only asked about witnessing sexual violence against women. In one-on-one interviews, when appropriate, we did ask about personal experiences.

20.   Personal communication, May 13, 2010.

21.   While we have been attempting to investigate more of the linkages between the *bajadores* and the other actors in border crime, it has become difficult since reports of robberies dropped sharply in the spring of 2009. On April 24 and May 13, 2009, bodies were found on the outskirts of Nogales, Sonora, Mexico. The two men had each been killed by strangulation and wrapped in plastic or *entamalado* (made into a *tamal*, a steamed corn-based food typical in Mexico) in the local slang, with a note attached from the cartels threatening to kill more bandits for their behavior. The first note read "esto les va a pasar a todos los que anden de bajadores, de ratas y los que apoyen con ranchos a estas personas ya los tenemos ubicados se los va cagar la madre" (This will happen to all *bajadores* or *ratas* as well as the people that help them by letting them use their ranches, we know where and who they are, you are screwed). *El Diario de Sonora*, April 24, 2009. There have been many similar murders since this event, but only one included a *narco-mensaje* (note).

22.   Figure based on three interviews with self-described *burreros*.

23.   Excerpt adapted from Jeremy Slack's field notes, September 4, 2009.

24.   There is a legal distinction between voluntary repatriation and deportation.

25.   Personal communication, September 4, 2010.

26.   Personal communication, September 4, 2009.

REFERENCES

Andreas, Peter. 2001. *Border Games: Policing the U.S.-Mexico Divide.* Ithaca, N.Y.: Cornell University Press.

Arendt, Hannah. 1970. *On Violence.* New York: Harvest Books.

Bourdieu, Pierre. 2000. *Pascalian Meditations.* Cambridge: Polity.

Bourdieu, Pierre, and Loïc J. D. Wacquant. 1992. *An Invitation to Reflexive Sociology.* Chicago: University of Chicago Press.

Bourgois, Philippe. 2001. "The Power of Violence in War and Peace: Post–Cold War Lessons from El Salvador." *Ethnography* 2 (1): 5–37.

———. 2009. "Recognizing Invisible Violence: A Thirty-Year Ethnographic Retrospective." In *Global Health in Times of Violence,* edited by Barbara Rylko-Bauer, Linda Whiteford, and Paul Farmer, 17–40. Santa Fe, N.Mex.: School of Advanced Research.

Bourgois, Philippe, and Jeff Schonberg. 2009. *Righteous Dopefiend.* Berkeley: University of California Press.

Comisión Nacional de los Derechos Humanos. 2007. *Todos saben, nadie sabe: Trece años de muerte de migrantes; reporte sobre impunidad y muerte en la frontera sur de Estados Unidos.* Annual Report. Mexico City: Comisión Nacional de los Derechos Humanos.

———. 2009. "Informe especial de la Comisión Nacional De Los Derechos Humanos sobre los casos de secuestro en contra de migrantes." June (accessed April 21, 2010; no longer posted). http://www.cndh.org.mx/INFORMES/Especiales/infEspSec Migra.pdf.

Cornelius, Wayne A. 2001. "Death at the Border: Efficacy and Unintended Consequences of United States Immigration Control Policy." *Population and Development Review* 27 (4): 661–85.

———. 2005. "Controlling 'Unwanted' Immigration: Lessons from the United States, 1993–2004." *Journal of Ethnic and Migration Studies* 31 (4): 775–94.

Cornelius, Wayne, and Jessa Lewis, eds. 2007. *Impacts of Border Enforcement on Mexican Migration: The View from Sending Communities.* La Jolla, Calif.: California Center for Comparative Immigration Studies.

Department of Homeland Security. 2010. "Performance and Accountability Report 2009." https://www.dhs.gov/publication/annual-financial-report-fiscal-year-2009.

Dunn, Timothy J. 2009. *Blockading the Border and Human Rights: The El Paso Operation That Remade Immigration Enforcement.* Austin: University of Texas Press.

Farmer, Paul. 1996. "On Suffering and Structural Violence: A View from Below." *Daedalus: Proceedings of the American Academy of Arts and Sciences* 125 (1): 261.

———. 2003. *Pathologies of Power: Health, Human Rights, and the New War on the Poor.* Berkeley: University of California Press.

———. 2004. "An Anthropology of Structural Violence." *Current Anthropology* 45 (6): 305–17.

Fassin, Didier. 2009. "A Violence of History: Accounting for AIDS in Post-Apartheid South Africa." In *Global Health in Times of Violence*, edited by Barbara Rylko-Bauer, Linda Whiteford, and Paul Farmer, 113–36. Santa Fe, N.Mex.: School of Advanced Research.

Galtung, Johan. 1969. "Violence, Peace, and Peace Research." *Journal of Peach Research* 6 (3): 167–91.

Green, Linda. 2008. "A Wink and a Nod: Notes from the Arizona Borderlands." *Dialectical Anthropology* 32: 161–67.

Hagan, Jacqueline. 2008. *Migration Miracle: Faith, Hope, and Meaning on the Undocumented Journey.* Cambridge, Mass.: Harvard University Press.

Instituto Nacional de Estadisticas y Geografia. 2005. "Conteo de Población y Vivienda." http://www.beta.inegi.org.mx/proyectos/ccpv/2005/.

Instituto Nacional de Migración. 2005. "Boletín de estadísticas migratorias." http://www.politicamigratoria.gob.mx/work/models/SEGOB/CEM/PDF/Estadisticas/Boletines_Estadisticos/2005/Cuadros2005/cuadro5.1.xls.

Levi, Primo. 1988. *The Drowned and the Saved.* New York: Summit Books.

Lopez Castro, Gustavo. 1998. "Factors That Influence Coyotes and Alien Smuggling." Accessed May 7; no longer posted. http://www.utexas.edu/lbj/uscir/binpapers/v3a -6lopez.pdf.

Martínez, Daniel. 2016. "Migrant Deaths, Border Enforcement, and Migrant Abuse." In *No Vale Nada la Vida*, edited by Rubio Goldsmith, 97–119. Tucson: University of Arizona Press.

Massey, Douglas S., Jorge Durand, and Nolan J. Malone. 2002. *Beyond Smoke and Mirrors: Mexican Immigration in an Era of Free Trade*. New York: Russell Sage Foundation.

McCombs, Brady. 2010. "Nearly 1,700 Bodies, Each One a Mystery." *Arizona Daily Star*, August 22, 2010.

Nevins, Joseph. 2005. "A Beating Worse Than Death: Imagining and Contesting Violence in the United States-Mexico Borderlands." *AmeriQuests* 2 (1): 1–25.

———. 2008. *Dying to Live: A Story of US Immigration in an Age of Global Apartheid*. New York: City Lights.

O'Leary, Anna Ochoa. 2009. "The ABCs of Migration Costs: Assembling, Bajadores, and Coyotes." *Migration Letters* 6 (1): 27–35.

Payan, Tony. 2006. *The Three United States-Mexico Border Wars: Drugs, Immigration, and Homeland Security*. Westport, Conn.: Praeger Security International.

Riches, David, ed. 1986. *The Anthropology of Violence*. Oxford: Basil Blackwell.

Rubio-Goldsmith, Raquel, M. Melissa McCormick, Daniel Martínez, and Inez Magdalena Duarte. 2006. "The Funnel Effect and Recovered Bodies of Unauthorized Migrants." Paper for the Pima County Board of Supervisors.

Scheper-Hughes, Nancy. 1992. *Death Without Weeping: The Violence of Everyday Life in Brazil*. Berkeley: University of California Press.

Schneider, Ben Ross, and Leandro Wolfson. 2005. "La organización de los intereses económicos y las coaliciones políticas en el proceso de las reformas de mercado en América Latina." *Desarrollo Económico* 45 (179): 349–72.

Secretaria de Relaciones Exteriores. 2006. "Evaluaciones del programa de repatriaciones al interior Mexico-Estados Unidos." Accessed May 12, 2010; no longer posted. http://www.sre.gob.mx/servicos/documentos/eva_finalo5.dos.

Soto, Gabriella, and Daniel E. Martínez. 2018. "The Geography of Migrant Death: Implications for Policy and Forensic Science." In *Sociopolitics of Migrant Death and Repatriation: Perspectives from Forensic Science*. Edited by Krista Latham and Alyson O'Daniel. N.p.: Springer.

Spener, David. 2009. *Clandestine Crossings: Migrants and Coyotes on the Texas–Mexico Border*. Ithaca, N.Y.: Cornell University Press.

Steinberg, Paul. 2000. *Speak You Also: A Survivor's Reckoning*. New York: Picador.

Stratfor. 2008. "Mexican Drug Cartels: Government Progress and Growing Violence." Accessed October 21, 2010; no longer posted. http://www.stratfor.com/memberships /128691/analysis/20081209_mexican_drug_cartelsgovernment_progress_and_growing _violence.

Whiteford, Linda, and Scott Whiteford. 2005. "Paradigm Change." In *Globalization, Water, and Health: Resource Management in Times of Scarcity*, edited by Linda Whiteford and Scott Whiteford, 3–16. Santa Fe, N.Mex.: School of American Research.

Wolseth, Jon. 2008. "Everyday Violence and the Persistence of Grief: Wandering and Loss Among Honduran Youths." *Journal of Latin American and Caribbean Anthropology* 13 (2): 311–35.

3

METHODS OF VIOLENCE

Researcher Safety and Adaptability in Times of Conflict

JEREMY SLACK, DANIEL E. MARTÍNEZ,
AND PRESCOTT VANDERVOET

INTRODUCTION

DURING OUR RESEARCH, we faced the difficult decision of whether to continue our fieldwork following several high-profile incidents of violence near our research site. There were a variety of opinions among the researchers involved. In this chapter, we include three different researchers' voices and opinions. These perspectives lead us to address broader issues involved with our responsibility as researchers to document the most prominent issues affecting our research localities in a reasonable albeit methodological manner.

Beginning in 2007, a group of graduate student researchers participated in a quantitative study known as the Migrant Border Crossing Study (MBCS, Wave 1) to document the experiences of migrants who had crossed through the desert in Arizona and had been apprehended by U.S. immigration authorities and returned to Mexico. Daniel E. Martínez had been the principal investigator (PI) since the fall of 2007, and Prescott Vandervoet and Jeremy Slack joined the project in October 2007 and January 2008, respectively.

The MBCS research team gathered for an emergency meeting in early October 2008. We rarely met as an entire group, as our hour-long carpooling from Tucson to our research site in the northern Mexican city of Nogales allowed for ample discussion regarding any study-related issues.[1] The survey was an attempt to gather generalizable data about the experiences of undocumented migrants during their border-crossing attempts and apprehension by U.S. authorities.

However, an incident near our research site (a shelter catering to returned and deported migrants) on October 3 raised questions about our team members' safety: a shooting occurred across the street from the shelter while four students were in the process of interviewing migrants. One person was assassinated and two others were shot and wounded. The cracking of automatic rifles was unmistakable even to those unaccustomed to the sound of gunfire. The drug war had been escalating for quite some time throughout the border region, and Nogales was experiencing levels of violence never before seen. High-profile public shootings between rival cartels had become a daily occurrence, and decapitated heads or mutilated bodies frequently appeared on the front pages of the local papers. That fall, federal and state police as well as Mexican military were deployed to Nogales, Sonora. Police helicopters and roadblocks suddenly bombarded once calm neighborhoods.

We were faced not only with the dilemma of cutting our research short but also of failing to record how drug violence affected migration. In this article, the three authors discuss the issues involved for anthropologists conducting research in a potentially dangerous environment as well as the need to create flexible research designs that do not neglect the most prominent issues affecting our research. In the sections below, we focus on the voices of three team members involved with the project to illustrate different opinions from the internal debate about whether or not to continue the research. Our analysis focuses on the challenges posed by working in dangerous situations and the need to do so in order to contribute to a broader understanding of the violence that occurs from the perspective of the researcher. The widespread concern that we were exposing ourselves to an unacceptable risk came from faculty, administration, and students. As a team, we engaged in a spirited debate with concerns from all sides being voiced. While there was (thankfully) never a formal mandate by the University of Arizona to halt all research on the border, many projects did cease or reduce their activities along the Mexican side of the border during this time. This raises a critical point: How is "danger" assessed, and when is it ethically acceptable to abandon a project for "safety" reasons?

THE MIGRANT BORDER CROSSING STUDY

The MBCS is a research project with the aim of gaining a better understanding of the sociological mechanisms and circumstances that shape migrants' most recent unauthorized crossing experiences through southern Arizona. At the time, southern Arizona had become the most important area for unauthorized crossings along the U.S.-Mexico border, as increased border enforcement efforts rerouted migration flows into the region (Rubio-Goldsmith et al. 2006). As such, a study systematically examining the unauthorized crossing experience in southern Arizona was crucial.

We conducted Wave I of the MBCS between October 2007 and August 2009. We collected many stories of kidnappings in U.S. "safe houses" or "drop houses" and of migrants forced to smuggle drugs at gunpoint. We caught glimpses of huge currents of violence that flow under the migrant stream and, in many ways, are as powerful in shaping people's experiences as the efforts of the border patrol and U.S. policy makers. A question that arises is how can one get a deeper and accurate understanding of the forces at work, and types of pressure exerted, on the average individual who attempts to work in the United States without documents? Particularly, how can one conduct this research without exposing project participants and researchers to even greater danger?

THE DILEMMA POSED BY EVENTS AND CONDITIONS IN NOGALES

Because of the differing opinions among researchers, the October 2008 events in Nogales posed several important challenges and questions for our research team. First, what is our responsibility to our research? How much danger can we legitimately accept, and how does it reflect on those around us? What are the possible legal implications for a university? Is conducting research purely an individual (and, it is to be hoped, well-informed) decision, or are there benchmarks and standards for deciding when to continue or stop researching? And perhaps most important, what is our obligation to the issues that have the greatest impact on our research area? When violence is raging and directly affects the issues that we are examining, regardless of a prior intellectual desire to specifically focus on violence or crime, do we not have a responsibility to document it to the best of our ability?

From the three statements below, and through the comments of the other active research team members, it is clear that there is both agreement and disagreement among the researchers. And while we would like to think that we are free to arrive at the answers to these questions independently, as academic researchers we are embedded within an institutional structure of a university for all of the good and bad which that entails. This leads us to the next question: When is it ethically acceptable to leave a research site?

PERSPECTIVE ONE: DANIEL E. MARTÍNEZ

In addition to my duties as the PI, I was in charge of transporting team members from Tucson, Arizona, to our research site in Nogales, Sonora. I felt I was personally responsible for our team members' safety from the time we left campus until the time we returned in the late hours of the night. I have my personal perspective regarding the issue of violence in Nogales as well as my beliefs and responsibilities as a PI. At times, these feelings have deviated substantially from one another and have been difficult to balance. Before proceeding, I must mention that team members who went on trips to survey went of their own accord; we never forced anyone to go to Nogales if they felt uncomfortable.

During my informal conversations with our friends at the research site, it quickly became evident that the city's residents had never experienced such a high level of violence as they had over the past few months. Some thought we should discontinue our research because it was not worth the risk. However, others felt that the risk was relatively low considering the cartels were not targeting residents and were especially uninterested in targeting foreigners. Honestly, until the evening in question, I never felt like we were in any danger while in Nogales.

Despite the uptick in violence, we continued our surveying trips with team members who felt comfortable going to Nogales. However, that quickly changed the night that someone was killed in a cartel-related shoot-out across the street from the shelter. This had a chilling effect and suddenly made the issue of violence a very real concern. I was present the night of the shooting; it is one thing to talk about violence, it is another thing to be so close to it.

After a lengthy discussion with one of my mentors at the university, we decided that it was best to temporarily suspend our data-collection process. I feel that it was the right decision. I could not imagine having to call a student's parents to inform them that their son or daughter had been seriously injured or killed after being hit by a stray bullet while conducting research.

My position is that no research is worth losing one's life. Sure, we can idealize the thought of conducting embedded research and illustrating the sociological implications of such acts of violence that may otherwise be overlooked.

However, it becomes a very different situation when you are responsible for the safety of others. Even if scholars are willing to participate in high-risk research, they must stop and consider that their endeavors may have consequences not only for themselves but also for the people in their lives who care about them.

A SECOND PERSPECTIVE: JEREMY SLACK

Having worked as a researcher in Nogales since 2003, I was adamant that we not halt our research after the shooting. My rationale was that as long as we are not facing any undue risks that locals are not also dealing with it is difficult to justify halting our activities so as to avoid exposure to violence that the people we talk to, the people we work with, cannot avoid. If foreigners were being targeted, I would have reconsidered it. As it stood, our risk of getting caught in the crossfire was still slim, as we made only one or two trips per week. In contrast, hundreds of thousands of people that live in the city were at greater risk. Because I was familiar with various groups of people throughout the city and frequently spent the night in the urban peripheral neighborhoods known as marginal *colonias*, I was well aware of the frequency of the violence.

Obviously, I was not trying to impose my decision on everyone in the research team. Two of my colleagues had already chosen to refrain from fieldwork until the situation changed. I simply did not want a mandate saying that I had to stop what I was doing. We were all adults conducting research of our own free will. Moreover, as volunteers there would have been no monetary penalty for opting out of researching, which lessens the burden on administration and faculty who could be accused of penalizing us for avoiding Nogales if we were employees.

I left the group meeting thinking that I had swayed the group and that we would be allowed to continue our research, but later that day I got a phone call saying that another professor, who frequently helped to advise on the project, had convinced the PI that we should stop. Despite the pretext of attempting to make the decision as a group in our meeting, it came down to an executive decision based on the opinions of external faculty. It was a difficult decision for me to accept and, honestly, I maintained a presence in Nogales for a variety of projects and to keep in contact with people at the research sites. For me, this was an important gesture to convince the staff and owners of the migrant shelter that we were committed to continuing our work and that we were not going to abandon our project or our friends during a difficult period.

THE THIRD PERSPECTIVE: PRESCOTT VANDERVOET

At the time of our meeting, my feeling was that the violence occurring in Nogales and other parts of the state was strictly targeted at a particular sector of the population—namely, those involved in narcotics trafficking. Also, it appeared clear that a battle was occurring for space between rival factions and that it behooved them not to engage other groups, as that would call heightened attention to the situation. Indeed, while many locals understood the escalating situation, most Arizonans who did not live in border communities were unaware of the imploding public safety structure in their neighboring state. This was evident in the time it took the University of Arizona and the U.S. State Department to issue travel advisories and warnings. In general, I considered the cartels to be playing by rules that would make the situation less dangerous for people not involved with the drug issues.

Nonetheless, innocent Nogales residents were eventually caught in the middle of shoot-outs. I was present at the shelter the night of the shooting across the street, and there was a real feeling of vulnerability on the part of everyone in the building, as the automatic rifle fire was very close. Just a few weeks later, while in Tijuana with a friend, we witnessed a single person gunned down with an automatic rifle on the sidewalk directly in front of a bar that we were visiting. It was a crazy sight to watch approximately one hundred people in the room duck down in response to the gunfire ringing out, cutting through the sound of the music. While this incident strengthened my feeling that the violence wracking Mexico was specifically targeted, it also increased my feeling of insecurity, as the violence could occur in any place and at any time. For me, the issue of violence came to a head a couple of months later as I was leading a group of teachers through Sásabe, Sonora. We were threatened by an individual with a semiautomatic rifle as we sat eating lunch in front of the Mexican customs building. The feeling of complete vulnerability was like a slap in the face, and I realized that even if most of those involved in this conflict play by some sort of "rules of engagement," the insecurity could be omnipresent. Ultimately, my feeling toward research in Nogales was that it didn't pose a direct threat to researchers, but during that time of heightened violence occurring in public (autumn and winter 2008), security was not guaranteed in any region of the Sonoran border. Thus, it ultimately caused considerable and unnecessary risk to our research team.

The border wall in the Imperial Dunes National Park in California.

The border wall outside of Ambos Nogales.

The border wall outside of Ambos Nogales.

The border wall ends in the Pacific Ocean, in Playas de Tijuana, where people splash in the waves, fish, and sell popsicles.

An altar for sixteen-year-old Jose Antonio Elena Rodríguez, who was shot and killed by border patrol agent Lonnie Schwartz in 2012.

The spot where Jose Antonio Elena Rodríguez was shot and killed.

El Bordo, Tijuana, the paved river that runs along the U.S.-Mexico border, where deportees and drug addicts congregate.

Deportees being dropped off at night at the Nogales port of entry.

Deportees praying before eating lunch at the comedor run by the Kino Border Initiative in Nogales, Sonora.

The border wall between El Paso, Texas, and Ciudad Juárez, Chihuahua.

Grupos Beta, the government agency tasked with providing aid to migrants along the border, picks up deportees from the Juan Bosco shelter in Nogales, Sonora.

Deportees leaving the Juan Bosco shelter in Nogales, Sonora.

DISCUSSION

These sentiments represent only a few of the opinions in our research team. Two people dropped out of the project, while the other six agreed to accept whatever collective decision was given. Unfortunately, after the period of inaction (October 2008–March 2009), we never regained the full momentum of the research team, and the majority of the final data collected for the first wave of the MBCS during the spring and summer of 2009 fell to Martínez and Slack. However, the mere need for this discussion and the consequences of our decisions raised a new set of questions about the ultimate goal of our research and our responsibility to record the drastic changes that exerted a strong influence on our research context.

RESEARCHER RESPONSIBILITY

While some of the issues shaping the context surrounding our research may be too dangerous, volatile, or sensitive to ever fully investigate in a way that would satisfy academic rigor, how do we balance the need for a basic understanding with the need to satisfy methodological standards? In this sense, the purpose of this article recycles issues of danger and fieldwork, applying them to our particular field site that happens to be one hour away from the university. The specific situation of border researchers requires attention because there is an increasing administrative pressure to discontinue research on the border because of the frequent media reports of violence.

This issue also takes us to another concern: treating the impacts of drug-related violence on our research in a nuanced, methodologically sound way. While there were some questions on our survey that specifically addressed issues of abuse (by the border patrol, police, thieves, and guides), issues of kidnapping and drug trafficking came up frequently but were originally not documented, leading us to believe that there is still much to be understood about the nature of undocumented migration and violence. As a research team, we noticed an undeniable yet confusing link between human smuggling, drug smuggling, and border banditry (*bajadores*). The migrants themselves, frequently the most vulnerable people along the border, were being sucked into the violent and costly drug war at the time in part because of the tightening of crossing spaces by border enforcement, which causes more suffering and danger throughout the entire crossing experience (Nevins 2008).

Can this type of research be conducted in a methodologically sound way? Through more than four hundred one-hour surveys with people who had recently attempted a crossing, we realized that there is still a lot to learn about how these clandestine forces operate. The survey instrument was not designed to capture these issues, and therefore much of our analysis will not address it. However, a survey is not the best way to get at issues so hidden and potentially dangerous. This is because the majority of the migrants understand very little about the structure of the system (e.g., human trafficking, drugs, bandits, etc.) with which they have gotten involved. Migrants arrive at the border with the intention of crossing into the United States but are immediately confronted with individuals who have decidedly different agendas. Moreover, overlap between drug runners, human smugglers, human traffickers, and bandits who prey on migrants is on the rise in response to militarization of the border and crackdowns on the flow of drugs within and from Mexico. How do you identify a target population and focus directly on this topic in a quantitative or qualitative way? The short answer is that one cannot.

The ethnographic tool kit offers several answers to the methodological approach, but there are also pitfalls. By casting a broad net and meticulously recording all of our interactions and conversations, as some of us began to do around the time of the rise in violence, we can absorb the nuances of migration and the social dynamics surrounding the driver of border commerce. This is by no means sufficient, but it represents the flexibility necessary to adapt to a changing field site and, therefore, a better methodological approach.

The ultimate disservice is to fail to document or anticipate these massively detrimental changes. Orin Starn (1992) writes about how social scientists completely missed the arrival of the Shining Path guerrilla war in Peru. For Starn, anthropologists were caught up in cultural ecology and ritual practices relating to understanding a general "Andeanism." The social scientists, therefore, failed to see the rising discontent and signs of an impending civil war. For us, this is the ultimate cautionary tale. Theoretical arguments and thematic areas of study are meant to illuminate aspects of a culture, group, or issue and not blind us from what is truly important.

As immigration and border scholars, we must ensure that we do not let our academic pursuits obscure the truly relevant and pertinent issues that are taking place and fail to forewarn the possibility of darker things to come. A strong focus on human rights and a broad understanding of how people react to the marginalization imposed by U.S. security and immigration policies illuminates the true costs of undocumented migration. However, we also need to individually determine what risks we are willing to take for our work. Administrative mandates imposed from on high will be extremely detrimental to the long-term commitments made by researchers and only serve to distance academics from the grounded realities that are needed to shape useful and pertinent research. We will never be able to develop a rubric for determining how dangerous is too dangerous, but an involved understanding of the situation combined with new and innovative methodological approaches will advance the study and understanding of violence.

CONCLUSIONS

The authors truly hope that the University of Arizona and other institutions do not institute travel bans. The administrative need to address and minimize risk and the ramifications for personnel in potentially dangerous environments is real. Waivers can be a useful tool to ensure that individuals affiliated with a university recognize the dangers of the setting they will enter. At the same time, researchers who have spent years learning about these places are often in a far better position than administrators to assess the unique situations of potentially dangerous environments and to make the ultimate decision about whether or not to conduct research. The authors of this chapter frequently give advice to other students and faculty planning their own travel and research along the border. This is a useful service, but it is far from ideal. As a team of investigators it is easy to get lost in our own research with our circle of contacts and not see all the changes going on around us.

When massive changes occur where we do research, as has happened along the border since the mid-2000s, we need the will to engage these events on a deeper level that can expand the picture painted by journalists who are often only concerned with providing a body count. We need to confront the challenges of working in these environments head on and recognize new and important issues that are influencing our field sites. Yes, it is scary. Yes, it is dangerous. Yes, it is more work. But it is necessary if we want our research to take a prominent place in debates about human rights, abuse, and the nature of conflicts.

POSTSCRIPT: JEREMY SLACK

In September of 2010, I scoped out the possibility of bringing a similar project to Ciudad Juárez, the city most affected by the drug violence in Mexico. While there, I was able to see the full impacts of a university policy that prohibits travel to its sister city in Mexico. The University of Texas system prohibited any university-related trips to Juárez in May of 2010. It was clear that this policy has real effects for relationships along the border and also has huge symbolic ramifications. The researchers at the Universidad Autónoma de Ciudad Juárez expressed their frustration at the inability to attract U.S. scholars to events on campus and that the travel ban at a university, once the model for community involvement and transborder relations, was yet another blow to those who continue to live and work in Juárez. The ban is yet another reminder that "where you live is too dangerous for me to even go."

Anthropologists and other social scientists who engage in long-term research are uniquely positioned to combine accounts based on extreme events with a deeper understanding of everyday life. The wide variety of voices and opinions that go into ethnographic accounts as well as the luxury of developing an opinion over longer periods of research are key in dispelling or tempering more sensationalistic accounts. Even more importantly, this knowledge is key for administrative staff concerned about issues of safety and liability in research.

NOTES

Reproduced by permission of the Society for Applied Anthropology from J. Slack, D. Martínez, and P. Vandervoet, "Methods of Violence: Researcher Safety and Adaptability in Times of Conflict," *Practicing Anthropology* 22, no. 1 (2011): 4.

1. Unless otherwise specified, we are referring to the city of Nogales in the Mexican state of Sonora rather than to the Arizona city of the same name.

REFERENCES

Nevins, Joseph. 2008. *Dying to Live: A Story of US Immigration in an Age of Global Apartheid.* New York: City Lights.

Rubio-Goldsmith, Raquel, M. Melissa McCormick, Daniel Martínez, and Inez Magdalena Duarte. 2006. "The Funnel Effect and Recovered Bodies of Unauthorized Migrants." Paper for the Pima County Board of Supervisors.

Starn, Orin. 1992. "Missing the Revolution: Anthropologists and the War in Peru." In *Re-reading Cultural Anthropology*, edited by George Marcus, 152–80. Durham, N.C.: Duke University Press.

4

IN HARM'S WAY

Family Separation, Immigration Enforcement Programs, and Security on the U.S.-Mexico Border

JEREMY SLACK, DANIEL E. MARTÍNEZ,
SCOTT WHITEFORD, AND EMILY PEIFFER

INTRODUCTION

THIS CHAPTER EXPLORES the recent changes to border and immigration enforcement enacted by the Consequence Delivery System (CDS). As described by U.S. Border Patrol chief Michael Fisher, the CDS "guides management and agents through a process designed to evaluate each subject uniquely and identify the ideal consequences to impede and deter future entry."[1] We ask how and whether this program functions to deter migration while we explore the potential harmful impacts of the CDS. Specifically, we examine the demographics and family ties of recently deported migrants and their experiences with immigration enforcement practices and programs under the CDS, including issues of due process and treatment of deportees in U.S. custody. The analysis focuses on two CDS programs:[2] (1) Operation Streamline, which criminally prosecutes illegal entrants en masse in particular border patrol sectors and crossing corridors, and (2) the Alien Transfer and Exit Program (ATEP), which deports unauthorized migrants apprehended in one region to another part of the border (Danielson 2013; De León 2013).

To answer these research questions, we draw on Wave II of the Migrant Border Crossing Study (MBCS). The MBCS differs from previous quantitative studies that focus on people's propensity to migrate conducted in sending communities in Mexico (Massey, Durand, and Malone 2002; Durand and

Massey 2004; Cornelius and Lewis 2007) or border flows (Bustamante 2002). The MBCS allows scholars and policy makers to better understand who is being deported, what they experience during their northward journeys, and what happened while they were processed through the programs that make up the CDS. The goal is to provide an empirical basis with which to bring the questions and concerns generated by two bodies of literature into the policy arena. First, literature based on qualitative, historical, and metatheoretical interpretations of border enforcement procedures has focused on the human and social costs of migration, especially migrant deaths in the desert (Andreas 2009; Nevins 2002; Nevins and Aizeki 2008; Heyman 2008; Martínez, Cantor, and Ewing 2014). The second, more recent body of literature has developed around deportation, especially interpreting the potential deportability of both authorized and unauthorized immigrants as a form of social control (Coleman 2007, 2009; Núñez and Heyman 2007; Varsanyi 2008; De Genova and Peutz 2010; Varsanyi 2010; Coleman and Kocher 2011).

RESEARCH METHODOLOGY AND SAMPLE CHARACTERISTICS

The data utilized in this analysis is from Wave II of the MBCS. It is based on survey interviews by U.S. and Mexican researchers with 1,109 recent deportees between 2009 and 2012,[3] covering their experiences crossing the border, being apprehended by U.S. authorities, and being repatriated to Mexico.[4] Interviews took place at ports of entry immediately following deportation and in migrant shelters in Tijuana and Mexicali, Baja California; Nogales, Sonora; Ciudad Juárez, Chihuahua; Nuevo Laredo, Tamaulipas; and Mexico City.[5]

Table 4.1 provides descriptive statistics for the survey respondents. The average person interviewed was a thirty-two-year-old male with eight years of formal education who earned a median household income of $346 per month before attempting to cross into the United States.

About one-half of the survey respondents spoke at least some English, and one in ten spoke an indigenous language in addition to Spanish. Sixty-two percent were employed before deciding to leave Mexico, and 42 percent were the sole income provider for their families. Three-quarters of deportees had previously lived or worked in the United States. Among those who had lived or worked in the United States, the median time spent in the country was nine years.

TABLE 4.1 Demographic characteristics and ties to the United States

VARIABLE	PERCENT/MEAN
Male	90%
Female	10%
Age (years)	32
Formal educational attainment (years)	8
Monthly household income before crossing (US$)	346
English speaking ("at least some")	47%
Indigenous language speaking	8%
Sole economic provider for household	42%
Employed before crossing	62%
Have lived or worked in the United States	75%
Years in the U.S. (among people with U.S. experience)	9
U.S.-citizen family members	49%
U.S.-citizen child	23%
U.S.-citizen minor child	20%
Current home located in the United States	30%
Intended to emigrate permanently after last crossing (10 years or longer)	46%

Source: Migrant Border Crossing Study, Wave II (N = 1,109), weighted data.

One-half had at least one U.S.-citizen family member, and about one in five had at least one child under the age of eighteen with U.S. citizenship. Almost one-half of those interviewed stated that they intended to settle permanently during their last crossing, and 30 percent stated that their current home was in the United States.

This is a strikingly different portrait of deportees than the common conception of seasonal laborers and young single men with no real ties to the United States. Julieta, a twenty-four-year-old deportee, explained, "As a mother it is very difficult to leave your children over there—I feel really bad about that. My daughter lives there with her father. He was abusive to me, so I am afraid to leave her there with him."

One might assume that family connections to the United States would generate legal options for immigration, but this is rarely the case. Under the Immigration and Naturalization Act, there are three broad categories for potential immigrants seeking lawful permanent residence.[6] Each of these categories is subject to direct numerical limitations each fiscal year and additional limits by country.[7] This quota system, combined with the use of a lottery "for increasing the diversity of immigrants," makes legal immigration in any given year more likely for an individual from a country with a low historical flow of immigrants than for an individual from a country with a high historical flow such as Mexico.

While 49 percent of people surveyed had a U.S.-citizen family member, many do not fit into categories that allow for legal entry, and if they do, the queue can stretch twenty years or longer. For instance, the U.S. State Department's visa bulletin for January 2015 reveals a visa priority date of September 15, 1994, in cases involving a U.S. citizen who filed an immigrant visa petition for their unmarried adult son or daughter from Mexico. Family members cannot file for permanent residency until their visa priority date becomes current. Moreover, Operation Streamline prosecutes individuals who have crossed the border without authorization. Before this program, border officials commonly exercised their discretion to allow unauthorized migrants to voluntarily be repatriated to Mexico instead of subjecting them to formal removal proceedings, which could lead to criminal charges for subsequent reentry. A far higher percentage of people than in the past undergo removal proceedings and are therefore inadmissible to the United States.

For the average MBCS respondent, who likely possesses low levels of human and financial capital (see table 4.1), legal immigration under the current statutory scheme would be extremely difficult or impossible. For example, a thirty-two-year-old Mexican man with eight years of formal education, some work experience in Mexico and the United States, at least one U.S.-citizen family member other than a spouse, and a U.S.-citizen child under the age of twenty-one may never find a way to immigrate legally. While the executive action announced by President Obama in November 2014 would have extended temporary administrative relief to as many as 5.2 million individuals who lack immigration status (Warren 2014), certain previous immigration-related criminal charges would exclude potential beneficiaries from the Deferred Action for Childhood Arrivals (DACA) program, the Deferred Action for Parents of Americans and Lawful Permanent Residents (DAPA) program, and other future avenues to legal status.

THE CONSEQUENCE DELIVERY SYSTEM AND INTERIOR ENFORCEMENT

THE EFFECTS ON DETERRENCE OF REMOVAL PROGRAMS

Claims that CDS programs significantly decrease the likelihood that people will return have never been externally evaluated or proved using reliable data with the exception of recidivism rates, which have their own limitations (Rosenblum 2013).[8] The Government Accountability Office (GAO) has recommended that Immigration and Customs Enforcement (ICE) provide metrics for evaluating removal programs due in part to their high cost (Government Accountability Office 2012), which is illustrated by the combined budget of Customs and Border Protections (CBP) and ICE of $18.2 billion in the 2014 fiscal year (Department of Homeland Security 2013).

The MBCS data show that deterrence by arrest, incarceration, and removal is largely ineffective. The majority of respondents expressed that they intend to return to the United States sometime in the future (55%),[9] with the rate being 18 percentage points higher for people who consider their current home to be located in the United States (66% vs. 48%, $p < .001$). Among people who stated that their home is in the United States, only 12 percent said they would not return in the future. Antonio, a forty-two-year-old deportee, explained, "I have no choice, my family is there. I need to go back to my children who want me back." While it is important to note that future intention to cross is different from actually crossing the border, the data could just as easily undercount people who will return as overcount. Participants in the study were interviewed immediately following deportation, when experiences of incarceration and the dangers of crossing were fresh in their minds. Following their return to Mexico, the availability of work and other social or cultural pressures may cause people to reconsider their intentions to cross in the future. However, David Spener notes that migrants tend to downplay the negative aspects of migration as time passes (2009). It is possible that some people may decide not to migrate again, while others who stated they would not attempt another crossing may indeed decide to do so upon returning to their communities of origin.

Deterrence became the linchpin of U.S. border enforcement policy in the mid-1990s (Andreas 2009; Nevins 2002; Dunn 1996, 2009; Rubio-Goldsmith and Reineke 2010; Ewing 2014), and yet despite billions of dollars spent, thousands of deaths, and millions of people detained, only 26 percent of all respondents stated that they would never return. Figure 4.1 compares the decision to cross again with the specific removal program (i.e., Operation Streamline, ATEP, and Secure Communities). As shown, these programs do not correspond to a significantly lower rate of future crossing intentions. Operation Streamline is shown to cause a slight but not statistically significant decrease. However, people who have been laterally repatriated report intentions to cross again at higher rates when compared with people not processed through this program

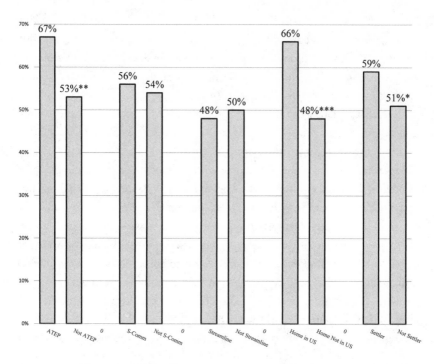

FIGURE 4.1 "Do you believe you'll cross again in the future?" ("Yes" responses by variable of interest). $^{†}p < .$10, $^{*}p < .$05, $^{**}p < .$01, $^{***}p < .$001 indicate that the difference is statistically significant. *Streamline* limited to people who crossed through sectors that have implemented the program. *Settlers* consist of respondents who had intended to permanently migrate to the United States.

($p < .$01). "Settlers"—those who state they intend to migrate permanently—also report that they will cross again at higher rates. These findings differ slightly from official statistics outlined in a report by the Congressional Research Service (CRS) that show a decline in recidivism for people who faced criminal prosecutions within a period of one fiscal year (Rosenblum 2013). However, we contend that statements about the intention to return are a more accurate indicator because they account for a more flexible and realistic time period to recuperate resources rather than the occurrence of repeat crossings within a period of one fiscal year. Furthermore, using recidivism statistics assumes that people will have the same likelihood of apprehension before and after a criminal prosecution. Our qualitative data show that people are likely to invest more time, effort, and resources in future crossings or take a riskier approach in order to avoid detection after prosecution. Moreover, nothing affects the decision to cross again as much as stating that one's home is in the United States, a factor not considered in the CRS report.

Considering the amount of taxpayer dollars being spent and the number of lives being affected, a serious evaluation of these programs is necessary to justify their continued operation. The following sections present survey findings on Operation Streamline, ATEP, and the interior immigration enforcement programs Secure Communities and 287(g).

OPERATION STREAMLINE

We all went in a big group in front of the judge . . . they put chains on us really tight . . . the whole time in there they made me feel like I killed someone.

—JAVIER

Operation Streamline is a coordinated program of immigration enforcement and criminal prosecution characterized by en masse plea agreements for immigration offenders who have illegally entered the United States, a misdemeanor offense. Those with previous convictions of criminal offenses can be charged with illegal reentry, which can be an aggravated felony if combined with other charges. The program officially began in the Del Rio border patrol sector (Texas) in 2005 and expanded to the Tucson sector (Arizona) by 2008 (Lydgate 2010). During our study period it was in operation in all but three sectors along the southern border.[10]

During our fieldwork, a defense attorney was provided for defendants in Operation Streamline, sometimes in groups and sometimes one-on-one, but the limited time allotted and complicated court setting raised concerns about due process and access to effective legal counsel. When asked "What did your lawyer inform you about your rights?" only 30 percent mentioned any sort of basic legal right such as the right to silence or a fair trial. Fifty-five percent of respondents stated that their lawyer simply informed them that they needed to sign their order of removal and plead guilty. Six percent reported that their lawyers did not tell them anything. Only one percent reported being informed

TABLE 4.2 Interaction with legal counsel during Operation Streamline

VARIABLE	PERCENT
Processed through Operation Streamline[a]	27
Shackled during Operation Streamline	95
"What did your lawyer tell you about your rights?"[b]	
Sign the form and do not fight the charges	55
Some mention of basic legal rights	30
Nothing or could not understand	6
Could not recall	3
Other	3
Asked to report abuses	1
Check for legal status of defendant	1
Prospect of being paroled while waiting for resolution of an immigration case	0

Source: Migrant Border Crossing Study, Wave II (*N* = 1,109), weighted data.
[a]Among all respondents. When people apprehended and repatriated in sectors not practicing Operation Streamline are omitted, the percentage increased to 35 percent.
[b]Among respondents who gave valid responses. Does not sum to 100 because of rounding.

that they could report abuses. And only three people stated that their lawyer screened for legal immigration options based on family connections, which is relevant to the subsequent removal process. Under the current immigration system, if more people were to fight the charges, the enormity of the caseload would quickly overwhelm the capacity of the courts.

Unauthorized entry carries a maximum six-month sentence, and those who are convicted have a criminal record based on an immigration offense, which hinders future legal residence or entry.[11] If apprehended again, they will be charged with illegal reentry, which generally carries a longer prison sentence. However, when asked what they understood about their sentence, only 71 percent of respondents processed through Operation Streamline mentioned that a judge had told them they would face some amount of jail time if they return to the United States after being deported. However, once people have pled to the criminal charges, even the misdemeanor plea options, it becomes almost impossible to pursue legal immigration avenues that may have been available in the past. Operation Streamline also diverts law enforcement and judicial resources away from prosecuting more serious offenders, including those who represent a public safety or security risk (see Lydgate 2010).

Federal criminal convictions for illegal entry have increased substantially over the past decade from 3,900 in FY 2000 to 92,215 in FY 2013 (Transactional Records Clearinghouse 2014). Federal convictions for illegal reentry increased from 6,513 in FY 2000 to 19,463 in FY 2012, while "other immigration" convictions increased from 1,032 to 1,504 during this same period (Light, Lopez, and Gonzalez-Barrera 2014). In FY 2000 only 17 percent of federal convictions were for immigration-related offenses, but by FY 2012 this share had increased to 30 percent (Light, Lopez, and Gonzalez-Barrera 2014). Operation Streamline has driven the increase in federal convictions for immigration-related offenses. For instance, 45 percent of all immigration-related prosecutions in southwest border districts between FY 2005—when Operation Streamline first began—to FY 2012 were a result of Operation Streamline proceedings (Rosenblum 2013).

The changes in prosecution brought about by Operation Streamline probably also account for a sizable proportion of "criminal aliens" who have been removed for immigration crimes. Among all "criminal aliens" removed in FY 2013, 31 percent were removed for immigration infractions (which includes unlawful entry and reentry), while the other largest categories were traffic violations (15%) and drug offenses (15%) (Simanski 2014).

As discussed, Operation Streamline has been criticized on the ground that mass trials are anathema to the justice system because of the lack of due process and the inability to effectively communicate the consequences of the conviction and future apprehensions. In addition, defendants are generally shackled before, during, and after their court appearances. Defendants reported being shackled at the feet, waist, and wrists for a median of six hours while they are transferred to and from the federal courthouse. Many women complained about not being able to go to the bathroom during this period because the shackles hold their pants up.

Because of Operation Streamline, the number of people who have been sent to federal prison for immigration violations has also increased tremendously. Thirty-eight percent of all survey respondents were criminally detained for more than one week, which means that they were not simply processed by border officials but were also sent to immigration detention or to federal prison where they served a sentence for illegal reentry.[12] For people who decide not to sign the removal order and who fight their cases, immigration detention can last for excessive periods, even years, because of a backlog in the system (Mountz 2010). There is an enormous cost associated with increased incarceration, with each detainee costing an estimated $119 per day (Department of Homeland Security 2013). The federal detention budget for ICE was $1.96 billion in FY 2013, excluding the cost of incarcerating people convicted of crimes who are sent to the federal prison system (Department of Homeland Security 2013). The legal implications of Operation Streamline will be experienced for decades in part because criminal records impede eligibility for immigration status, employment, and full participation in U.S. society.

THE ALIEN TRANSFER AND EXIT PROGRAM: LATERAL REPATRIATION

ATEP is an enforcement program with the explicit directive of breaking smuggling networks (Government Accountability Office 2010).[13] Under this program, the border patrol deports migrants from a different sector along the border from the one in which they were apprehended (De León 2013). The MBCS found that 13 percent of deportees were laterally repatriated[14] and 20 percent were deported between the hours of 10:00 p.m. and 5:00 a.m. Despite the stated goal of ATEP to break up smuggling networks, people processed through the program reported that they will return to the United States at higher rates. Forty percent of people processed through ATEP reported that they planned on crossing again within the next week compared with just 28 percent of people not processed through the program. The MBCS findings also show that ATEP sends people away from the Arizona-Sonora border, which is the second busiest point of unauthorized crossing, to other areas where fewer people cross. Officially, only men are processed through ATEP. However, women who are separated from men during the deportation process are also deported alone. As a result, 17 percent of the people deported to Sonora, Mexico, are women versus 10 percent border wide due to men being sent to other parts of the border (Rodríguez and Martínez Caballero 2013). The separation of women from male family or friends with whom they are traveling places them at increased risk of theft, violence, and abuse (Danielson 2013, 11).

Mexico's northeastern border region is home to the criminal organization Los Zetas. While by no means an exception among criminal organizations, Los Zetas has been known to kidnap, extort, and kill migrants on a large scale. The infamous massacre of 72 migrants in August 2010 and the discovery of mass graves containing hundreds of migrants have raised concerns about the ethics of continuing deportations to this area. In recent years Tamaulipas has become one of the top states for deportations, with tens of thousands more deportations than the number of people apprehended in the corresponding area (Meyer and Isacson 2013; Slack 2015). Many people are also sent to cities in this region in the middle of the night. Twenty percent of all survey respondents were deported to the border between the hours of 10:00 p.m. and 5:00 a.m, although recent policy changes have officially put a stop to this practice since our research. When evaluating the CDS as an immigration enforcement strategy, we must ask if it is justifiable to put people's lives in danger to punish them for unauthorized entry.

INTERIOR ENFORCEMENT:
SECURE COMMUNITIES AND 287(G)

Twenty-five percent of MBCS respondents were apprehended as a consequence of interior enforcement programs such as the Secure Communities program[15] (S-Comm) or 287(g).[16] Interior enforcement targets people who are already settled in the United States and have established a life there, making it a particularly traumatic experience. Studies have shown that these programs lead to a racialized form of policing, generating extreme distrust between minority communities and the police (Coleman and Kocher 2011). Research has also illustrated that the S-Comm program had no impact on alleviating index crime rates at the local level (Miles and Cox 2014). The rollout of S-Comm marked the end of the highly visible spectacle of workplace raids, such as the 2008 Postville Raid in Iowa, which provoked an outcry from human rights organizations, businesses, and religious groups alike. S-Comm was far less visible and caused a less concentrated economic impact as compared to workplace raids, which have the potential to shut down whole businesses and even sectors of the economy.

Almost half of the people deported through interior enforcement measures stated that their home is in the United States versus only a quarter of other deportees (see table 4.3). They had also spent an average of 8.2 years in the United States versus 6.0 for other deportees, further illustrating that interior enforcement programs target people who have established ties and roots in the United States, including children. This creates consequences for children who not only witness their families physically torn apart but who must live with the absence of a parent.

Besides having a devastating impact on families, interior immigration enforcement efforts invariably turn law enforcement officers into immigration officials in the minds of immigrants in many communities. This hinders the ability of a police force to investigate crimes, which generally requires the trust and cooperation of receptive communities. People fear any interaction with

TABLE 4.3 Difference between number of people apprehended through interior immigration enforcement programs and through other means

VARIABLE	INTERIOR ENFORCEMENT PROGRAMS (25%)	OTHER REMOVAL PROGRAMS (75%)	DIFFERENCE
U.S.-citizen family members	43%	51%	8%[†]
U.S.-citizen children	28%	22%	6%
Current home in United States	47%	25%	22%[***]
Total years in United States	8.2	6.0	2.2[***]

Source: Migrant Border Crossing Study, Wave II (N = 1,109), weighted data.
[†] $p < .10$, [***] $p < .001$

law enforcement, be it a simple traffic stop or the reporting of serious crimes, because they could end up being deported. Because of this fear, they avoid authorities at all costs.

TREATMENT OF DEPORTEES IN U.S. CUSTODY

DUE PROCESS ABUSE

Many nongovernmental organizations and immigrant rights groups have expressed concern that the USBP's removal procedures, including Operation Streamline, do not meet basic due process requirements (No More Deaths 2011). The MBCS sought to uncover how people understood their experiences in U.S. custody. Nearly all respondents (96%) indicated they signed a removal order while in U.S. custody, whether a voluntary return or a formal removal.[17] Among those who signed, 28 percent reported that no one explained the documents they had signed, and 27 percent responded "no" or "don't know" when asked if they knew what they had signed. Thirty-three percent reported feeling forced or pressured to sign a removal order. This occurred largely while in the custody of the USBP.

There is little transparency about what happens to immigrants in the U.S. justice and immigration systems. Signing documents while in U.S. custody can have long-term and far-reaching consequences for people's future ability to immigrate legally.[18] Individuals facing deportation have a right to due process including notice and a hearing.[19] Dense, complex forms that fail to provide

TABLE 4.4 Mistreatment while in U.S. custody

VARIABLE	PERCENT
Reported physical abuse by U.S. authorities	12
Reported verbal abuse by U.S. authorities	20
Did not receive sufficient food while in U.S. custody	41
Had possessions taken and not returned by U.S. authorities[a]	27
Were carrying identifying Mexican documents and had at least one document taken and not returned	19

Source: Migrant Border Crossing Study, Wave II (*N* = 1,109), weighted data.
[a]Excludes mentions of food or water.

adequate, clear information on remedies and consequences of action or inaction may violate constitutionally guaranteed due process rights.[20]

The increased use of expedited removal, a summary deportation without the benefit of a trial before an immigration judge, has also raised concerns about people's knowledge of and access to legal counsel. The logic behind not incorporating removal proceedings into the criminal justice system has a long and complicated history but largely hinges on the ruling that deportation is not considered a criminal punishment (Kanstroom 2007). It is important to reevaluate the role of border officials in processing, sentencing, and removing unauthorized migrants. Border officials cannot reasonably be expected to perform the tasks of arresting officer, judge, prosecutor, and defense attorney all at once. Moreover, incentives for the USBP and ICE are focused on increasing deportations. In order to ensure that reasonable protections exist, the processing, sentencing, and removal of unauthorized migrants must be excised from the authority of border officials and ICE and returned to the already overwhelmed and underfunded court system.

CONCLUSION: WHAT IS SECURITY?

Increased border enforcement has dominated recent discussions about immigration reform. The idea that reform can only happen once the border is secure raises the question of what security might mean for different groups. Is a secure border one through which nothing and no one that is unauthorized can pass, or is it one where quality of life and a clear, just, and transparent process of border enforcement is ensured for people who live in its shadow (Heyman 2013)? An impermeable border is impossible if the United States and Mexico expect to maintain or expand trade and economic development. There are other ways to stem the flow of migrants, such as promoting economic development in Mexico and Central America, which would provide people with the option not to migrate, commonly referred to as "el derecho de no migrar." Rather than assert that more border enforcement is necessary in order to proceed with immigration reform, we would like to revisit what border enforcement aims to accomplish.

While the official mission of CBP is to prevent terrorism,[21] this is hardly its day-to-day task. The replacement of the Immigration and Naturalization Services (INS) by the Department of Homeland Security as the umbrella organization for the USBP emphasizes its security-oriented function. The rise of the CDS illustrates the extent to which enforcement has become more punitive. The MBCS sheds light on what is happening under the guise of security along the border. Does Operation Streamline or ATEP increase security? Does family separation and detention increase security? To conflate all immigration enforcement with security distorts the nature of these programs. Any discussion of reforms needs to address the explicit and implicit goals of specific enforcement programs as well as their unintended consequences.

As shown by the MBCS, more and more of the people who are being expelled from the United States have very strong ties to the country as the family members of U.S. citizens. A deportation should not be seen as an event affecting only the deportee but as one affecting their family members and community as well. Family reunification is one of the primary goals of the U.S. immigration system.[22] Immigration reform must first and foremost provide pathways to citizenship for the family members of U.S. citizens already living and working in the United States. Lawmakers should also reevaluate people with minor infractions, such as immigration-related offenses and traffic violations that result in deportations, who would otherwise be eligible for relief under DACA, DAPA, or the proposed Development, Relief, and Education for Alien Minors (DREAM) Act. Moreover, it is important to reduce or eliminate penalties for false claims of citizenship, which currently lead to a permanent bar from legal entry. In our research, we found that the vast majority of people who attempt to cross the border by talking their way through ports of entry claiming to be U.S. citizens are young people who have spent significant time living in the United States and are unaware of the repercussions of doing so.[23] These individuals often have little or no connection to Mexico and find themselves in an extremely difficult and precarious position upon deportation to Mexico. For instance, an eighteen-year-old deportee, Julian, stated, "I have been in the United States since I was five. I got in a fight right after I turned 18 and the judge deported me. I don't know anyone in Mexico. I don't exist here or in the United States."

Some scholars have recently claimed that mass labor migration from Mexico to the United States has ended because of the economic downturn, the impact of anti-immigrant policies in the United States, and economic improvements, declining fertility rates, and an aging population in Mexico (Durand 2013; Massey and Gentsch 2014). While the United States may not experience the same levels of migration from Mexico as it did in the early to mid-2000s, we are not entirely convinced that this is a permanent decline in unauthorized Mexican migration given the tenuous and often volatile nature of macroeconomic processes. Further, the MBCS findings highlight that a shift toward family-oriented migration is becoming a more significant portion of the unauthorized stream.

The MBCS findings suggest that the United States may be experiencing a new era of migration stemming directly from the rise of an enforcement regime, which has led to high rates of family separation. Academic and political discourses based on neoclassical, rational actor models were instrumental in developing the policies of deterrence that have failed so many and cost so much. While family-based migrants may not necessarily behave in drastically different ways than economic migrants, the idea that the cost of migration can be too great, the danger too perilous, and the punishments too harsh to keep people from reuniting with their loved ones needs to be rejected. The MBCS shows that people who consider the United States their home are willing to endure hardships at the border, discrimination in the United States, and the harsh penalties of an increasingly criminalized immigration system (Martínez and Slack 2013). The impacts of the current approach to immigration enforcement will be felt for generations, including migrants' family members who are citizens of the United States, and will not deter those who are most adversely affected. We are currently at a juncture where we can change course and adopt a humane immigration system and inclusive approach to security that addresses our needs as one society connected by family, economics, and the desire to make a better life for ourselves and our loved ones.

NOTES

Originally published as J. Slack, D. E. Martínez, S. Whiteford, and E. Peiffer, "In Harm's Way: Family Separation, Immigration Enforcement Programs and Security on the US-Mexico Border," *Journal on Migration and Human Security* 3 (2): 109–28. Adapted and reprinted by permission.

1. Testimony of Michael J. Fisher, Chief, U.S. Border Patrol, U.S. Customs and Border Protection, before the House Committee on Homeland Security, Subcommittee on Border and Maritime Security: "Does Administrative Amnesty Harm Our Efforts to Gain and Maintain Operational Control of the Border?" October 4, 2011. http://www.dhs.gov/news/2011/10/04/written-testimony-cbp-house-homeland-security-subcommittee-border-and-maritime.

2. The CDS includes the following programs: Operation Streamline, Alien Transfer and Exit Program (ATEP), Mexican Interior Repatriation Program (MIRP), and Operation Against Smugglers Initiative on Safety and Security (OASISS). Additional initiatives that represent examples of the CDS include expedited removal proceedings, reinstatement of removal, voluntary return, efficient immigration court hearings, and warrant of arrest/notice to appear (see Fisher Testimony, sup.). We include a discussion of interior enforcement in this article because the removal of people who have established homes in the United States is vital to the continued functioning of this enforcement strategy. The analysis also examines experiences of deportees with Secure Communities, an interior enforcement program that between October 2008 and November 2014 screened virtually all people who were arrested against the Department of Homeland Security's (DHS's) Automated Biometric Identification System (IDENT) database for immigration violations. We ask (1) Who is most affected by these programs? and (2) What is the overall impact and efficacy of increased punishments for unauthorized migrants? The findings show that border enforcement practices over the past two decades have led to longer stays and therefore increased ties to the United States. The current approach to immigration enforcement has caused disproportionately negative impacts on people who have been removed who have family in the United States.

3. Wave II of the MBCS included 27 interviews during 2009, 14 during 2010, 999 during 2011, and 73 during 2012.

4. Wave I was conducted with 421 deportees in Nogales, Sonora, from 2007 to 2009.

5. Interviews in Mexico City were with participants of the Mexican Interior Repatriation Program (MIRP), which offers people a flight to Mexico City or a bus ticket home out of the Tucson sector during the summer months instead of being dropped off at the border. The program did not operate in 2012, and the future of this program is uncertain. Formally launched in 2011, its component initiatives were all functioning before that date. Operation Streamline began in 2005, and ATEP has been documented in some form or another throughout the history of the U.S. Border Patrol (USBP) (Hernandez 2010). While migration and border enforcement are constantly evolving and changing, the MBCS captures all official border enforcement measures in place at the time this article was written. An important goal of the MBCS is to provide generalizable findings about abuses and hardships of the border-crossing experience that will be useful to scholars, nongovernmental organizations, and policy makers.

6. Family-sponsored immigrants, employment-based immigrants, and diversity immigrants may qualify for lawful permanent residence. INA § 201, 8 U.S.C. § 1151.

7.   INA § 201, 8 U.S.C. § 1151; INA § 202, 8 U.S.C. § 1152.

8.   Recidivism assumes that people will have the same probability of being apprehended again rather than taking a more costly or risky route that guarantees greater likelihood of success.

9.   Although intentions many not necessarily translate into actual behavior, the theory of planned behavior suggests intentions are the most proximate determinant of behavior (Ajzen 1991).

10. The El Centro and San Diego sector (California) do not participate in Operation Streamline, and the Big Bend sector (Texas) experiences too few apprehensions to warrant the use of the program.

11. INA § 275, 8 U.S.C. § 1325.

12. Those who are convicted of a federal offense are sent to a federal prison alongside the general population. People attempting to fight an immigration case are held in immigration detention.

13. The survey defined ATEP recipients as individuals who were apprehended by the border patrol while crossing and returned to Mexico in a different, nonadjacent border patrol sector. It excluded individuals who went to long-term detention and/or successfully arrived at their desired destination. It also excluded people who were deported to adjacent sectors in order to eliminate people that might have walked into another sector before being apprehended ($N = 505$).

14. This is a conservative estimate that does not include people who arrived at their desired destination or were detained for more than one week. To be counted, individuals must have crossed and been deported in different and nonadjacent sectors.

15. DHS announced the discontinuation of the Secure Communities program on November 20, 2014. The program will be replaced by the Priority Enforcement Program (PEP), through which ICE will continue to rely on fingerprint-based biometric data submitted during bookings by state and local law enforcement agencies but should only seek the transfer of an alien in the custody of state or local law enforcement when the alien poses a demonstrable risk to national security or has been convicted of specific crimes. See memorandum from DHS secretary Jeh Johnson regarding secure communities, November 20, 2014, http://www.dhs.gov/sites/default/files/publications/14_1120_memo_secure_communities.pdf.

16. For the MBCS sample, people included in this category must have been apprehended by police outside of the border zone and subsequently deported. It is often difficult to determine whether people apprehended inside the border zone were processed through an interior enforcement program or one of the many informal arrangements between police and the border patrol. For instance, in southern Arizona the police frequently call border patrol agents when they suspect someone might be unauthorized rather than going through formal channels, charging them with a crime or processing them. However, according to ICE statistics, 20 percent of all removals in 2011 stemmed from Secure Communities (Government Accountability Office 2012).

17. The remaining 4 percent most likely refused to sign. They were still removed but were required (often forcibly) to put a thumbprint in a box marked "refused to sign."

18. For example, an immigration offense such as entering without inspection may be an "aggravated felony" with harsh immigration consequences if an individual was previously deported for another offense. INA § 101(a)(43)(O), 8 U.S.C. § 1101(a) (43)(O). Individuals who were previously removed from the United States are ineligible to receive visas and ineligible to be admitted to the United States for certain periods of time. INA § 212(a)(9)(A), 8 U.S.C. § 1182(a)(9)(A).

19. See, e.g., Landon v. Plasencia, 259 U.S. 21, 32–33 (1982).

20. Walters v. Reno, 145 F.3d 1032 (9th Cir. 1998).

21. In 2015, the mission of CBP is to "protect the American public against terrorists and the implements of terror." There is no mention of unauthorized migrants. http://www.cbp.gov/xp/cgov/about/mission/guardians.xml (no longer posted).

22. See generally INA § 201(a)(1), 8 U.S.C. § 1151(a)(1) (describing family-sponsored immigrants); INA § 201(a)(2)(A)(i), 8 U.S.C. § 1151(a)(2)(A)(i) (exempting immediate relatives from direct numerical limitations); INA § 240A, 8 U.S.C. § 1229b (describing cancellation of removal based on hardship to U.S. citizen or lawful permanent resident family members); INS v. Errico 385 U.S. 214 (1966) (evaluating the legislative history of the INA to find that family unity is a primary goal, often trumping either enforcement of quota provisions or keeping potentially harmful people out of the U.S.); Fiallo v. Bell 430 U.S. 787 (1977) (recognizing the underlying intention and goal of immigration law to be family unity as demonstrated by legal preference for the immigration of certain family members); Holder v. Martinez Gutierrez 132 S. Ct. 2011 (2012) (affirming the fact that goals of family unity underlie or inform immigration law while declining to interpret every provision in the statute in the most family-friendly light).

23. See INA § 212(a)(6)(C)(ii), 8 U.S.C. 1182(a)(6)(C)(ii) (describing a false claim to U.S. citizenship for any purpose or benefit under any federal or state law as a ground of inadmissibility); INA § 237(a)(1)(H), 8 U.S.C. 1227(a)(1)(H) (allowing for a waiver of certain misrepresentations at the discretion of the attorney general but not allowing waiver of a false claim); Sandoval v. Holder 641 F.3d 982 (2011) (reviewing specifically whether an unaccompanied minor falsely claiming citizenship should be subject to the nonwaivable permanent bar but deferring to the Board of Immigration Appeals to explain the statutory provisions); Jaen-Chavez v. US Atty. Gen. 415 Fed.Appx. 964 (11th Cir. 2011) (finding no reversible error in the Bureau of Immigrant Affairs' determination of inadmissibility for a false claim on Form I-9 and no available waiver for this misrepresentation).

REFERENCES

Ajzen, Icek. 1991. "The Theory of Planned Behavior." *Organizational Behavior and Human Decision Processes* 50 (2): 179–211.

Andreas, Peter. 2009. *Border Games Policing the US-Mexico Divide.* 2nd ed. Ithaca, N.Y.: Cornell University Press.

Bustamante, Jorge A. 2002. "Immigrants' Vulnerability as Subjects of Human Rights." *International Migration Review* 36 (2): 333–54.

Coleman, Mathew. 2007. "Immigration Geopolitics Beyond the Mexico-US Border." *Antipode* 39 (1): 54–76.

———. 2009. "What Counts as the Politics and Practice of Security, and Where? Devolution and Immigrant Insecurity After 9/11." *Annals of the Association of American Geographers* 99 (5): 904–13.

Coleman, Mathew, and Austin Kocher. 2011. "Detention, Deportation, Devolution and Immigrant Incapacitation in the US, Post-9/11." *Geographical Journal* 177 (3): 228–37.

Cornelius, Wayne. 2001. "Death at the Border: Efficacy and Unintended Consequences of US Immigration Control Policy." *Population and Development Review* 27 (4): 661–85.

———. 2005. "Controlling 'Unwanted' Immigration: Lessons from the United States, 1993–2004." *Journal of Ethnic and Migration Studies* 31 (4): 775–94.

Cornelius, Wayne A., and Jessa M. Lewis. 2007. *Impacts of Border Enforcement on Mexican Migration: The View from Sending Communities.* La Jolla, Calif.: Center for Comparative Immigration Studies.

Danielson, Michael. 2013. *Documented Failures: The Consequences of Immigration Policy on the U.S. Mexico Border.* Nogales, Ariz.: Jesuit Relief Services and the Kino Border Initiative. http://www.jesuit.org/jesuits/wp-content/uploads/Kino_FULL -REPORT_web.pdf.

De Genova, Nicholas, and Nathalie Mae Peutz. 2010. *The Deportation Regime: Sovereignty, Space, and the Freedom of Movement.* Durham, N.C.: Duke University Press.

De León, Jason. 2013. "The Efficacy and Impact of the Alien Transfer Exit Programme: Migrant Perspectives from Nogales, Sonora, Mexico." *IMIG International Migration* 51 (2): 10–23.

Deming, W. Edwards, and Frederick F. Stephan. 1940. "On a Least Squares Adjustment of a Sampled Frequency Table When the Expected Marginal Totals Are Known." *Annals of Mathematical Statistics* 11 (4): 427–44.

Department of Homeland Security. 2013. "Budget-in-Brief: Fiscal Year 2014." https:// www.dhs.gov/sites/default/files/publications/FY%202014%20BIB%20-%20FINAL %20-508%20Formatted%20%284%29.pdf.

Dunn, Timothy J. 1996. *The Militarization of the US-Mexico Border, 1978–1992: Low-Intensity Conflict Doctrine Comes Home.* Austin: CMAS Books, University of Texas at Austin.

———. 2009. *Blockading the Border and Human Rights: The El Paso Operation That Remade Immigration Enforcement.* Austin: University of Texas Press.

Durand, Jorge. 2013. "Nueva fase migratoria." *Papeles de Población* 19 (77): 83–113.

Durand, Jorge, and Douglas S. Massey. 2004. *Crossing the Border: Research from the Mexican Migration Project.* New York: Russell Sage Foundation.

Eschbach, Karl, Jacqueline Hagan, Nestor Rodriguez, Ruben Hernandez-Leon, and Stanley Bailey. 1999. "Death at the Border." *International Migration Review* 33 (2): 430–54.

Ewing, Walter A. 2014. "'Enemy Territory': Immigration Enforcement in the US-Mexico Borderlands." *Journal on Migration and Human Security* 2 (3): 198–222.

Government Accountability Office. 2010. *Alien Smuggling: DHS Needs to Better Leverage Investigative Resources and Measure Program Performance Along the Southwestern Border*. Washington, D.C.: Government Accountability Office. http://www.gao.gov /assets/310/304610.pdf.

———. 2012. *Secure Communities: Criminal Alien Removals Increased, but Technology Planning Improvements Needed*. Washington, D.C.: Government Accountability Office. http://www.gao.gov/assets/600/592415.pdf.

Hernandez, K. L. 2010. *Migra! A History of the U.S. Border Patrol*. Berkeley: University of California Press.

Heyman, Josiah McC. 2008. "Constructing a Virtual Wall: Race and Citizenship in US-Mexico Border Policing." *Journal of the Southwest* 50 (3): 305–33.

———. 2013. "A Voice of the US Southwestern Border: The 2012 'We the Border: Envisioning a Narrative for Our Future' Conference." *Journal on Migration and Human Security* 1 (2): 60–75.

Kanstroom, Dan. 2007. *Deportation Nation: Outsiders in American History*. Cambridge, Mass.: Harvard University Press, 2007.

Light, Michael T., Mark Hugo Lopez, and Ana Gonzalez-Barrera. 2014. "The Rise of Federal Immigration Crimes." Washington, D.C.: Pew Research Center. http://www .pewhispanic.org/2014/03/18/the-rise-of-federal-immigration-crimes/.

Lydgate, Joanna. 2010. "Assembly-Line Justice: A Review of Operation Streamline." The Chief Justice Earl Warren Institute on Race, Ethnicity and Diversity, Policy Brief. Berkeley: University of California, Berkeley Law School. https://www.law.berkeley .edu/files/Operation_Streamline_Policy_Brief.pdf.

Martínez, Daniel E., Guillermo Cantor, and Walter Ewing. 2014. *No Action Taken: Lack of CBP Accountability in Responding to Complaints of Abuse*. Washington, D.C.: Immigration Policy Center. https://www.americanimmigrationcouncil.org/sites/default /files/research/No%20Action%20Taken_Final.pdf.

Martínez, Daniel, and Jeremy Slack. 2013. "What Part of 'Illegal' Don't You Understand? The Social Consequences of Criminalizing Unauthorized Mexican Migrants in the United States." *Social and Legal Studies* 22 (4): 535–51.

Massey, Douglas S., Jorge Durand, and Nolan J. Malone. 2002. *Beyond Smoke and Mirrors: Mexican Immigration in an Era of Economic Integration*. New York: Russell Sage Foundation.

Massey, Douglas S., and Kerstin Gentsch. 2014. "Undocumented Migration to the United States and the Wages of Mexican Immigrants." *International Migration Review* 48 (2): 482–99.

Meyer, Maureen, and Adam Isacson. 2013. *Unsafe Deportation Practices That Put Migrants at Risk*. Washington, D.C.: Washington Office on Latin America. http://www.wola .org/commentary/unsafe_deportation_practices_that_put_migrants_at_risk.

Miles, Thomas J., and Adam B. Cox. 2014. "Does Immigration Enforcement Reduce Crime? Evidence from 'Secure Communities.'" *Journal of Law and Economics* 57 (4): 937–73.

Mountz, Alison. 2010. *Seeking Asylum: Human Smuggling and Bureaucracy at the Border.* Minneapolis: University of Minnesota Press.

Nevins, Joseph. 2002. *Operation Gatekeeper: The Rise of the "Illegal Alien" and the Making of the US-Mexico Boundary.* New York: Routledge.

Nevins, Joseph, and Mizue Aizeki. 2008. *Dying to Live: A Story of US Immigration in an Age of Global Apartheid.* San Francisco: City Lights.

No More Deaths. 2011. *A Culture of Cruelty: Abuse and Impunity in Short-Term U.S. Border Patrol Custody.* Tucson, Ariz.: No More Deaths. http://forms.nomoredeaths.org /wp-content/uploads/2014/10/CultureOfCruelty-full.compressed.pdf.

Núñez, Guillermina, and Josiah Heyman. 2007. "Entrapment Processes and Immigrant Communities in a Time of Heightened Border Vigilance." *Human Organization* 66 (4): 354–65.

Rodríguez, Ernesto Chavez, and Graciela Martínez Caballero. 2013. *Síntesis 2012: Estadística migratoria.* Mexico City: Secretaría de Gobernación, Centro de Estudios Migratorios, Unidad de Política Migratoria, Subsecretaría de Población, Migración y Asuntos Religiosos.

Rosenblum, Marc. 2013. *Border Security: Immigration Enforcement Between Ports of Entry.* Washington, D.C.: Congressional Research Service.

Rubio-Goldsmith, Raquel, and Robin Reineke. 2010. "Border Deaths and Federal Immigration Enforcement." *NACLA Report on the Americas* 43 (6): 48–49.

Simanski, John. 2014. *Immigration Enforcement Actions: 2013.* Report Prepared for the Office of Immigration Statistics. Washington, D.C.: Department of Homeland Security. http://www.dhs.gov/sites/default/files/publications/ois_enforcement_ar _2013.pdf

Slack, Jeremy. 2015. "Captive Bodies: Migrant Kidnapping and Deportation in Mexico." *Area* 48 (3): 271–77.

Spener, David. 2009. *Clandestine Crossings: Migrants and Coyotes on the Texas-Mexico Border.* Ithaca, N.Y.: Cornell University Press.

Transactional Records Clearinghouse. 2014. *Despite Rise in Felony Charges, Most Immigration Convictions Remain Misdemeanors.* Syracuse, N.Y.: Syracuse University. http:// trac.syr.edu/immigration/reports/356/.

Varsanyi, Monica. 2008. "Rescaling the 'Alien,' Rescaling Personhood: Neoliberalism, Immigration, and the State." *Annals of the Association of American Geographers* 98 (4): 877–96.

———. 2010. *Taking Local Control: Immigration Policy Activism in US Cities and States.* Stanford, Calif.: Stanford University Press.

Warren, Robert. 2014. "Democratizing Data About Unauthorized Residents in the United States: Estimates and Public-Use Data, 2010 to 2013." *Journal on Migration and Human Security* 2 (4): 305–28.

5

THE GEOGRAPHY OF BORDER MILITARIZATION

Violence, Death, and Health in Mexico and the United States

JEREMY SLACK, DANIEL E. MARTÍNEZ,
ALISON ELIZABETH LEE, AND SCOTT WHITEFORD

INTRODUCTION

IN 2013, the U.S. Congress was locked in a contentious battle over immigration, border security, and the desire for a militarized surge to close off the border. The Senate passed a comprehensive immigration reform (CIR) bill (S. 744) that included nearly $30 billion in additional spending on border security and calls for 20,000–30,000 new U.S. Border Patrol (USBP) agents in addition to the 20,863 agents already employed as of FY 2014 (Customs and Border Protection 2015b). Despite its hardline militarization, the bill stalled in the House, where more conservative politicians claimed it did not go far enough. Nevertheless, President Donald J. Trump seems poised to continue this escalation as signaled by two executive orders signed in January 2017 (executive orders 13767, 13768). Among other changes, the executive orders increase border and interior immigration enforcement, explore the feasibility of an expanded border wall, and terminate deportation relief afforded to some immigrants during the last two years of the Obama administration. Talks of an additional surge in border enforcement funding are omnipresent in Washington, D.C., and come on the heels of an unprecedented buildup along the border that tripled the size of the USBP between FY 2004 and 2012.

Despite the billions of dollars spent each year, how these funds, as well as any proposed increases, are spent in terms of the day-to-day activities of agents, specific enforcement programs, and technological interventions have rarely been analyzed. Most scholarship on border militarization and enforcement centers on the "prevention through deterrence strategy" (e.g., Operation Hold the Line, Operation Gatekeeper, etc.), which consisted of the buildup of enforcement in urban centers that pushed people to remote and dangerous border zones (Dunn 2009, 1996; Nevins 2002; Andreas 2000; Cornelius and Lewis 2007). While this body of work has been attentive to the increased lethality of undocumented migration,[1] this article compares enforcement practices in the San Diego, El Centro, Tucson, El Paso, and Laredo sectors of the border. Our goal is to develop a more geographically nuanced perspective, one that interrogates the role of violence within an increasingly militarized and violent border region.[2] We contend that violence, not security objectives, guides border enforcement strategies. In recent years, border enforcement strategy has centered on the development of a militarized logic and a strategic plan for enforcement that emphasizes pain, suffering, and trauma as deterrents to undocumented migration. Vital to understanding enforcement practices are the ways in which the instrumental use of natural hazards, criminalization and incarceration of migrants, and the institutionalized abuse of power contribute to state policy.

By approaching the border not as one homogenous geographic region but rather as a series of highly interconnected and yet disparate zones, we will show how enforcement practices are enormously varied across border patrol sectors. Not only does the specific physical geography of these areas result in unique sets of challenges and concerns, but behavioral patterns emerge that illuminate the institutional cultures of the border patrol.

While there is a large body of literature that examines the discursive (Brown 2010) or performative aspects of militarization and the state (Secor 2007), these are not the goals of this article. Rather, we are interested in the effects of previous waves of militarization and how these impacts may affect the future of subsequent border enforcement measures. For example, while the previous rounds of border militarization through the "prevention through deterrence" strategy and Operation Gatekeeper in the mid-1990s have been associated with an increase in migrant deaths (Nevins and Aizeki 2008; Eschbach et al. 1999), the next wave may increase deaths or it may not. Much of this is contingent on how proposed increases to militarized enforcement (something we take as inevitable for the purposes of this article) are actually manifested on the ground. However, if the past is any indication of the future, increased border militarization is likely to lead to an increase in migrant deaths and escalated violence perpetrated by human smugglers and border bandits known as *bajadores* (Slack and Whiteford 2011; Nevins 2005). This occurs not only through formal policies such as the funneling of people into remote and dangerous zones and increasing the criminal penalties for undocumented migration but also through informal sets of practices such as rampant abuse and a lack of accountability of U.S. authorities perpetuating such abuses. We contend that the formal and informal practices of enforcement are intimately linked by the centrality of violence in border enforcement strategy.

We begin with a discussion of important definitions and aggregate figures provided by scholars examining border militarization and clandestine migration from Mexico. After a discussion of our methodology, we present our findings, which draw on two research projects: a border-wide postdeportation survey and a series of in-depth interviews with migrants who had returned to their hometowns in Puebla, Mexico. We examine the dangers of the crossing experience through different border sectors, the practices and procedures of U.S. authorities that create different forms of violence for undocumented migrants, and the trauma produced for families waiting on family members who may never return.

AN INCREASINGLY MILITARIZED BORDER

Unprecedented investment by the United States in immigration and border enforcement has transformed the region. Timothy Dunn used the term *militarization* to describe enhanced border policing with the specific aim of highlighting "the use of military rhetoric and ideology, as well as military tactics, strategy, technology, equipment and forces" that in turn conflicts with the human rights of border crossers and residents (Dunn 1996, 3). U.S. border militarization efforts of the 1990s and early 2000s—often described by scholars as the Gatekeeper Era—have received substantial attention in the literature (Dunn 1996; Andreas 2000). But less attention has been given to the more recent exponential increase in resources allocated to enforce the U.S.-Mexico border. Funding for the Secure Border Initiative increased from $38 million in 2005 to $800 million in 2010, totaling almost $4.5 billion in spending over this time period (Government Accountability Office 2010). Political discourse in Congress and in mainstream media frames security as almost synonymous with militarization, stressing that a secure border is one that necessitates more equipment, agents, and fortifications. However, academics have problematized the militarization-securitization nexus, aiming to refocus the concept of security on an inclusive understanding of human life (Fukuda-Parr and Messineo 2012; Kaldor 2007; Kaldor, Martin, and Selchow 2007). The concept of "human security" is an attempt to distance understandings of security from those of war by focusing explicitly on the range of needs for a healthy, productive life that is free from direct violence perpetuated by others, including agents of the state. While the human security framework has grown in popularity among European academics—emphasizing the rights to local, sustainable, and inclusive frameworks for livelihoods—this project has largely been neglected in the United States because of the prevalence of post–September 11, 2001, frameworks for militarized security (Hale 2008; for an exception, see the relatively new policy-oriented *Journal of Migration and Human Security*, edited by the Center for Migration Studies of New York). However, aside from human security, others use feminist geopolitics as a way to examine how "security" is an entirely subjective concept, creating insecurity and violence for some while protecting the rights of the powerful in a racialized and gendered manner (Boyce and Williams 2012). It is important to acknowledge that other formulations of secure borderlands could exist beyond the militarized version we see on Mexico's northern border and the increasingly closed borders of the European Union.

Despite the fact that no U.S. politician has been able to adequately describe what constitutes a "secure border,"[3] in 2010 the United States spent $17.1 billion on border enforcement, with Immigration and Customs Enforcement (ICE) receiving $5.8 billion and Customs and Border Protection (CBP) receiving $11.3 billion (Department of Homeland Security 2013). The construction of the border fence between 2006 and 2010 cost taxpayers between $3.9 million to $16 million per mile for a total of $2.4 billion (Dear 2013). The 2010 deployment of 1,299 National Guard troops on the U.S.-Mexico border by President Obama cost taxpayers $660 million before they were withdrawn in 2011 (Meissner et al. 2013). In a short time the U.S.-Mexico border changed from relatively calm, highly interconnected border cities into a heavily patrolled border with more than twenty thousand USBP agents, long wait times, new entry and exit requirements, and a variety of border barriers monitored by drones and other high-tech devices (Boyce 2015).

A well-developed literature links border militarization to the increase in deaths at the border. While scholars have noted that the border-crossing experience was lethal before the 1990s, enforcement practices drastically changed the distribution of mortality, concentrating it in southern Arizona (Eschbach et al. 1999). Others note that migrant deaths have increased exponentially since the early 2000s, particularly in southern Arizona and South Texas (Nevins and Aizeki 2008; Nevins 2002; Cornelius and Lewis 2007; Andreas 2000; Eschbach et al. 1999; Hagan 2008; Martínez et al. 2014; Rodríguez and Hagan 2004). As illustrated in figure 5.1 (below), these trends have continued unabated in southern Arizona, with the rate of death remaining high even as apprehensions have slowed in recent years. Figure 4.1 also illustrates the notable increase in migrant death rates in the area after the implementation of the "prevention through deterrence" strategy of the mid-1990s and early 2000s (See Martínez 2016 for a full discussion). Others have linked economic and social factors to a system of enforcement that has done little to stem overall flows or deter future crossers (Massey, Durand, and Malone 2002; Fernandez-Kelly and Massey 2007; Durand and Massey 2004; Cornelius and Lewis 2007; Heyman 2008). Although scholars have long disproven the immigration-crime nexus (Orrenius and Coronado 2005), security and crime, notably through the guise of the "war on terror" and the "war on drugs," continue to drive rationales for channeling money into border enforcement.

In addition to the military equipment employed, there are several other ways in which the border has become increasingly militarized according to former USBP agents (Miller 2014). First, the increased hiring of former military personnel as USBP agents has changed the organizational culture of the agency. One problem with this approach is that military forces are trained to engage enemy combatants. But undocumented migrants are not enemy combatants. USBP officers commonly refer to migrants as "tonks." This is a derogatory term referring to the sound of large flashlights striking migrants' heads. This not only dehumanizes migrants but also normalizes and naturalizes acts of physical abuse (Heyman 2004). Second, politically laden idioms such as the "war on drugs," "war on terror," and "war to control the border" have transformed the border debate from one about sensible immigration to one about protecting the state from "alien invaders" as a military mandate.

CBP officials frequently evoke images of terrorists and foreign threats materializing at the U.S.-Mexico border. While this has occurred most recently with an unsubstantiated claim by Judicial Watch of an Islamic State training camp near Ciudad Juárez along the Texas border with Mexico (Judicial Watch 2015), it has a longer and more entrenched history within the organization. In fact, the mission statement for CBP does not mention immigration at all but rather focuses explicitly on terrorism. As stated on the CBP website as

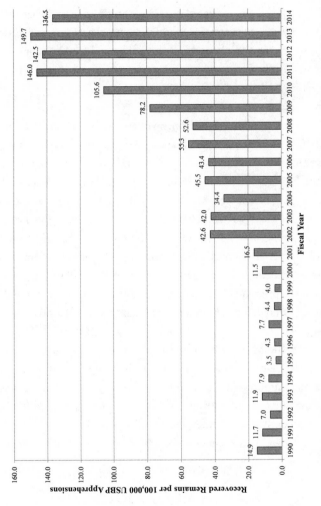

FIGURE 5.1 Approximate death rate in the Tucson sector using Pima County Office of the Medical Examiner deaths coded as undocumented border crossers, FY 1990–2014 (*N* = 2,533).

recently as 2015, their mission is "to safeguard America's borders thereby protecting the public from dangerous people and materials. . . . We protect the American people against terrorists and the instruments of terror" (Customs and Border Protection 2015a). The disconnect between the day-to-day activities of CBP officials and their stated mission is one of our principal areas of concern. The only way to fulfill this mission is by a steadfast assertion that undocumented migrants are dangerous people and synonymous with terrorists despite a widespread understanding that migrants are largely driven by economic and family-oriented factors. This rationale reinforces the need, or at the very least the tolerance, for violence against migrants as an acceptable or necessary aspect of border enforcement.

A final dimension of militarization involves the institutional rearrangement of CBP. The Immigration and Naturalization Service (INS), the former umbrella organization for CBP, was dissolved in November of 2002 with the creation of the Department of Homeland Security (DHS). This led to a drastic change in the strategic plan for border security. Instead of relying on the natural physical hazards of the desert and physical barriers—including the border wall and border patrol checkpoints—to deter immigrants, the inauguration of the Consequence Delivery System (CDS) in 2011 marked a new era of enforcement (Martínez and Slack 2013). This set of practices includes escalating punishments for undocumented migrants apprehended along the southern border and plays a key role in the "whole of government" approach that involves all levels of law enforcement across several agencies in immigration enforcement (De Genova and Peutz 2010). The most visible result of these programs, largely stemming from Operation Streamline, has been increased incarceration rates and lengths of sentences for immigration offenders (Martínez and Slack 2013; Lydgate 2010). This has fundamentally reshaped how migrants experience the border as well as conveniently framed an ever-expanding majority as "criminal aliens" because of the changes in prosecution brought about by Operation Streamline.

RESEARCH METHODOLOGY

The data discussed in this chapter come from two independent yet complementary projects: Wave II of the Migrant Border Crossing Study (MBCS) and the Economic Crisis and Response in Migrant Communities in Puebla Study, hereafter referred to as the Puebla study. In the Puebla study, researchers conducted 120 in-depth interviews in four communities in Puebla, Mexico, with undocumented migrants who returned to their hometowns between 2007 and 2010. While the study originally focused on the impact of economic crisis on migratory flows, border violence emerged as a major theme in the interviews, revealing negative physical and psychological health effects from the violence people experienced during their journey. Together these two studies document the various forms of violence among one of North America's most vulnerable populations—undocumented Mexican migrants.

DEMOGRAPHIC PROFILE

While scholars have noted an increase in female migration (O'Leary 2009; Staudt, Payan, and Kruszewski 2009), data show that 86 percent of people apprehended (U.S. Border Patrol 2013a) and 90 percent of those deported to Mexico in 2012 were male (Instituto Nacional de Migracion 2013). These figures are consistent with estimates gathered through the MBCS, with about 85 percent of the sample being male (see chap. 1 for an overview of the demographic characteristics of migrants surveyed in Wave II of the MBCS). Of 120 migrants interviewed in the Puebla study, twelve were deported; only one deportee was female. Approximately a quarter of the migrants experienced violence along the border or hardships resulting from border militarization.

VIOLENT JOURNEYS: THE CONTEMPORARY CROSSING EXPERIENCE

The journey itself is an arduous and dangerous one regardless of treatment by U.S. authorities. Temperatures along the border, particularly in the Sonoran Desert, where almost half of all apprehensions occurred during the study period, frequently reach 110 degrees Fahrenheit (43°C) during the summer and drop well below freezing (30°F/0°C) at night during winter months. For example, the following vignette represents a common experience for many undocumented migrants:

> Andrés' food ran out on the third day of a six-day trek through the desert. He rationed his only bottle of water for the remainder of the journey. On the final

day, the USBP chased the group, scattering and separating the migrants. Augustín avoided capture but fell and twisted his knee badly during the pursuit. He painfully limped for several hours to reach the pickup point. Using a cell phone, he called the coyote, who instructed him to wait for a vehicle. More than a day passed with no signs of his ride; then the cell phone battery died, cutting him off from the guide. Weak and hopeless, Augustín staggered along the highway for an hour in broad daylight, trying to flag down drivers who might have something to drink. Eventually a USBP truck stopped, gave him water and took him into custody. Augustín reflected on how fortunate he had been to be near the highway when the pernicious effects of dehydration set in.[4]

While this interview illustrates a typical experience of dangerous desert crossings, there has been notable controversy around USBP not responding to migrants actively searching for their help. This has been a frequent topic of conversation in our interviews, as respondents report being left by the road for hours even after making contact with agents, and it was also explored in depth by the award-winning *Need to Know* documentary on PBS (Frey 2013).

Enforcement practices that push people into physically dangerous border terrain have killed thousands of people. The concept of structural violence is frequently deployed to understand how the state, while not directly inflicting violence on people, is nonetheless creating structural conditions that lead to death and increased mortality (Martínez et al. 2014; Holmes 2013; Nevins and Aizeki 2008). According to the USBP, 463 migrants were found deceased along the border in 2012 alone (U.S. Border Patrol 2013b). In southern Arizona the remains of over 2,100 migrants have been recovered since 2000, 6 percent of whom were children under the age of 18 (Martínez et al. 2013). Even more disturbing, many bodies are never recovered because of the extreme isolation of areas along the border. Martínez and colleagues found that nearly 34 percent of migrant remains recovered in southern Arizona between 1990 and 2012 were unidentified. In a similar vein, the Missing Migrants Project, led by Robin Reineke of the Tucson-based Colibrí Center for Human Rights, has compiled a database with thousands of missing persons reports from the families of undocumented border crossers (Martínez et al. 2014). This has left thousands of family members in Mexico, Central America, and in the United States to deal with an agonizing sense of "ambiguous loss" of loved ones (Boss 1999, 2002). Not finding a loved one's remains and the torture of not having a definitive answer about what happened to a loved one creates its own set of emotional and psychological issues for family members of the missing.

Jorge and Leo's stories suggest how easy it has become for migrants to be abandoned in the Arizona-Sonora desert. "The coyote told [the three female migrants] if you don't keep going, you're not going to make it. He gave them drugs to help them keep walking all day. And well, they didn't make it. The coyote left them in the desert. They were abandoned in the desert."[5] "Leo had trouble sleeping for months after meeting a man in an Arizona 'safe house' who cried inconsolably because coyotes left his snake-bitten nephew in the desert. The guides would not return the man to the area."[6]

While the number of deaths along the border remains high despite decreases in migrant flows, it appears that border militarization has once again rearranged this lethal geography. Although Arizona became the principal undocumented crossing point along the border in the mid-1990s (Andreas 2000), there has been a recent increase in crossings through South Texas that has led to increased fatalities in an area that previously received little attention from activists and the USBP, as evidenced by the significantly greater number of agents currently stationed in the Tucson sector (Martínez et al. 2014). This shift can be explained

TABLE 5.1 Context of respondents' most recent crossing experience

MBCS II SURVEY QUESTION	ALL RESPONDENTS	MALES	FEMALES	DIFFERENCE
Total lifetime crossing attempts	4.8	5.2	2.9	2.3
Total lifetime apprehensions	2.9	3.2	1.7	1.5
First-time crossers (%)	16.6	14.5	26.2	11.7***
Had previously crossed or attempted to cross the border (%)	83.4	85.5	73.8	11.7***
Used a coyote or guide to cross the border (%)	71.7	69.1	84.2	15.1***
Cost of coyote (in 2011 US$)	2,400	2,289	2,902	613***
Number of days walking through the desert	2.3	2.4	1.8	0.6**
Ran out of water (%)	39.2	40.1	34.4	5.6
Ran out of food (%)	30.7	31.8	25.0	6.8†
Known migrant deaths (FY 2012)				
Border wide	463	–	–	–
Southern Arizona[a]	171	137	14	–

Source: Migrant Border Crossing Study, Wave II (N = 1,109).
[a]The biological sex of ten decedents was unknown because of advanced decomposition or skeletonization.
† $p < .10$, ** $p < .01$, *** $p < .001$

by two interrelated factors. The first is the relative buildup of border enforcement in southern Arizona. There are over four thousand USBP agents in the Tucson sector alone, up from three hundred agents in 1992 (U.S. Border Patrol 2013a). Data suggest that the danger of crossing through the remote Arizona desert has been compounded by the costs as well as the likelihood of failure over the past decade (Slack et al. 2015). The second contributing factor is the recent increase in Central American migration. The journey to the South Texas border is at least two weeks shorter than to the Arizona border because one must travel thousands of miles farther to the west and north. This has caused an influx of migrants into a part of the border with significantly less enforcement but a deceptively deadly climate.

Table 5.2 compares the experiences of individuals who crossed in different border zones. The journey through the Tucson desert is by far the most arduous, with a mean of 3.3 days crossing as compared with 1.7 through Tijuana and Nuevo Laredo. Nearly half of all respondents report running out of water, and 39 percent report running out of food on this journey. The Tucson sector also exhibits the highest level of abandonment in the desert (either of the respondent or another member of their group), a factor that no doubt contributes to the historically high number of deaths in this region. In contrast, the sectors along South Texas show much lower levels of abuse by U.S. authorities but the highest percentage of respondents who used a coyote, suggesting either a greater amount of control by organized crime (Izcara Palacios 2012) or a lack of previous knowledge of the region. These differences highlight the uneven nature of militarization across the border; immigration enforcement was prioritized in Southern Arizona, escalating violence in that sector, while South Texas received less impetus for control, leading to a relatively lower rate of abuses.

U.S. AUTHORITY ABUSE

When trying to understand the role of direct state violence committed by U.S. authorities, we also need to understand its regional variations. There are distinct patterns that emerge when investigating physical and verbal abuse as well as abuses of due process such as the removal of personal items. If this violence is simply a routine aspect of the apprehension process, then why is there such variance across regions? A constant refusal to investigate fatal instances or share documentation with the public regarding these cases highlights the punitive

TABLE 5.2 Mean (SD) comparison of crossing experience by U.S. Border Patrol sector (west to east)

MBCS II SURVEY QUESTION	SAN DIEGO (N = 167)	EL CENTRO (N = 86)	TUCSON (N = 440)	EL PASO (N = 134)	LAREDO (N = 154)	RIO GRANDE (N = 72)
Days traveled	1.73 (2.46)	1.51 (1.49)	3.32 (2.84)	1.05 (2.65)	1.73 (1.80)	1.40 (1.64)
Successful crossing	.37 (.48)	.22 (.42)	.21 (.41)	.24 (.43)	.51 (.50)	.54 (.50)
Ran out of water	.45 (.50)	.41 (.49)	.48 (.50)	.15 (.35)	.34 (.48)	.28 (.45)
Ran out of food	.47 (.50)	.29 (.46)	.39 (.49)	.14 (.35)	.15 (.36)	.16 (.37)
Used a coyote or guide	.57 (.50)	.65 (.48)	.76 (.43)	.64 (.48)	.84 (.37)	.83 (.38)
Abandoned by group	.11 (.32)	.13 (.33)	.19 (.39)	.11 (.32)	.07 (.25)	.11 (.31)
Group abandoned others	.18 (.39)	.11 (.32)	.22 (.41)	.11 (.32)	.08 (.27)	.15 (.36)
Physical abuse by U.S. authorities	.18 (.39)	.08 (.28)	.11 (.32)	.04 (.19)	.09 (.29)	.11 (.32)
Verbal abuse by U.S. authorities	.35 (.48)	.11 (.31)	.30 (.46)	.25 (.44)	.06 (.23)	.11 (.32)

Note: SD = standard deviation. All associations are statistically significant beyond the .005-level. Yuma, Big Bend, and Del Rio sectors omitted because of low number of observations.

Source: Migrant Border Crossing Study, Wave II (N = 1,053).

nature of the USBP, an institution long endowed with a sense of entitlement and exceptionality (Heyman 2004). While a hesitance to regulate and investigate misconduct or provide public information is common to most bureaucracies, scholars have argued that the unique political circumstances of the U.S.-Mexico border exacerbate this situation.

Lack of transparency and accountability continues to be a widespread problem within CBP and other authorities involved with enforcing immigration (e.g., ICE, USBP, and many police departments). One of the challenges is determining which abuses stem from day-to-day practices by individual officers versus organizational policies that prevent reporting or reprimanding infractions. The USBP has tripled in size since 2004 to 20,863 agents as of FY 2014 (Customs and Border Protection 2015b). The Trump administration has proposed adding an additional 15,000 border agents (USBP and ICE). The USBP is already the largest police force in the United States. This rapid expansion has raised concerns about training, especially in light of abuses. As noted in table 5.3, 10 percent of migrants report some form of physical abuse during their last apprehension, and one in five report verbal abuse. Another report by the nongovernmental organization No More Deaths found a physical abuse rate of 10 percent (No More Deaths 2011), which has also been corroborated in a study of Central American deportees to El Salvador, which also reported a physical abuse rate of about 20 percent during the apprehension process and 10 percent during detention (Phillips, Hagan, and Rodríguez 2006). While this rate may not seem alarming, we emphasize that the USBP has apprehended approximately 400,000 people each year over the past several years. And many individuals cross multiple times, increasing the likelihood that they will encounter an abusive situation. Furthermore, this trend has remained consistent over time, indicating that this is a systematic problem. These manifestations of violence help us understand how violence is being used as part of the enforcement toolbox. The USBP has for years lamented the propensity of return migration among undocumented border crossers (Heyman 2001). This led to the "prevention through deterrence" strategy and, more recently, to one that is aimed at delivering a direct "consequence" for undocumented migrants. Overall, this prioritizes pain and suffering as integral to immigration enforcement. We contend that state violence committed against migrants is an extension of this institutional mandate. This helps explain why there have been almost no attempts to limit, reprimand, or curtail this violence. Moreover, it demonstrates that the stated mission of CBP is used to justify violence, providing another

TABLE 5.3 Mistreatment while in U.S. custody (%)

MBCS II SURVEY QUESTION	ALL RESPONDENTS	MALES	FEMALES	DIFFERENCE
Reported physical abuse by U.S. authorities	10.3	10.2	10.6	.4
Reported verbal abuse by U.S. authorities	22.8	21.2	31.2	10.0**
Did not receive sufficient food while in U.S. custody	44.5	42.8	52.2	9.4*
Needed medical attention while in U.S. custody	23.0	20.9	33.9	13.0***
Needed medical attention and asked for it (N = 268)	66.8	69.8	58.5	11.3†
Needed medical attention and asked for it but did not receive it (N = 185)	37.3	36.7	39.5	2.8

Source: Migrant Border Crossing Study, Wave II (N = 1,109).
† p < .10, * p < .05, ** p < .01, *** p < .001

way of reinforcing the perceived dangerous and violent nature of undocumented migrants.

A general lack of oversight and transparency has led to numerous complaints against the USBP with no available criteria for understanding how and when agents are allowed to use force (Martínez, Cantor, and Ewing 2014). Furthermore, the forty-three documented cases of lethal force by the USBP, fifteen of which were U.S. citizens between 2005 and 2013 (Nevins 2014), as well as other cases of severe beatings have enraged border communities and devastated families. In none of these cases are agents known to have faced any consequences (Ortega and O'Dell 2013). The shooting of sixteen-year-old José Antonio Elena Rodríguez on October 10, 2012, in Nogales, Sonora, sparked intense outrage on both sides of the border. Autopsy reports show that he was shot between eight and eleven times in the back while he was lying on the ground. Officials reported that there was suspected drug trafficking in the area and later that rocks were thrown, a frequent justification for use of lethal force. While an internal investigation cleared all agents of culpability, USBP agent Lonnie Schwartz was indicted for second-degree murder on October 9, 2015, three years after the shooting (Burnett 2015). This is the first indictment of a border patrol agent who shot into Mexico at a suspect despite similar instances, like the shooting of Sergio Adrian Hernández Güereca in Ciudad Juárez, where judges ruled that people in Mexico are not protected by the U.S. Constitution for civil purposes (Tanfani, Bennett, and Savage 2015). The Supreme Court recently reviewed this case, but it was sent back to the fifth circuit courts for more consideration.

CUSTOMS AND BORDER PROTECTION: A ROGUE AGENCY?

Attempts to understand the centrality of violence in shaping and enacting border enforcement measures needs to take into account the disconnect between official policies and material practices on the border. A congressional order, prompted by the high-profile death of Anastasio Hernández, a migrant who was filmed being beaten and tazed to death at the San Ysidro port of entry, mandated external review of CBP's use-of-force protocols. The Police Executive Research Forum (PERF) conducted an external review of CBP, but the final report was released in redacted form, with officials from CBP accepting only the most limited suggestions and subsequently redacting the most damning criticisms. However, a nonredacted version was leaked several months later. The redacted passages were highly critical of current procedures—namely, shooting at rock throwers, and people driving cars, rather than first attempting to step out of harm's way. The suggestion that agents not step in front of vehicles to shoot at the driver were summarily rejected, stating that drug-trafficking organizations would now try to run them over if they knew that U.S authorities could not fire (Bennett 2014). This report, as well as other complaints about enforcement procedures, directly challenges assertions by USBP press secretaries that problems are the results of "a few bad-apples" rather than the institutional mandate of immigration enforcement. The lack of official and explicit ways of dealing with violence perpetrated by agents against a highly vulnerable population is emblematic of the current approach to enforcement.

One report found that 97 percent of all complaints against CBP agents result in no action taken, suggesting that this multibillion-dollar agency has no formal system for receiving and addressing complaints (Martínez, Cantor, and Ewing 2014). Other documents have shown that there is a pervasive problem of alcohol abuse among agents leading to an average of two alcohol-related arrests per week within CBP (Blacher 2013). When the nonredacted version of the congressionally commissioned PERF report was finally leaked (Bennett 2014), a revised statement was issued by USBP chief Mike Fisher acquiescing to a reassessment of their use-of-force doctrine (Bennet 2014). Moreover, the much sought after use-of-force manual was quietly leaked by the Center for Investigative Reporting (CIR), and to the surprise of the activist community, it contained no mention of rock throwers (Becker and Schulz 2014). The only truly remarkable thing about the use-of-force manual is the fact that CBP refused to release it. The document not only fails to address the use of lethal force against rock throwers but also neglects other common practices by border patrol. While the use-of-force manual has since been updated, the most disturbing problem is that the practices of this multibillion-dollar agency do not relate to any official policy.

The documented evidence of abuses and irregularities shows the blurred line between institutional policies and practices, suggesting that these violent actions are not in fact aberrations but part of the systemic process of border and immigration enforcement. It is important to note, however, that not everyone reports negative experiences with the USBP (see table 5.4). Many of those who get lost in the desert, for example, express gratitude at being saved by the USBP. The vast range in people's experiences with the USBP helps further contextualize that this is not an issue that can be reduced to individual behaviors from bad faith actors. Instead, this is a systemic, institutional problem, one directly produced by the militarization occurring along the border and its accompanying security discourse represented by CBP's mission statement, which constructs undocumented migrants as terrorists and justifies the violence against them.

TABLE 5.4 Treatment while in U.S. custody

RESPONSE	PERCENT
Everyone treated me with respect	28
The majority treated me with respect	30
About half treated me with respect	28
The majority did not treat me with respect	9
No one treated me with respect	5

Note: The question asked in the study was "In general, how were you treated by US immigration officials during your most recent encounter with them?"
Source: Migrant Border Crossing Study, Wave II (N = 1,109), weighted data.

BORDER VIOLENCE AND COLLECTIVE
TRAUMA IN SENDING COMMUNITIES

The effects of this militarization and violence have far-reaching impacts not limited to solely to those migrating. Before the border buildup began in the mid-1990s and escalated post–September 11, 2001, researchers often reported that informants viewed the border-crossing process as a rite of passage or coming-of-age event, especially for young males, a somewhat difficult, occasionally dangerous event that helped one gain social status back home (Spener 2009; Brigden and Vogt 2014; Dunn 1996, 2009; Andreas 2000; Kandel and Massey 2002). However, the Puebla study suggests that this view is changing because of the accumulation of migrants' violent border experiences that increase their sense of the border as chaotic, dangerous, and unpredictable (Lee 2014). Accounts of run-ins with *bajadores*, coyotes that abuse or abandon migrants, and prolonged detentions followed by deportation travel quickly through migrants' hometowns, heightening migrants' and their families' sense of vulnerability. Even if a person did not experience the violence directly, what happened to family members and friends is internalized, forms painful memories, and sows fear and frustration in the community. The border, which has always been viewed as a risk, is seen as increasingly impenetrable and dangerous. "I think you just have to definitively say good bye to your family if you decide to go [to the United States]," Ignacio declared, preparing both himself and his family for the worst.[7]

Border violence produces not only individual trauma but also collective trauma through the ongoing physical and psychological assaults on people's ability to maintain social bonds and a sense of community (Erikson 1994; Robben and Suarez-Orozco 2000). Trauma is one product of the structural violence created out of quotidian injustices at the border and perpetrated on marginalized populations simply hoping to improve their chances to distance themselves from pernicious poverty. Migrant families, long divided by borders, now agonize even more over whether or not spouses and children should accompany their families across the border for a permanent relocation. While considerations of the economic costs of maintaining one's family in the north and the impact of U.S. culture on children's socialization continue to be important, now parents must face an increased possibility that their children will witness or experience violent acts in the border region. Stories of child kidnappings and parents and children being separated during the crossing are especially terrifying. Some parents simply decide that their children will remain in Mexico despite the problems that long-term separation has on family and community dynamics (Suarez-Orozco and Louie 2002), including depression and anxiety among parents and children and behavioral problems in young and adolescent children (Cavazos-Rehg, Zayas, and Spitznagel 2007). To avoid or ameliorate these problems, migrants cited family reunification as the most important reason for returning to Puebla despite the fact they knew they would have to face a dangerous border if they were to migrate in the future.

CONCLUSION

Violence, whether structural or directly perpetrated by the state, has become central to the militarized strategy for border enforcement. With the proposed increases to border security, we need to disentangle the different practices that make up immigration enforcement to determine what aspects are causing which specific types of violence. We found that the Tucson sector, which has seen the largest buildup of the USBP in the past two decades, also has the highest levels of violence in terms of abuse by U.S. authorities and the most border deaths over the past decade. However, as an increasing number of Central Americans now cross through South Texas, what will be the results of a shift in border buildup to this region? The high death toll in South Texas over the past few years shows how a strategy of neglect and isolation is also highly lethal. This does not explain the lower levels of reported abuse in this region. With additional agents and resources arriving in South Texas, will levels of abuse and violence accompany this escalation? Continued research will be required to understand the intraregional variations in border militarization and how these practices produce and manage different forms of violence.

Previous research on migration has tended to obscure geographical variations by taking a meta-approach to the border as a geopolitical phenomenon, one that can conveniently be relocated or expanded (Gregory 2011). Or, conversely, empirical studies have had difficulty connecting across border regions, and localized studies in one area are presented as representational of some sort of universal border politic (see Johnson et al. 2011 for a full discussion). This is understandable, as working along the entire border is extremely difficult, not only because transportation between cites is limited but also because of the complicated safety situation in each location. Researchers concerned with empirical studies of migration have run into the material and institutional challenges of drug violence on the border. This leaves many unanswered questions: How does the institutional mission and attitude shape abuse in different sectors? How do enforcement protocols lead to different forms of violence such as kidnapping by coyotes and gangs (Slack 2016)? Moreover, with the increases in militarization on the Mexican side of the border, how has it reshaped patterns of violence for those moving through this terrain? Future research needs to be done to determine how drug-related violence in Mexico reshaped the geography of migration as a whole.

For many in the political sphere, "secure" is synonymous with militarized, but this is not true for the majority of the people who live on the border. Harassment, long queues to cross the border, and impediments to social and economic activities contradict what a "human security" framework for the border would require (Hale 2008; Kaldor, Martin, and Selchow 2007). Enforcement actions such as the Consequence Delivery System increase the punishments and vulnerability of people looking for work or to reunite with family and contribute to twisting the logic of border enforcement away from economic and family-based migration into an antiterrorism mission. Moreover, the very fact that they are applied with such variation across the border region, as evidenced by wide variations in abuses among border patrol sectors, shows the ad hoc nature of this multibillion-dollar agency. It is hard to fathom how a militarized border can ever result in greater security. Rather, by understanding the role of public policy and institutional frailty in structuring geographies of violence, we can clearly see how militarization produces pain, death, and trauma in the border region.

NOTES

Originally published as J. Slack, D. E. Martínez, A. E. Lee, and S. Whiteford, "The Geography of Border Militarization: Violence, Death and Health in Mexico and the United States," *Journal of Latin American Geography* 15, no. 1 (2016): 7–32. Adapted here from the original.

1.   For this article we use the terms *undocumented* and *migrants* specifically because the sample we interviewed for this article as part of the MBCS must have crossed the border without proper documentation. Other scholars have noted that there are complexities of legality within the population of immigrants and therefore use the term *unauthorized*. Because of our methodological approach, this distinction does not apply. We also use the term *migrant* instead of *immigrant* to denote the different motivations present within the population. Some intend to immigrate permanently, while others simply plan on migrating to work for a specific period of time. However, we also discuss various "immigration authorities" in the United

States, as the official perspective does not distinguish these intentions. Moreover, these institutions are officially titled "immigration authorities."

2. We would like to thank the Ford Foundation for their support of the MBCS and Mexico's Council for Science and Technology (Consejo Nacional de Ciencia y Tecnología [CONACYT]) for the Puebla study (CV-22008–01–00102222, "Crisis económica global y respuesta en tres comunidades de reciente migración"). We would also like to thank the Puentes Consortium for funding this collaborative effort as well as the thousands of people who shared their stories and their lives with us during this research.

3. Discussions about the need to define a secure border led to the proposal of a metric (turnbacks + apprehensions) / (got aways + turn backs + apprehensions). However, there was a lack of standardized data, questions about the feasibility in documenting "turnbacks" (i.e., when groups turn around and return to Mexico) or "got aways" (especially because this implies that everyone crossing the border was being tracked at some point), and no agreement on what level this would take (Government Accountability Office 2013).

4. Andrés, Puebla study, interview June 19, 2011.

5. Puebla study, Jorge, June 10, 2011.

6. Puebla study, Leo, June 6, 2011.

7. Puebla study, June 23, 2011.

REFERENCES

Andreas, Peter. 2000. *Border Games: Policing the U.S.-Mexico Divide.* Ithaca, N.Y.: Cornell University Press.

Arendt, Hannah. 1970. *On Violence.* New York: Harcourt, Brace, Jovanovich.

Becker, Andrew, and G. W. Schulz. 2014. "Border Agency Watchdog Censors Recommendations to Curb Deadly Force." *Center for Investigative Reporting Online,* January 29, 2014 (no longer posted). http://cironline.org/reports/border-agency-watchdog -censors-recommendations-curb-deadly-force-5761.

Bennett, Brian. 2014. "Border Patrol's Use of Deadly Force Criticized in Report." *Los Angeles Times,* February 27, 2014. http://articles.latimes.com/2014/feb/27/nation/la-na -border-killings-20140227.

Blacher, Mitch. 2013. "US Border Patrol Has 'Alarming' Alcohol Problem, Says Internal Memo and Source." *ABC 10 News,* San Diego, November 14.

Boss, P. 1999. *Ambiguous Loss.* Cambridge, Mass.: Harvard University Press.

———. 2002. "Ambiguous Loss: Working with Families of the Missing." *Family Process* 41 (1): 4–17.

Bourdieu, Pierre. 2001. *Male Domination.* Vol. 1. Oxford: Blackwell.

Bourdieu, Pierre, and Loïc J. D. Wacquant. 1992. *An Invitation to Reflexive Sociology.* Chicago: University of Chicago Press.

Bourgois, Philippe. 2009. "Recognizing Invisible Violence: A Thirty Year Ethnographic Retrospective." In *Global Health in Times of Violence,* edited by Barbara Rylko-Bauer,

Linda Whiteford, and Paul Farmer, 17–40. Santa Fe, N.Mex.: School for Advanced Research Press.

Boyce, Geoffrey A. 2015. "The Rugged Border: Surveillance, Policing and the Dynamic Materiality of the US/Mexico Frontier." *Environment and Planning D: Society and Space* 34 (2): 245–62.

Boyce, Geoffrey, and Jill Williams. 2012. "Intervention: Homeland Security and the Precarity of Life in the Borderlands." AntipodeFoundation.org, December 10. http://antipodefoundation.org/2012/12/10/intervention-homeland-security-and-the -precarity-of-life-in-the-borderlands/.

Brigden, Noelle Kateri, and Wendy A. Vogt. 2014. "Homeland Heroes: Migrants and Soldiers in the Neoliberal Era." *Antipode* 47 (3): 303–22.

Brown, Wendy. 2010. *Walled States, Waning Sovereignty.* New York: Zone Books.

Burnett, John. 2015. "In a First, Border Agent Indicted for Killing Mexican Teen Across Border." *Morning Edition*, National Public Radio, October 9. http://www.npr.org /2015/10/09/446866267/in-a-first-border-agent-indicted-for-killing-mexican-teen -across-fence.

Cavazos-Rehg, Patricia A., Luis H. Zayas, and Edward L. Spitznagel. 2007. "Legal Status, Emotional Well-Being and Subjective Health Status of Latino Immigrants." *Journal of the National Medical Association* 99 (10): 1126.

Chatterjee, I. 2009. "Violent Morphologies: Landscape, Border and Scale in Ahmedabad Conflict." *Geoforum* 40 (6): 1003–13.

Coleman, Mathew, and Austin Kocher. 2001. "Death at the Border: Efficacy and Unintended Consequences of US Immigration Control Policy." *Population and Development Review* 27 (4): 661–85.

———. 2005. "Controlling 'Unwanted' Immigration: Lessons from the United States, 1993–2004." *Journal of Ethnic and Migration Studies* 31 (4): 775–94.

———. 2011a. "Detention, Deportation, Devolution and Immigrant Incapacitation in the US, Post 9/11." *Geographical Journal* 177 (3): 228–37.

———. 2011b. "Does Border Enforcement Matter? U.S. Immigration Policy from Clinton to Obama." Paper presented at the Global Innovation and Immigration, San Jose State University.

Cornelius, Wayne A., and Jessa M. Lewis. 2007. *Impacts of Border Enforcement on Mexican Migration: The View from Sending Communities.* La Jolla, Calif.: Center for Comparative Immigration Studies.

Customs and Border Protection. 2015a. "About CBP." http://www.cbp.gov/about.

———. 2015b. "United States Border Patrol: Sector Profile—Fiscal Year 2014." Washington, D.C.: Customs and Border Protection.

Dear, Michael. 2013. *Why Walls Won't Work: Repairing the US-Mexico Divide.* Oxford: Oxford University Press.

De Genova, Nicholas, and Nathalie Mae Peutz. 2010. *The Deportation Regime: Sovereignty, Space, and the Freedom of Movement.* Durham, N.C.: Duke University Press.

De León, Jason. 2013. "The Efficacy and Impact of the Alien Transfer Exit Programme: Migrant Perspectives from Nogales, Sonora, Mexico." *International Migration* 51 (2): 10–23.

Department of Homeland Security. 2013. "FY 2011 Budget in Brief." Washington, D.C.: Department of Homeland Security.

Dunn, Timothy J. 1996. *The Militarization of the U.S.-Mexico Border, 1978–1992: Low-Intensity Conflict Doctrine Comes Home.* Austin: CMAS Books, University of Texas at Austin.

———. 2009. *Blockading the Border and Human Rights: The El Paso Operation That Remade Immigration Enforcement.* Austin: University of Texas Press.

Durand, Jorge, and Douglas S. Massey, eds. 2004. *Crossing the Border: Research from the Mexican Migration Project.* New York: Russell Sage Foundation.

Erikson, Kai. 1994. *A New Species of Trouble: Explorations in Disaster, Trauma, and Community.* New York: W. W. Norton.

Eschbach, Karl, Jacqueline Hagan, Nestor Rodríguez, Ruben Hernandez-Leon, and Stanley Bailey. 1999. "Death at the Border." *International Migration Review* 33 (2): 430–54.

Farmer, Paul. 1996. "On Suffering and Structural Violence: A View from Below." *Daedalus* 125 (1): 261–83.

———. 2003. *Pathologies of Power: Health, Human Rights, and the New War on the Poor.* Berkeley: University of California Press.

Fassin, Didier, and Richard Rechtman. 2009. *The Empire of Trauma: An Inquiry into the Condition of Victimhood.* Princeton, N.J.: Princeton University Press.

Fernandez-Kelly, Patricia, and Douglas Massey. 2007. "Borders for Whom? The Role of NAFTA in Mexico-U.S. Migration." *Annals of the American Academy of Political and Social Science* 610 (1): 98–118.

Frey, John Carlos. 2013. "Crossing the Line at the Border: Dying to Get Back." *Need to Know*, PBS, May 17. http://www.pbs.org/wnet/need-to-know/video/border-patrol-part-3/16916/.

Fukuda-Parr, Sakiko, and Carol Messineo. 2012. "Human Security: A Critical Review of the Literature." In Centre for Research on Peace and Development Working Paper no. 11. Leuven, Belgium: Centre for Research on Peace and Development.

Galtung, Johan. 1969. "Violence, Peace, and Peace Research." *Journal of Peace Research* 6 (3): 167–91.

Garmany, Jeff. 2011. "Drugs, Violence, Fear, and Death: The Necro- and Narco-geographies of Contemporary Urban Space." *Urban Geography Urban Geography* 32 (8): 1148–66.

Government Accountability Office. 2010. *DHS Needs to Strengthen Management and Oversight of Its Prime Contractor.* Washington, D.C.: U.S. Government Accountability Office.

———. 2013. *Border Patrol Goals and Measures Not Yet in Place to Inform Border Security Status and Resource Needs.* Washington, D.C.: U.S. Government Accountability Office.

Gregory, Derek. 2011. "The Everywhere War." *Geographical Journal* 177 (3): 238–50.

Gregory, Derek, and Allan Pred. 2007. *Violent Geographies: Fear, Terror, and Political Violence.* New York: Routledge.

Hagan, Jacqueline Phillips Scott. 2008. "Border Blunders: The Unanticipated Human and Economic Costs of the U.S. Approach to Immigration Control, 1986–2007." *Criminology and Public Policy* 7 (1): 83–94.

Hale, Charles R. 2008. *Engaging Contradictions: Theory, Politics, and Methods of Activist Scholarship.* Berkeley: University of California Press.

Heyman, Josiah McC. 2001. "Class and Classification at the US-Mexico Border." *Human Organization* 60 (2): 128–40.

———. 2004. "The Anthropology of Power-Wielding Bureaucracies." *Human Organization* 63 (4): 487–500.

———. 2008. "Constructing a Virtual Wall: Race and Citizenship in U.S.-Mexico Border Policing." *Journal of the Southwest* 50 (3): 305–33.

Holmes, Seth. 2013. *Fresh Fruit, Broken Bodies: Migrant Farmworkers in the United States.* California Series in Public Anthropology, vol. 27. Berkeley: University of California Press.

Instituto Nacional de Migracion. 2013. *Estadística Migratoria: Síntesis 2012.* Mexico City: Instituto Nacional de Migracion.

Izcara Palacios, Simón Pedro. 2012. "Coyotaje y Grupos Delictivos en Tamaulipas." *Latin American Research Review* 47 (3): 41–61.

Johnson, Corey, Reece Jones, Anssi Paasi, Louise Amoore, Alison Mountz, Mark Salter, and Chris Rumford. 2011. "Interventions on Rethinking 'The Border' in Border Studies." *Political Geography* 30 (2): 61–69.

Judicial Watch. 2015. "ISIS Camp a Few Miles from Texas, Mexican Authorities Confirm." *Judicial Watch*, April 14. https://www.judicialwatch.org/blog/2015/04/isis-camp -a-few-miles-from-texas-mexican-authorities-confirm/.

Kaldor, Mary. 2007. *Human Security.* Cambridge: Polity Press.

Kaldor, Mary H., Mary E. Martin, and Sabine Selchow. 2007. "Human Security: A New Strategic Narrative for Europe." *International Affairs* 83 (2): 273–88.

Kandel, William, and Douglas S. Massey. 2002. "The Culture of Mexican Migration: A Theoretical and Empirical Analysis." *Social Forces* 80 (3): 981–1004.

Le Billon, Philippe. 2001. "The Political Ecology of War: Natural Resources and Armed Conflicts." *Political Geography* 20 (5): 561–84.

Lee, Alison Elizabeth. 2014. "Crisis económica global, vigilancia/violencia fronteriza y sobreexplotación: Cambios en los patrones migratorios internacionales en Zapotitlán Salinas, Puebla." In *¿Todos vuelven? Migración acelerada, crisis de la economía estadounidense y retorno en cuatro localidades del estado de Puebla, México,* edited by María Eugenia D'Aubeterre and María Leticia Rivermar, 117–64. Puebla: Instituto de Ciencias Sociales y Humanidades, Benemérita Autónoma Universidad de Puebla.

Lydgate, Joanna Jacobbi. 2010. "Assembly-line Justice: A Review of Operation Streamline." *California Law Review* 98 (2): 481–544.

Martínez, Daniel E. 2016. "Migrant Deaths in the Sonora Desert: Evidence of Unsuccessful Border Militarization Efforts from Southern Arizona." In *Migrant Deaths in the Arizona Desert: No vale nada la vida*, edited by R. Rubio-Goldsmith, C. Fernandez, J. F. Finch, and A. Masterson, 97–119. Tucson: University of Arizona Press.

Martínez, Daniel, Guillermo Cantor, and Walter Ewing. 2014. "No Action Taken: Lack of Accountability in Responding to Complaints of Abuse." In *Special Report*. Washington, D.C.: American Immigration Council.

Martínez, Daniel, Robin Reineke, Raquel Rubio-Goldsmith, Bruce Anderson, Gregory Hess, and Bruce Parks. 2013. "A Continued Humanitarian Crisis on the Border: Undocumented Border Crossers Deaths Recorded by the Pima County Office of the Medical Examiner 1990–2012." Tucson: Bi-National Migration Institute, University of Arizona.

Martínez, Daniel E., Robin C. Reineke, Raquel Rubio-Goldsmith, and Bruce O. Parks. 2014. "Structural Violence and Migrant Deaths in Southern Arizona: Data from the Pima County Office of the Medical Examiner, 1990–2013." *Journal on Migration and Human Security* 2 (4): 257–86.

Martinez, Daniel, and Jeremy Slack. 2013. "What Part of 'Illegal' Don't You Understand? The Social Consequences of Criminalizing Unauthorized Mexican Migrants in the United States." *Social and Legal Studies* 22 (4): 535–51.

Massey, Douglas S., Jorge Durand, and Nolan J. Malone. 2002. *Beyond Smoke and Mirrors: Mexican Immigration in an Era of Economic Integration*. New York: Russell Sage Foundation.

Meissner, Doris, Donald Kerwin, Muzaffar Chishti, and Claire Bergeron. 2013. *Immigration Enforcement in the United States: The Rise of a Formidable Machinery*. Washington, D.C.: Migration Policy Institute.

Miller, Todd. 2014. *Border Patrol Nation: Dispatches from the Front Lines of Homeland Security*. San Francisco: City Lights.

Nevins, J. 2014. "Killing with Impunity on the U.S.-Mexico Border: The Global Color Line." *Border Wars*, nacla.org, February 25, 2014. https://nacla.org/blog/2014/2/26/killing-impunity-us-mexico-border-global-color-line.

Nevins, Joseph. 2002. *Operation Gatekeeper: The Rise of the "Illegal Alien" and the Making of the U.S.-Mexico Boundary*. New York: Routledge.

———. 2005. "A Beating Worse Than Death: Imagining and Contesting Violence in the US-Mexico Borderlands." *AmeriQuests* 2 (1): 1–25.

Nevins, Joseph, and Mizue Aizeki. 2008. *Dying to Live: A Story of U.S. Immigration in an Age of Global Apartheid*. San Francisco: Open Media / City Lights.

No More Deaths. 2011. *Culture of Cruelty: Abuse and Impunity in U.S. Border Patrol Short-Term Detention*. Tucson: No More Deaths.

O'Leary, Anna Ochoa. 2009. "Mujeres en el Cruce: Remapping Border Security Through Migrant Mobility." *Journal of the Southwest* 51 (4): 523–42.

Orrenius, Pia M., and Roberto Coronado. 2005. *The Effect of Illegal Immigration and Border Enforcement on Crime Rates Along the US-Mexico Border*. San Diego: Center for Comparative Immigration Studies, University of California.

Ortega, Bob, and Rob O'Dell. 2013. "Deadly Border Agent Incidents Cloaked in Silence." *Arizona Republic,* December 16. http://www.azcentral.com/news/politics/articles/20131212arizona-border-patrol-deadly-force-investigation.html.

Peluso, Nancy Lee, and Michael Watts. 2001. *Violent Environments*. Ithaca, N.Y.: Cornell University Press.

Phillips, Scott, Jacqueline Maria Hagan, and Nestor Rodríguez. 2006. "Brutal Borders? Examining the Treatment of Deportees During Arrest and Detention." *Social Forces* 85 (1): 1.

Richardson, Chad, and Rosalva Resendiz. 2006. *On the Edge of the Law: Culture, Labor, and Deviance on the South Texas Border*. Austin: University of Texas Press.

Robben, Antonius C. G. M., and Marcelo M. Suarez-Orozco. 2000. *Cultures Under Siege: Collective Violence and Trauma*. Cambridge: Cambridge University Press.

Rodríguez, Nestor, and Jacqueline Maria Hagan. 2004. "Fractured Families and Communities: Effects of Immigration Reform in Texas, Mexico, and El Salvador." *Latino Studies* 2 (3): 328–51.

Scheper-Hughes, Nancy. 1992. *Death Without Weeping: The Violence of Everyday Life in Brazil*. Berkeley: University of California Press.

Scheper-Hughes, Nancy, and Philippe I. Bourgois. 2004. *Violence in War and Peace*. New York. Blackwell.

Secor, Anna J. 2007. "Between Longing and Despair: State, Space, and Subjectivity in Turkey." *Environment and Planning D* 25 (1): 35–52.

Slack, Jeremy. 2016. "Captive Bodies: Migrant Kidnapping and Deportation in Mexico." *Area* 48 (3): 271–77. doi:10.1111/area.12151.

Slack, Jeremy, Daniel E. Martínez, Scott Whiteford, and Emily Peiffer. 2013. "In the Shadow of the Wall: Family Separation, Immigration Enforcement and Security." Report, Center for Latin American Studies, University of Arizona. https://las.arizona .edu/sites/las.arizona.edu/files/UA_Immigration_Report2013web.pdf.

———. 2015. "In Harm's Way: Family Separation, Immigration Enforcement Programs and Security on the US-Mexico Border." *Journal on Migration and Human Security* 3 (2): 109–28.

Slack, Jeremy, and Scott Whiteford. 2011. "Violence and Migration on the Arizona-Sonora Border." *Human Organization* 70 (1): 11–21.

Spener, David. 2009. *Clandestine Crossings: Migrants and Coyotes on the Texas-Mexico Border*. Ithaca, N.Y.: Cornell University Press.

Staudt, Kathleen A., Tony Payan, and Z. Anthony Kruszewski. 2009. *Human Rights Along the U.S.-Mexico Border: Gendered Violence and Insecurity*. Tucson: University of Arizona Press.

Suarez-Orozco, C., I. Todorova, and J. L. Louie 2002. "Making Up for Lost Time: The Experience of Separation and Reunification Among Immigrant Families." *Family Process* 41 (4): 625–43.

Tanfani, Joseph, Brian Bennett, and David Savage. 2015. "Should Noncitizens Be Protected from Excessive Force at Border? Supreme Court to Consider Case." *Los Angeles Times*, November 6. http://www.latimes.com/nation/la-na-court-border-shooting -20151106-story.html.

Tyner, James A. 2012. *Space, Place, and Violence: Violence and the Embodied Geographies of Race, Sex and Gender*. New York: Routledge.

U.S. Border Patrol. 2013a. "Nationwide Illegal Alien Apprehensions: Fiscal Years 1925–2012." https://www.cbp.gov/sites/default/files/assets/documents/2016-Oct/BP%20Total%20Apps%20FY1925-FY2016.pdf.

———. 2013b. "United States Border Patrol Southwest Border Sectors: Southwest Border Deaths by Fiscal Year." https://www.cbp.gov/sites/default/files/assets/documents/2016-Oct/BP%20Southwest%20Border%20Sector%20Deaths%20FY1998%20-%20FY2016.pdf.

Watts, Michael J. 2013. *Silent Violence: Food, Famine, and Peasantry in Northern Nigeria.* Geographies of Justice and Social Transformation, vol. 15. Athens: University of Georgia Press.

Woodhouse, Murphy. 2013. "Autopsy Paints Troubling Picture in Border Patrol Shooting." *Border Wars*, nacla.org, February 21, 2013. https://nacla.org/blog/2013/2/22/update-autopsy-paints-troubling-picture-border-patrol-shooting.

6

WHAT PART OF "ILLEGAL" DON'T *YOU* UNDERSTAND?

The Social Consequences of Criminalizing Unauthorized
Mexican Migrants in the United States

DANIEL E. MARTÍNEZ AND JEREMY SLACK

INTRODUCTION

BETWEEN DRUG-RELATED VIOLENCE, state and federal anti-immigrant initiatives, and the Consequence Delivery System (CDS) aimed at punishing
undocumented migrants, the situation along the U.S.-Mexico border presents
a grim reality for the hundreds of thousands of people deported every year.
Although scholars have identified policy changes that have contributed greatly
to the criminalization of unauthorized immigrants in the United States (Boehm
2011; Coleman 2007; Golash-Boza 2009; Welch 2003, 2007), relatively little
work has focused on the social implications of this emerging criminalization
process. Controversial policies such as Arizona's Senate Bill 1070 and Alabama's
House Bill 56 as well as federal programs like Secure Communities, 287(g), and
Operation Streamline have all contributed to the increased incarceration of
unauthorized immigrants in addition to record numbers of interior apprehensions and formal removals by Immigration and Customs Enforcement (ICE).
We ask how these policies are contributing to the (re)production and perpetuation of another criminalized, subordinate class within the United States while
also placing people in danger upon return to Mexico, especially for those who
become involved in crime as a direct result of the contacts made while incarcerated for immigration violations or being deported.

Relying on data gathered through semistructured interviews with recent deportees, we detail how recent policy changes have not only figuratively but literally redefined what it means to be "illegal" in the United States. We stress that our intention is not to generalize to all unauthorized migrants and the contemporary migration experience, nor do we empirically test extant criminological theories. Rather, our goal is to draw on our conversations with deportees to illuminate the social harm arising from the systematic criminalization of unauthorized migrants as a politically motivated and profit-generating enterprise. This in itself is a challenging task. Friedrichs (2007) has called attention to the chasm between traditional and critical perspectives in explicating issues of crime and criminalization at a global level. We hope to indirectly contribute to bridging this gap by drawing on mainstream criminological theories to help highlight the consequences of treating violators of immigration law as criminals while simultaneously providing a critical analysis of the powerful entities that have deliberately reshaped immigration policy in the United States.

THE CRIMINALIZATION OF IMMIGRATION LAW AND INCREASED INCARCERATION

In this article, we interrogate the "immigration industrial complex" (Golash-Boza 2009) in order to identify the implications of big business and lawmakers generating what we believe to be a major social problem—the social criminalization of migrants. The process of questioning the immigration-industrial complex involves theorizing the intersections between individuals, the state, and the corporations in securing the border, be it inside the United States or directly at the two-thousand-mile border with Mexico. Three interrelated factors, among others, have contributed significantly to the rise of the immigration-industrial complex: the "criminalization of immigration law" (Coleman 2007, 56), a shift toward an incarceration-oriented approach to immigration control, and the emergence of the CDS (Fisher 2011)—the latter having largely emerged out of the aforementioned processes.

During the 1990s and 2000s, the United States attempted to address the issue of unauthorized migration by adopting the "prevention through deterrence" strategy, which relied largely on militarizing the U.S.-Mexico border (Andreas 1998, 2009; Dunn 2009; Massey, Durand, and Malone 2002; U.S.

Border Patrol 1994). After being apprehended, migrants typically agreed to a voluntary repatriation to a Mexican border town. This approach resulted in the "voluntary departure complex" (Heyman 1995) in which the migrants simply kept attempting to cross the border until they avoided detection.

Around the same time, policy makers seized windows of opportunity created by moral panics over the 1993 and 2001 terrorist attacks on the World Trade Center to enact tougher immigration legislation (Coleman 2007; Golash-Boza 2009; Welch 2003, 2007). In the process, policy makers have coupled "immigration control to criminal law enforcement," a course of action that Coleman (2007, 56) has described as the "criminalization of immigration law." Immigration infractions have historically been treated as federal civil administrative matters; however, an increasingly anti-immigrant political climate and worries surrounding potential terrorist attacks have shifted policies toward criminal prosecution for unauthorized entry (Coleman 2007; Welch 2003, 2007). This has led to an increased risk of apprehension, incarceration, and deportation stemming from interactions with law and immigration enforcement officials.

The 1996 Illegal Immigration Reform and Immigration Responsibility Act expanded the list of deportable offenses and "aggravated felonies—a specific class of crimes committed by non-citizens, applicable only in the context of immigration law, and warranting deportation from the U.S." (Coleman 2007, 58). In certain cases, this can include illegal reentry. The newly enacted immigration policies were also made retroactive, meaning that immigrants could be deported for crimes for which they were previously adjudicated, including instances where individuals pled guilty to certain offenses in exchange for probation rather than risk serving jail time and even in cases where no formal sentence was given (Coleman 2007; Welch 2007). This meant that "individuals could be identified as deportable aggravated felons without an explicit conviction for an aggravated felony" (Coleman 2007, 58). The growing incongruences between immigration law and criminal law have increased, whereby immigrants are essentially tried twice for the same crime, once in a criminal court and again in an immigration court. This has resulted in the need for immigration lawyers to undergo training in criminal law and for public defenders to familiarize themselves with immigration law when defending immigrants in criminal court. The *Padilla v. Kentucky* Supreme Court ruling requires individuals to be counseled on the immigration-related consequences of criminal convictions (Kanstroom 2011).

Perhaps most disturbing is that the lines between immigration policy and criminal law have become increasingly blurred while the judicial review process for immigration violations has become increasingly limited (Coleman 2007). This restricts the ability of unauthorized migrants to defend themselves legitimately against charges during the judicial process and increases the likelihood of an unfavorable outcome compared with citizens—most notably deportation.

The use of private detention facilities to house violators of immigration law has increased significantly over the past ten years (Wides-Muñoz and Burke 2012), a trend that appears to have paralleled increased penalties associated with unauthorized reentry. Today, about half of all people held on immigration violations are serving time in private detention facilities (Wides-Muñoz and Burke 2012). The extent to which the private prison lobby was involved in crafting Arizona's SB 1070 received increased public scrutiny because of a radio news story by National Public Radio (Robbins 2010). In December 2009, four months before the bill was signed into law, the American Legislative Exchange Council held a conference in Washington, D.C. At the conference, former senator Russell Pearce (R-Ariz.) and other lobbyists drafted a piece of legislation titled "Support Our Law Enforcement and Safe Neighborhoods Act," the exact name given to the bill signed into law by Arizona governor Jan Brewer in 2010 (Sullivan 2010). The connections between the policy makers who drafted the bill and private prison interests are undeniable yet completely legal (Wides-Muñoz and Burke 2012). Of the bill's thirty-six cosponsors, thirty received donations from prison lobbyist groups, and two of Governor Brewer's top aides were former lobbyists for private prisons (Sullivan 2010). CoreCivic, which at the time was called Corrections Corporation of America (CCA), was on the verge of bankruptcy in 2000 (Wides-Muñoz and Burke 2012) and openly pursued detention of immigrants as a primary source of revenue generation. "Last year, they wrote that they expect to bring in 'a significant portion of our revenues' from Immigration and Customs Enforcement, the agency that detains illegal immigrants" (Sullivan 2010). In 2011, CCA reported a net income of US\$162 million, with federal contracts making up 43 percent of the company's total revenues.

Clandestine migration to the United States has slumped to twenty-year lows, which has coincided with an economic downturn that has been particularly devastating for construction and service sectors of the economy (Cornelius 2010). This trend threatened to leave private detention centers half empty and the more than twenty thousand border patrol agents (U.S. Department of Customs and Border Protection 2011) tending empty processing centers or patrolling an empty desert. We contend that part of the impetus to increase criminal penalties for immigration violations comes from the need to maintain this revenue stream from the federal government (for private industries as well as federal agencies). CoreCivic has purchased detention facilities across the United States and in many states garnered contracts pledging minimum 90 percent occupancy (Pavlo 2012). While the Department of Justice canceled their contracts with private detention facilities during the Obama administration, the Trump administration has signaled their willingness to restart these relationships, causing stock prices for Geo Group and CoreCivic to soar (Long 2017).

The exploitation and extraction of capital from undocumented workers in the United States has expanded beyond low wages and few benefits and now includes the emergence of an industry—one that is paid to take control of this labor force in times of economic contraction when demand for it has decreased. Today, this approach is neatly packaged and touted to the public as the CDS. The CDS has also increased incarceration time for undocumented migrants and increased the number of people who are now considered "criminal aliens," thereby maintaining the status quo in terms of justification for the record number of detention facilities and border patrol agents. Therefore, in addition to being profitable, increasing the arrests and incarceration of undocumented migrants has become politically valuable.

TOWARD AN ETHNOGRAPHY OF REMOVAL

Scholars have begun to take interest in processes of removal and deportation of immigrants. Although not a fully fledged subtopic of academic inquiry, the examination of modes and manners of removal provides an important supplement to studies of migration. However, deportation and removal as processes are almost always intertwined, not only with migration but with imprisonment as well. For De Genova and Peutz (2010), the question becomes, why does the state deport? Why remove people en masse? We follow by asking why systematically criminalize and incarcerate an entire segment of the population, especially when they will almost inevitably be removed to another part of the world afterward? The answers to these questions rest in part on the control of surplus labor (Marx [1867] 1978). By providing the constant potential for deportation or "deportability" (De Genova and Peutz 2010; Nuñez and Heyman 2007), a docile workforce is created with limited engagement outside the sites of capital extraction. Although insightful, we contend that this theoretical approach may not be as applicable during times of economic contraction when there is decreased demand for undocumented labor.

Rather than merely deporting the surplus labor force in times of economic downturn, systematic criminalization and incarceration ensures that excess undocumented labor is economically exploited to its full potential before being removed. Detention facilities have become sites of capital extraction beyond the surplus value of labor, ultimately extending to the commodification of the imprisoned body, especially in its extreme form with the exponential growth of for-profit private prisons. We follow Loïc Wacquant (2000) in his characterization of the prison as a surrogate ghetto where incarceration is a new legal regime—one that logically extends slavery, Jim Crow laws, and the ghettoization of the inner city as a place to house unwanted labor. The dialectical relationship of capital, labor, and now the imprisonment of that labor force has created a system of immense social consequences that stays with people for years or decades after they are released, especially for people intent on reuniting with families in the United States.

The criminalization of unauthorized migrants and all the intricacies this process entails creates multiple layers of marginality, highlighting the flexibility of the state and the need to create new criminal categories. The fact that immigration offenders are frequently incarcerated in the same spaces with criminal offenders, coupled with the desperation of people who need to find a way to support family members either in Mexico or in the United States, means engaging in criminal activity is becoming increasingly common.

The practice of incarcerating violators of immigration law has exposed many unauthorized migrants to criminal offenders in detention facilities where norms and values that are favorable to criminal behavior can be acquired and reproduced (Sutherland 1947; Burgess and Akers 1966). The social consequences of criminalizing and incarcerating people for immigration violations include (1) significantly reducing migrants' chances of gaining legal permanent resident status (or having this status revoked) and (2) introducing migrants into illegitimate means structures (Cloward 1959; Cloward and Ohlin 1960) that may precipitate involvement in narcotics and human smuggling by incarcerating them alongside serious criminal offenders. These experiences are especially destructive for young migrants who are determined to remain in the United States because they have incorporated into American society and have more social ties and life experiences there than in their countries of origin.

We document the ways in which incarceration for immigration violations increases migrants' exposure to cross border illicit activities, such as human or drug smuggling, that are normally distinct from clandestine border crossings (Spener 2009). Drawing from our qualitative interviews with recently deported migrants, we highlight the different ways that subsectors of the migrant stream are targeted. While circumstances facing the vast majority of undocumented migrants include lack of adequate legal counsel, the incongruence between immigration and criminal law, the extreme repercussions for menial offenses, and the tremendous variation in consequences, treatment, and abuse creates a difficult and confusing scenario for research.

METHODOLOGY

The data in this article come from 210 in-depth interviews with recently deported migrants in a shelter in Nogales, Sonora, Mexico. The interviews are derived mainly from deportees who spent time in Arizona's state and federal penal systems or were held in one of many private detention facilities across the state. Our qualitative data consist of a subsample from Waves I and II of the MBCS. Among 415 respondents surveyed in Wave I, we found that nearly 25 percent were sent to a detention center after being processed by the border patrol. This figure increased notably to nearly 40 percent of respondents in Wave II. Most were held in detention facilities that had a gang task force. While most people charged with immigration offenses are housed in separate units away from gang members and violence, transfers and appointments for court appearances mix the populations, sometimes for days at a time, creating experiences that many people relate with fear and shock. A closer examination of the social repercussions of criminalizing and incarcerating unauthorized economic migrants for political and economic gain is imperative.

THE RAMIFICATIONS OF A PENAL APPROACH TO UNAUTHORIZED IMMIGRATION

In order to maintain the security apparatus and its economic prominence, a subsection of migrants must be created that will continually remain in contact with the state. This subsection consists of the individuals who have established a home and family in the United States and will continue to attempt to gain entry regardless of the punishment handed down. We have interviewed people who have spent years in detention for immigration violations and are determined to enter the United States yet again. In one case, one of our respondents spent two years in detention, was deported, crossed again, was apprehended and deported without being detained, and then, upon crossing again, was detained for six months before being interviewed.[1] Despite this demoralizing and highly confusing experience, he was dead set on returning to be with his family. The process of crossing—hoping for a successful attempt, and then upon failure, hoping that sentencing will be lenient—is a defining factor in his life. Moreover, if he arrives at his destination, he will live in constant fear of any contact with authorities because of his status.

FROM BUSINESS OWNER AND FAMILY MAN TO "CRIMINAL"

The following vignette provides firsthand examples of the incongruences between immigration policies and criminal law and how they can create a hidden disadvantage for unauthorized migrants who are simultaneously caught in the judicial, immigration, and penal systems. Luis's story also demonstrates exactly how perilous an incarceration-oriented approach to dealing with unauthorized immigration can be for individuals without legal status and their families.

Luis Alvaro Rodriguez had been in the United States for fifteen years.[2] He operated his own business doing minor construction projects as a repairperson and landscaper in Tucson, Arizona. In April 2009, Luis was driving his brother to the bus station so that he could catch a ride to the border and then to the central Mexican state of Guanajuato. He was carrying US$4,000 in cash for their parents back home, a common way to send remittances to Mexico. Police officers pulled over their car in a random traffic stop and searched their belongings. The officers found the cash and accused Luis of laundering money. Luis protested that he could prove he obtained it legally, but they confiscated the money and sent him to jail. He was given a receipt for the cash, but because he was immediately deported to Mexico, neither he nor his family recovered the money despite handing over documentation of his income.

Luis was prosecuted through Operation Streamline, a mass trial for immigration violators, which occurs five days a week at the Tucson federal courthouse downtown. About seventy people are tried and convicted of entering the country illegally, given a misdemeanor or felony charge (depending on prior violations), and formally deported to Mexico. Luis had never imagined such a process existed in the United States. He was adamant that there should be criminal prosecution for *mulas* (drug smugglers), coyotes (human smugglers), and *sicarios* (cartel hitmen), but Luis made it clear that he is not a criminal and has never done anything except to work hard to support his family. Luis's experience in the courtroom terrified him. When he was called in front of the judge to plead guilty, Luis said that he could not even physically speak; the words would not come out. "It is too intimidating. For normal people like me who never thought we would be in this situation, how do you respond? I felt like crying," said Luis.

Upon leaving court, he was taken to the border patrol processing center. His lawyer insisted that he not sign the deportation form because his children and the amount of time he spent in the United States gave him a legitimate claim for residency. Luis said that the agents began threatening him, telling him that he would go to jail for years if he did not sign and, eventually, he caved. Luis's lawyer advised him to come back to the United States as soon as possible so that he could demonstrate continued residence. This is just one of the many ways that the lack of immigration reform has led to a confusing and contradictory system in which people are often required to break one law in order to remain in compliance with another while putting their lives at risk in the process.

Luis crossed back into the United States on April 17, 2009. Along the way, border bandits, known locally as *bajadores*, robbed him at gunpoint, stealing all of his food, Mex$500, and US$30. Despite spending three more days walking without food, he made it back to Tucson and began working again. Six months later, a police officer stopped Luis after work because the officer claimed his van was suspiciously weighted down. After the officer looked inside and noticed the tools and building materials, he said that he did not need to look around but asked Luis to wait for a minute. Soon a U.S. Border Patrol agent showed up and apprehended Luis.

Once again, he was processed through Operation Streamline, and this time he was sentenced to sixty days in a privately owned and operated CCA detention facility in Florence, Arizona. He was convicted of a felony for unlawful reentry, essentially eliminating his claims for residency.

Detention had a profound impact on Luis. He claimed to only have met two or three people who were there for unlawful reentry; the rest were incarcerated for drug offenses, gang-related matters, or domestic violence charges. He said that the *burreros* (a common term for people who carry marijuana through the desert in backpacks) were constantly talking about the amount of drugs they were carrying—10 kg of marijuana in the tire of a car, 5 pounds of heroin, 50 pounds of marijuana in a backpack—one person even told Luis that he was caught carrying a load of drugs and that the border patrol confiscated it and simply returned him to Mexico. Luis was upset that the people whose drugs are confiscated or "lost" get off without a charge. He said that the people that had drugs would get out in five days, while he and the two others incarcerated for reentry stayed for months. "It makes me want to just go with drugs next time. If they get five days when they have drugs and I get sixty days for nothing, why shouldn't I?" he asked.

The people Luis described were most likely not being charged with drug trafficking because U.S. authorities realize that they are merely *mulas* (drug mules) rather than high-ranking cartel members and, therefore, do not warrant the expenditure of necessary resources to prosecute them. Rather, in these cases, the contraband is seized and the individuals are processed as unauthorized migrants and given a voluntary repatriation or formal deportation. Luis's perception that these individuals receive less severe punishments than migrants should be taken with a grain of salt, as it has become common to process everyone through Operation Streamline in order to save time, which means that charges will be roughly the same. It is also likely that the U.S. officials are willing to be more lenient on *mulas* if they agree to provide information that could lead to arrests of other members higher up in the cartel pecking order. However, *mulas* are often unfamiliar with the chain of command in what have become increasingly decentralized smuggling networks and, therefore, provide few leads for prosecutors. Although Luis may not be aware of the intricacies between voluntary repatriations, drug trafficking prosecutions, and Operation Streamline proceedings, his perception is that he is being incarcerated alongside *mulas* and *burreros* who are punished less punitively than migrants prosecuted for unlawful reentry. He is, however, well aware that not all unauthorized migrants are processed through Operation Streamline, which adds to his frustration. Luis is not alone in his perception of and frustration with this situation, as numerous respondents have brought such inconsistencies to our attention.

Luis was again deported to Nogales, Sonora, after being forced to sign another deportation order. It is a common practice for the U.S. authorities to repatriate unauthorized Mexican migrants to a border town rather than to their communities of origin—a practice that carries numerous potential consequences in and of itself. When they dropped Luis off two nights before our interview on December 9, 2009, it was midnight, and he was wearing the same shirt that he had been wearing two months ago when he was apprehended. He did not have any money or know of anywhere to sleep. He found a pile of trash and wrapped himself in it for the night. Groups Beta, a Mexican agency that provides assistance to migrants, helped him get shoes and a jacket the next day and took him to the shelter where he was able to eat and sleep. Although grateful, these small comforts did little to assuage his main fear of losing his family. Luis's lawyer informed him that he would be incarcerated for anywhere from six months to one year if he were apprehended again. Despite this risk, Luis said that he would try to cross again in February.

OPERATION STREAMLINE AND DETENTION: THE "SOLUTION" TO THE VOLUNTARY DEPARTURE COMPLEX

There are numerous ways for migrants to be removed from the United States that do not involve a criminal proceeding; however, there has been a notable shift away from the administrative process of removal, such as a voluntary repatriation, in favor of criminal prosecution. At the time of our fieldwork, most unauthorized Mexican immigrants apprehended while attempting to cross the border sign paperwork and are repatriated within a day or two, usually to a Mexican border town. First-time offenders in Operation Streamline, however, typically are convicted or plead guilty to unauthorized entry and face anywhere from time served to 180 days of detention (La Coalición de Derechos Humanos 2008; Lydgate 2010; McCombs 2008; Stanton 2008; U.S. Department of Customs and Border Protection 2005). If a person is caught a second time and has already been through Operation Streamline or previously deported, they can be charged with felony reentry under 8 U.S.C. § 1326, which generally carries a 2-year maximum penalty but can involve up to a 20-year maximum if the migrant has a criminal record (Lydgate 2010).

The overwhelming majority of people incarcerated as a result of Operation Streamline proceedings are held in private detention facilities. The increased reliance on privately owned detention centers confirms Wacquant's analysis of the prison industry's "frenetic development of a private incarceration industry . . . which has taken on a national and even international scope to satisfy the state's demand for expanded punishment" (Wacquant 2009, xv). We also follow Wacquant in his analysis of the incarceration system as another technology of control and extraction that mirrors the trajectory from slavery to Jim Crow laws to the ghetto all as places to store reserve labor when it is undesirable (Wacquant 2000; see also Alexander 2010). Although illegal entry and reentry have been considered federal immigration crimes since the early 1920s, Operation Streamline is the first major attempt to systematically charge and convict border crossers entering the United States without authorization. Despite the magnitude of this shift, very little academic work has studied people's experiences with Operation Streamline proceedings.

Although only an hour long, the Operation Streamline proceeding can have negative long-term legal, social, and psychological implications for people who undergo the process.

A forty-one-year-old man stated about his experience during the court proceeding, "They shouldn't treat us that way. They treat us like animals. It's inhumane." Another twenty-two-year-old from Tlaxcala, Mexico, said succinctly, "They kill us psychologically." Benjamín, a forty-five-year-old fisherman from Michoacán, has crossed over thirteen times to work in the United States and has even been apprehended five times. Yet this was his first experience with Operation Streamline. He stated, "I felt bad when it happened (the court proceeding). . . . That has never happened to me, I have never been chained up like that. . . . Now they treat you like an animal." Javier, a twenty-two-year-old originally from Chiapas who had been working at a factory in Tijuana, recalls, "We all went in a big group in front of the judge. . . . They put chains on us really tight. . . . The whole time in there they made me feel like I killed someone." The shock expressed here shows how alien this entire experience is for these individuals. These comments also help illustrate that not only has the legal criminalization process begun for these migrants but the psychological criminalization process has as well. It is not uncommon to hear statements from respondents justifying their own detention or criminal prosecution under the same anti-immigrant adage, "We broke the law." "We came illegally." These are labels, images, and experiences they have begun to internalize and will carry with them throughout their lives. The criminalization of migrants is also a symbolic process of violence that internalizes and naturalizes the identity of "criminal" (Bourdieu 2001; Bourdieu and Wacquant 1992). These symbolic dimensions contribute to the social processes of criminalization that have concerned critical criminologists for decades.

SOCIAL IMPACTS OF CRIMINALIZATION: DESPERATION, STRAIN, AND ACCESS TO ILLEGITIMATE MEANS STRUCTURES

Scholars have long suggested that crime is caused in part by strain stemming from various negative social experiences or the inability to achieve certain commonly held goals in the society (Agnew 1992; Cloward and Ohlin 1960; Cohen 1955; Merton 1938). Access to the means needed to pursue certain commonly held goals is not available to many members of the society because of certain economic and social restrictions, and it is precisely this disconnect that can lead to criminal behavior (Merton 1938). Individuals may seek out illegitimate means that society deems deviant to pursue and achieve their desired goals or to alleviate other forms of strain such as poverty (e.g., Agnew 1992; Cloward and Ohlin 1960; Merton 1938). This perspective offers great insight into the social criminalization of unauthorized migrants, especially those who have served time in close proximity with human and drug smugglers.

The notion of illegitimate means structures can be applied to the case of unauthorized immigration in two ways: the first relates to the act of unauthorized migration itself, while the second speaks to the social contacts that unauthorized migrants develop while incarcerated alongside criminal offenders. An argument can be made that the need to migrate is a crucial social or economic goal for many unauthorized immigrants. Nevertheless, most do not possess the necessary human or economic capital to pursue legitimate immigration opportunities such as acquiring a visa. Therefore, the actual process of unauthorized migration itself can be viewed as an illegitimate means to an end goal (e.g., migrating to the United States to work or for family reunification).

This conceptual framework also proves fruitful when applied to the case of migrants who are apprehended and incarcerated for immigration violations. After multiple failed crossing attempts and months of incarceration, money is lost on hotels, food, travel to and from different crossing regions, and accumulated debts while families are left without income from at least one of their economic providers. Once incarcerated, the end goal of needing to migrate and to make money to support one's family has not changed. But the desire to achieve said goal intensifies because of the pressures resulting from an unsuccessful crossing attempt. At the same time, migrants' access to illegitimate means structures expands once they are incarcerated. Previously, an unauthorized immigrant may have only had access to an illegitimate means structure (social networks) to facilitate an unauthorized crossing and secure employment or housing in their desired destination. After being incarcerated for a considerable amount of time, people are exposed to completely different illegitimate means structures and social networks than they have had access to in the past. Couple this exposure with the labeling that takes place not only in the court system and detention centers but also by anti-immigrant politicians, pundits, and other public figures, and individuals' notions of who and what is crime drastically change. The concept of symbolic violence, an internalization of the structures of domination and abuse particular to a certain group, demonstrates how destructive these experiences can be (Bourdieu 2001).

Octavio, a nineteen-year-old migrant from the southern Mexican state of Chiapas, developed close ties to a criminal organization while he was incarcerated in a federal detention facility for a recent immigration violation. He explained, "There are more Sureños (a Mexican / Mexican American gang) in jail than any other group. They protect us because we are all *paisanos* (countrymen). You have to join with them, and they make sure no one touches you. All the groups keep to themselves. There are the blacks, the Chicanos, and the whites. The only ones that are separate and you don't go near are Las Letras." We were unfamiliar with this group and asked who they were. He looked over his shoulder nervously and said, "Los Zetas," a brutal and feared Mexican drug cartel that began kidnapping deported migrants along the border in recent years, forcing them to smuggle drugs, work as hit men, or work in marijuana fields in northern Mexico.[3] Octavio said that during the six months he spent incarcerated, someone messed with a Sureño and "we pounded him." We asked whether he had joined them, and he said that he had.

Octavio first came to the United States as a teenager and had been stopped by police officers in Phoenix because his friend was visibly intoxicated in public. The police roughed up Octavio and chipped his tooth. He intended to file a complaint, but when the police realized he was only seventeen, they immediately called ICE and repatriated him. Octavio said they never charged him with a crime. Upon reentering, he was again apprehended and sent to the Florence Correctional Center for six months, where he first came into contact with the Sureños.[4] Octavio's relationship with the Sureños was ironically facilitated by the recent criminalization of immigration law and the emergence of an incarceration-oriented approach to unauthorized immigration.

While CoreCivic (formally known as CCA) claims to separate violent offenders from the rest of those incarcerated, migrants' stories note that they still have a significant amount of contact with other types of criminal offenders. This often happens in long periods waiting to transfer to other facilities or to go to court as well as during work or recreational activities, if available. As Mercedes indicates "there is a lot of violence, drugs, and weapons inside. . . . People smoke weed there openly. . . . Someone even got stabbed right before I left." Miguel, a twenty-three-year-old self-described *campesino* from Guanajuato, echoes Mercedes's concerns: "I couldn't believe it, I felt like I was being kept in there with murderers." For Jaime, an unsuccessful reentry attempt and the experience of being in jail put him in contact with the violent conflicts of different gangs. "In CCA there were gangs, drug mules, human smugglers . . . everything." Jaime said that he stayed away from them by staying in his cell and drawing, forgoing recreation time. There were some fights, and other migrants wanted him to get involved, choose sides, and align with the existing gangs. For some, the line between economic migrant and gang member blurs because of the everyday social pressures people encounter while incarcerated. Jaime said he just wanted to get away and stay in his cell to get out faster.[5] Eusebio, a middle-aged man from Tabasco, also complained about how drug traffickers get let out faster than people who are charged with reentry. "It almost seems like they want us to take drugs."[6] Avoiding deviant activity behind bars becomes much more difficult as the frequency and duration of migrants' stays in detention facilities increase.

A twenty-four-year-old named Andres from Oaxaca relayed his experience of transitioning from migrant to drug trafficker. He had originally paid US$1,000 to cross into the United States, but after being apprehended twice, Andres moved to Sonora and began working in the fields earning only US$100 a week. However, this employment was sporadic. Although the details of exactly how he became involved with drug trafficking were unclear, he became *camaradas* (close friends) with drug smugglers while residing near the border after being deported. He explained that you have to meet the right people to get this type of work since it is physically demanding and also provides ample opportunities for gangs to lose valuable cargo. "I have taken marijuana across four times, but twice I had to abandon it in the desert," Andres said in choppy Spanish. On his most recent trip, he had run out of water and dumped the backpack with 40 pounds of marijuana and turned himself in to the nearest border patrol agent he could find. At US$1,800 per successful trip, he would be making 4.5 months' salary for a week's work. "I will keep crossing until I get caught, but once they give me eight months in jail I will have to find something else [other work] because it will be too much time away from my family," Andres said.

Every day, hundreds of Mexican migrants are put in precarious circumstances upon repatriation by the U.S. authorities to an unfamiliar town on the U.S.-Mexico border. All too often, individuals such as Luis, the focus of our vignette, find themselves with just the clothes on their backs and as far from their communities of origin as from their desired destination. For some, the only social capital from which they can draw are the contacts they have made while incarcerated with individuals who may already be involved with human and drug smuggling near and along the border. In these cases, the detention facilities and border region itself are perfect examples of the appropriate environments for the acquisition and reinforcement of values and skills associated with illicit behavior, as discussed by Cloward and Ohlin (1960). During his sixty-day stay in CCA, Luis recalled that drug mules were bragging about the amount of drugs that they had been carrying, and yet they were only given voluntary repatriations. Not only was this frustrating to Luis, but it also made him realize that while he was paying someone else to cross (a coyote or guide), others were being paid to cross with marijuana. He even went on to suggest that he would consider crossing with drugs the next time if the penalties were not much different.

Policies that systematically criminalize and incarcerate people at high rates, such as Operation Streamline, are exposing economic migrants to criminal networks and certain norms and values to which they may have otherwise never been exposed. With that said, we are aware that zero-tolerance, incarceration-oriented policies aimed at policing immigration enforcement may have a polarizing effect by deterring some migrants from ever attempting an unauthorized crossing while also funneling other migrants into the previously unfamiliar and violent world of drugs and crime.

CONCLUSION

The shift from a deterrence strategy toward a consequence approach (e.g., criminalization and incarceration) to dealing with immigration as well as the creation of a for-profit prison system akin to a modern slave trade has exponentially increased the ramifications for unauthorized economic or familial migration. The process of criminalizing a foreign population on American soil also creates problems for Mexico, especially as deportees from prisons are frequently being targeted either as potential recruits for the drug cartels or, conversely, as enemy combatants if they are from rival territories (i.e., someone from Sinaloa being deported to Tamaulipas). As we have shown, not only does this take the form of abuse of human rights but it also produces strain among migrants (Agnew 1992; Merton 1938) and can increase exposure to illegitimate means structures (Cloward and Ohlin 1960). Being in contact with a criminal element, perceiving that the penalties for more serious crimes are only slightly greater than for those related to immigration, and internalizing the treatment as a dangerous criminal for a civil violation all can increase the propensity to engage actively in criminal activity.

For people whose lives and families are now entirely situated in the United States, these decisions are the most pronounced and are exacerbated by increased exposure to crime while incarcerated. An increasing subsection of deportees will not stop trying to gain entry into the United States and, in the process, will become more likely to engage in illicit activities in their desperation to return to their day-to-day lives. The CDS labels people as criminal within the U.S. context, a destructive label for many whose homes and families are permanently located in the United States. The process of labeling people as criminal also has an impact as people negotiate the fact that much of the U.S. population has come to casually refer to them as "illegals" or worse. We argue that this process in turn generates further violence by exposing people to far more dangerous and destructive practices that would otherwise be absent from the undocumented migration experience. These practices include human smuggling or working as a guide, trafficking drugs as a *burrero*, or even working as a border bandit, kidnapper, or assassin for various drug cartels. Obviously not everyone is affected the same way. Some people reject outright the label of illegal or criminal, while others simply decide to leave the United States behind and return to Mexico regardless of the hardships implied by that choice. However, with hundreds of thousands of removals every year, the extent of this process both for the United States and for Mexico is a cause for great concern.

Unauthorized, economically driven migration is a largely benign phenomenon in and of itself. It is only when it is criminalized and couched within highly dangerous situations that it becomes a threat to people's lives and the safety and security of those living along the border. Ultimately, the United

States' current approach to unauthorized migration systematically criminalizes an entire segment of the U.S. population and contributes to the continued mass incarceration of people of color in a country with one of the highest incarceration rates in the entire world. Alexander (2010) has provided a convincing argument that the mass incarceration of young black men in American jails and prisons is a de facto continuation of Jim Crow. One cannot help but notice the striking parallels between the mass incarceration of African Americans and the criminalization of largely brown mestizo and indigenous undocumented migrants from Latin America. Juan Crow appears to be riding in on the tail feathers of Jim Crow.

NOTES

Originally published as D. Martínez and J. Slack, "What Part of 'Illegal' Don't You Understand? The Social Consequences of Criminalizing Unauthorized Mexican Migrants in the United States," *Social and Legal Studies* 22 (4): 535–51. Adapted and reprinted by permission.

1. He claimed that he had never been arrested except for immigration violations, although because of the anonymity of our project, it is impossible to fully verify.

2. The rest of this section is based on an interview conducted December 9, 2009.

3. The Zetas cartel was responsible for the 2010 kidnapping and brutal execution of 72 unauthorized migrants in San Fernando, Tamaulipas, Mexico, as well as other mass graves of murdered migrants found in northeastern Mexico.

4. Personal communication, February 16, 2011.

5. Field notes, June 15, 2010.

6. Personal communication, February 16, 2011.

REFERENCES

Agnew, R. 1992. "Foundation for a General Strain Theory of Crime and Delinquency." *Criminology* 30: 47–87.

Alexander, M. 2010. *The New Jim Crow: Mass Incarceration in the Age of Colorblindness.* New York: New Press.

Andreas, P. 1998. "The U.S. Immigration Control Offensive: Constructing an Image of Order on the Southwest Border." In *Crossings: Mexican Immigration in Interdisciplinary Perspectives*, edited by M. Suarez-Orozco, 343–56. Cambridge, Mass.: Harvard University Press.

———. 2009. *Border Games: Policing the U.S.-Mexico Divide.* 2nd ed. Ithaca, N.Y.: Cornell University Press.

Boehm, D. A. 2011. "US-Mexico Mixed Migration in an Age of Deportation: An Inquiry into the Transnational Circulation of Violence." *Refugee Survey Quarterly* 30 (1): 1–21.

Bourdieu, P. 2001. *Male Domination*. Oxford: Blackwell.

Bourdieu, P., and L. Wacquant. 1992. *An Invitation to Reflexive Sociology*. Chicago: University of Chicago Press.

Burgess, R., and R. Akers. 1966. "A Differential Association-Reinforcement Theory of Criminal Behavior." *Social Problems* 14 (2): 128–47.

Cloward, R. A. 1959. "Illegitimate Means, Anomie, and Deviant Behavior." *American Sociological Review* 24: 164–76.

Cloward, R. A., and L. E. Ohlin. 1960. *Delinquency and Opportunity*. New York: Free Press.

Cohen, A. K. 1955. *Delinquent Boys: The Culture of the Gang*. New York: Free Press.

Coleman, M. 2007. "Immigration Geopolitics Beyond the Mexico-US Border." *Antipode* 38 (1): 54–76.

Cornelius, W. A., ed. 2010. *Mexican Migration and the U.S. Economic Crisis: A Transnational Perspective*. San Diego, Calif.: Center for Comparative Immigration Studies.

De Genova, N. P., and N. P. Peutz 2010. *The Deportation Regime: Sovereignty, Space, and the Freedom of Movement*. Durham, N.C.: Duke University Press.

Dunn, T. J. 2009. *Blockading the Border and Human Rights: The El Paso Operation That Remade Immigration Enforcement*. Austin: University of Texas Press.

Fisher, M. J. 2011. "CBP U.S. Border Patrol Chief Michael J. Fisher Testifies Before House Committee on Homeland Security, Subcommittee on Border and Maritime Security: 'Does Administrative Amnesty Harm Our Efforts to Gain and Maintain Operational Control of the Border?'" Department of Homeland Security, October 4. https://www.dhs.gov/news/2011/10/04/written-testimony-cbp-house-homeland-security-subcommittee-border-and-maritime.

Friedrichs, D. O. 2007. "Transnational Crime and Global Criminology: Definitional, Typological, and Contextual Conundrums." *Social Justice* 34 (2): 4–18.

Golash-Boza, T. 2009. "The Immigration Industrial Complex: Why We Enforce Immigration Policies Destined to Fail." *Sociology Compass* 3 (2): 295–309.

Heyman, J. M. 1995. "Putting Power in the Anthropology of Bureaucracy: The Immigration and Naturalization Service at the Mexico-United States Border." *Current Anthropology* 36: 261–87.

Kanstroom, D. 2011. "The Right to Deportation Counsel in *Padilla v. Kentucky*: The Challenging Construction of the Fifth-and-a-Half Amendment." *UCLA Law Review* 58: 1461–1516.

La Coalición de Derechos Humanos. 2008. "Operation Streamline Call to Action!" Accessed April 29, 2008; no longer posted. http://www.derechoshumanosaz.net/index2.php?option=com_content&do_pdf=1&id=96.

Long, H. 2017. "Private Prison Stocks Up 100% Since Trump's Win." *CNN: Money*. February 24, 2017. http://money.cnn.com/2017/02/24/investing/private-prison-stocks-soar-trump/index.html.

Lydgate, J. 2010. "Assembly-Line of Justice: A Review of Operation Streamline." *California Law Review* 98 (2): 481–544.

Marx, K. (1867) 1978. "Capital, volume 1." In *The Marx-Engles Reader*, edited by R. Tucker. 2nd ed. New York: W. W. Norton.

Massey, D. S., J. Durand, and N. J. Malone. 2002. *Beyond Smoke and Mirrors: Mexican Immigration in an Era of Economic Integration*. New York: Russell Sage Foundation.

McCombs, B. 2008. "BP Targeting 40 Illegal Crossers a Day in Tucson Sector." *Arizona Daily Star*, January 24 (accessed April 29, 2008; no longer posted). http://www.azstar net.com/sn/printDS/221983.

Merton, R. K. 1938. "Social Structure and Anomie." *American Sociological Review* 3: 672–82.

Nuñez, G. G., and J. M. Heyman. 2007. "Entrapment Processes and Immigrant Communities in a Time of Heightened Border Vigilance." *Human Organization* 66 (4): 354–65.

Pavlo, W. 2012. "Corrections Corporation of America on a Buying Spree: State Prisons for Sale?" *Forbes*, February 14.

Robbins, Ted. 2010. "Claims of Border Program Success Are Unproven." *All Things Considered*, NPR, September 13. http://www.npr.org/templates/story/story.php?storyId =129827870.

Spener, D. 2009. *Clandestine Crossings: Migrants and Coyotes on the Texas-Mexico Border*. Ithaca, N.Y.: Cornell University Press.

Stanton, B. 2008. "Stanton: At the Federal Courthouse, the Immigration Show Goes On." *Tucson Citizen*, March 5.

Sullivan, Laura. 2010. "Prison Economic Help Drive Arizona Law Immigration Law." *Morning Edition*, NPR, October 28. http://www.npr.org/2010/10/28/130833741/prison -economics-help-drive-ariz-immigration-law.

Sutherland, E. H. 1947. *Principles of Criminology*. Chicago: Lippincott.

U.S. Border Patrol. 1994. *Border Patrol Strategic Plan: 1994 and Beyond*. Washington, D.C.: U.S. Border Patrol.

U.S. Department of Customs and Border Protection. 2005. "DHS Launches 'Operation Streamline II' Enforcement Effort Focusing on Prosecuting and Removing Illegal Aliens in Del Rio, Texas." Customs and Border Protection (accessed April 12, 2008; no longer posted). http://www.cbp.gov/xp/cgov/newsroom/news_releases/archives /2005_press_releases/122005/ 12162005.xml.

———. 2007. "Operation Streamline Nets 1,200-Plus Prosecutions in Arizona." Accessed April 27, 2008; no longer posted. http://www.cbp.gov/xp/cgov/newsroom/news _releases/ archives/2007_news_releases/072007/07242007_3.xml.

———. 2011. "CBP's 2011 Fiscal Year in Review." Accessed January 18, 2012; no longer posted. http://www.cbp.gov/xp/cgov/newsroom/news_releases/national/2011_news _archive/12122011.xml.

U.S. Department of Homeland Security. 2010. "Immigration Enforcement Actions: 2009." https://www.dhs.gov/sites/default/files/publications/Enforcement_Actions _2009.pdf.

Wacquant, L. 2000. "The New 'Peculiar Institution': On the Prison as Surrogate Ghetto." *Theoretical Criminology* 4: 377–89.

———. 2009. *Punishing the Poor*. Durham, N.C.: Duke University Press.

Welch, M. 2003. "Ironies of Social Control and the Criminalization of Immigrants." *Crime, Law and Social Change* 39: 319–37.

———. 2007. "Immigration Lockdown Before and After 9/11: Ethnic Constructions and Their Consequences." In *Race, Gender, and Punishment: From Colonialism to the War on Terror*, edited by M. Bosworth and J. Flavin, 149–63. Piscataway, N.J.: Rutgers University Press.

Wides-Muñoz, L., and G. Burke. 2012. "Immigrants Prove Big Business for Prison Companies." *Los Angeles Daily News*, August 2 (accessed September 12, 2012; no longer posted). http://www.dailynews.com/news/ci_21224243/ immigrants-prove-big -business-prison-companies.

7

COYOTE USE IN AN ERA OF HEIGHTENED BORDER ENFORCEMENT

New Evidence from the Arizona-Sonora Border

DANIEL E. MARTÍNEZ

INTRODUCTION

NUMEROUS JOURNALISTIC ACCOUNTS of unauthorized Mexican immigrants' border-crossing experiences exist, but fewer academic studies have addressed the facilitation, conditions, and circumstances surrounding the crossing experience itself (Singer and Massey 1998; Donato and Patterson 2004; Donato, Wagner, and Patterson 2008; Hagan 2008), especially crossings through southern Arizona (for an exception, see O'Leary 2009, 2012). Much of the research that does exist was completed when it was relatively less difficult to cross the border. Thus, the social process of contemporary border crossings in an era of increased border enforcement is probably different than in years past. Moreover, quantitative studies examining migrants' experiences have been rare in the case of southern Arizona, an area that has become one of the most important crossing corridors for unauthorized Mexican migrants since the mid-2000s.

Increased enforcement efforts in southern Arizona have resulted in numerous consequences and elevated risks for border crossers. Given these recent important changes along the border, in this chapter I ask the following questions: What sociological factors explain unauthorized Mexican migrants' crossing modes in southern Arizona? What role, if any, do individual-level factors such as social network ties, prior migration experience, age, and gender play in this process? What types of coyotes (i.e., human smugglers) do migrants tend to rely on in this heavily patrolled region of the U.S.-Mexico border? I address these questions by drawing on the first wave of the Migrant Border Crossing Study (MBCS), a unique data source on the experiences of Mexican migrants. In addition to focusing exclusively on southern Arizona, I specifically differentiate between coyote types. This is a distinction that qualitative studies have deemed crucial (Lopez Castro 1998; Spener 2009; O'Leary 2012) but that has yet to be made in quantitative studies of crossing modes. Distinguishing between coyote types is important to the sociological understanding of unauthorized migration, as human smuggling activities often operate within differential social contexts that can affect the conditions of migrants' crossing attempts.

LITERATURE REVIEW

INCREASED CROSSINGS AND HEIGHTENED RISKS IN SOUTHERN ARIZONA

Scholars have paid substantial attention to the role of risk and uncertainty in the migration process. Williams and Baláž (2011) note the migration process can be seen as being "informed by, generating, and ameliorating risk and uncertainty" (167). At the individual level, the decision to undertake an unauthorized border-crossing attempt can itself be perceived as risky and awash with uncertainty. The risk of physical injury and apprehension are real concerns during the journey, while the uncertainty of finding adequate housing and employment may also linger in one's mind (Williams and Baláž 2011). These risks are especially pronounced in systems of *unauthorized* migration throughout the world, including between the African continent and the European Union, Southeast Asia and Australia, and several marginalized regions and the United States (Brian and Laczko 2014; Donnelly and Hagan 2014). In the context of Latin American migration to the United States, crossing the U.S.-Mexico border without documentation in an era of increased enforcement presents a series of very real dangers, including apprehension, victimization, exploitation, injury, abandonment, and death (O'Leary 2009, 2012). Therefore, managing and reducing risk is an important part of the unauthorized journey for individuals, families, and communities (Singer and Massey 1998; Donato and Patterson 2004; Donato, Wagner, and Patterson 2008; Hagan 2008).

Increased enforcement along the U.S.-Mexico border in historical urban crossing points (e.g., San Diego, Calif., and El Paso, Tex.) has changed migration routes and forced people to traverse remote areas along the border to avoid apprehension, including through southern Arizona (Eschbach et al. 1999; Cornelius 2001; Rubio-Goldsmith et al. 2006; Andreas 2009; Martínez et al. 2014). The risk of death while crossing the border is a serious concern and has remained high in recent years with heightened border enforcement. Many migrants attempt to lower the risk of death by using the services of coyotes to cross the border.

Death is not the only risk migrants face while crossing the border. Increases in the number of border agents and the deployment of new technologies and equipment in the southwest have elevated the risk of apprehension at official ports of entry and in remote areas. One study notes "as the border has become more heavily patrolled than at any previous time in U.S. history, *polleros* [human smugglers] have become essential to a successful and relatively safe crossing" (Hicken, Cohen, and Narvaez 2010, 62–63). And despite the high costs of hiring a coyote, many unauthorized migrants do so in an attempt to lower the risk of apprehension (Fuentes et al. 2007). Others have noted that people "understand that hiring a coyote is illegal," but "many view it as necessary to evade apprehension and to mitigate the danger of crossing clandestinely" (Kimball, Acosta, and Dames 2007, 99).

Another significant but less understood consequence has been the heightened competition between drug-trafficking organizations, coyotes, and *bajadores* (border bandits) for control and access to less enforced crossing corridors (Felbab-Brown 2009; O'Leary 2012). Although some scholars have argued that drug trafficking and human smuggling are fundamentally different activities (Spener 2009; Izcara Palacios 2015; Sanchez 2015), the heightened competition between these actors for geographical space along the border has contributed to unauthorized migrants' increased vulnerability as they attempt to enter the United States (O'Leary 2012). Migrants may also seek to reduce this vulnerability by hiring a coyote to guide them across the border (Fuentes et al. 2007; Kimball, Acosta, and Dames 2007; Donato, Wagner, and Patterson 2008; Hagan 2008; Parks et al. 2009; Spener 2009; Hicken, Cohen, and Narvaez 2010; Sanchez 2015). Whether or not the effectiveness of using a coyote is real, a psychological artifact, or a social and logistic necessity in geographically contested spaces, relying on the services of a smuggling network is one way migrants and their families attempt to mitigate the risks of death, apprehension, and other dangers while crossing the border. Yet little is known about migrants' coyote use and other modes of crossing in southern Arizona.

EXISTING STUDIES ON MODE OF CROSSING
AMONG UNAUTHORIZED MEXICAN MIGRANTS

Previous studies have found that undocumented Mexican migrants typically cross the border in one of three ways: alone, with family or friends (usually experienced crossers), or with a paid coyote (Singer and Massey 1998; Donato and Patterson 2004; Donato, Wagner, and Patterson 2008), with the smallest proportion of people attempting the journey alone. As detailed below, substantial attention has been given to the influence that social capital, human capital, and demographic characteristics have on unauthorized migrants' crossing modes.

SOCIAL CAPITAL/SOCIAL TIES

Immigration scholars have highlighted the importance of social capital in the initiation, facilitation, and perpetuation of international migration (Massey et al. 1993). Social capital has been defined as "the ability of actors to secure benefits by virtue of membership in social networks or other social structures" (Portes 1998, 6). Thus, the ability to convert the value of social ties into other forms of capital is central to the sociological understanding of this resource. The donors and recipients of social capital are persuaded to comply with their respective roles in network exchanges through a series of principled or instrumental motivations centered around "value introjection," "reciprocity exchanges," "bounded solidarity," and "enforceable trust" (see Portes and Sensenbrenner 1993, 1323–25, and Portes 1998, 7–9, for extensive discussions of the sources of social capital).

General social capital in the migratory context has been operationalized as ties to siblings or friends in the United States, whereas migration-specific social capital consists of stronger ties, such as children or spouses (Massey and García España 1987; Espinosa and Massey 1997; Massey and Espinosa 1997; Singer and Massey 1998; Aguilera and Massey 2003). Using this approach, researchers have empirically illustrated how migrant network ties shape people's initial decisions to migrate (Grasmuck and Pessar 1991; Espinosa and Massey 1997), help facilitate unauthorized crossing attempts (Singer and Massey 1998), and direct newcomers to housing and employment during the initial stages of settlement (Bailey and Waldinger 1991; Aguilera and Massey 2003).

With regard to unauthorized border crossings, a number of studies have found that when controlling for all other factors, prospective migrants with experienced migrant parents are more likely to cross with family/friends and coyotes (relative to alone) than people without a parent with U.S. experience (Singer and Massey 1998; Donato, Wagner, and Patterson 2008). Singer and Massey (1998) demonstrated that migrants with siblings with U.S. experience are more likely to travel alone (relative to with family/friends or a coyote), while a more recent study by Donato, Wagner, and Patterson (2008) suggests that having a sibling with U.S migration experience increases the likelihood of traveling with a coyote but has the opposite effect on traveling with family/friends. Further, Singer and Massey (1998) find that male migrants with U.S. migrant spouses are less likely to travel with a coyote, while those with U.S. migrant children are more likely to travel with family/friends. Collectively, these studies strongly suggest that migrants with social ties to migrants with U.S. experience draw on these connections in different ways to cross the border.

Although "most research on social networks and immigrant incorporation focuses on the short-term and positive functions of networks" (Hagan 1998, 55), the "social capital" approach overlooks the fact that migrant networks can be asymmetrical, exploitative, yield negative consequences, and transform over time or across social contexts (Portes and Sensenbrenner 1993; Hagan 1998; O'Leary 2012). Hagan (1998), for example, found that social networks among Mayan immigrants in Houston tended to be gendered along occupational niches, with men working for one particular supermarket chain and women working as live-in domestics. Because of their occupational and neighborhood isolation, women's networks tended to be more closed and consisted of mostly strong ties. While men's networks were also characterized by strong ties, men were much more likely to establish weak ties with people outside of their network (Hagan 1998). These weak contacts ultimately helped men more than women make significant gains in the incorporation process, such as legalizing their immigration statuses (Hagan 1998).

The notions that social capital and network membership can have negative consequences, be exploitative, and result in asymmetrical relationships are important criticisms of the "social capital" approach in migration studies. However, for many unauthorized migrants—especially those with relatively little firsthand migration experience—social capital may be one of the few resources on which they are able to draw to facilitate a border-crossing attempt. Thus, the role of social capital in explicating modes of crossing during an era of increased border enforcement warrants further examination.

HUMAN CAPITAL

Scholars have extensively documented the importance of individual human capital in various stages of the migration process (Massey and Espinosa 1997; Espinosa and Massey 1997; Singer and Massey 1998; Aguilera and Massey 2003; Donato and Patterson 2004; Donato, Wagner, and Patterson 2008; Hagan 2008; Hagan, Hernández-León, and Demonsant 2015). With regard to Mexico-U.S. migration, general human capital has been operationalized to include factors such as age, education, sector of employment, labor market experience, and English-language proficiency. For instance, the literature has found that age is a particularly important form of general human capital in the social process of migration (Espinosa and Massey 1997; Singer and Massey 1998). With age comes a general increase in knowledge gained through lived experiences as well as a decrease in socially risky behavior. Cerrutti and Massey (2001) found that older married people are generally less likely to migrate than younger married people when controlling for all other factors. Among people who have migrated, previous research has found that older migrants are more likely to migrate alone than with family/friends or a coyote even when controlling for previous migration experience (Singer and Massey 1998; Donato and Patterson 2004; Donato, Wagner, and Patterson 2008).

However, scholars have emphasized an important difference between general and migration-specific human capital in the migration process. Whereas general human capital can include the aforementioned factors, migration-specific human capital has been operationalized as one's firsthand immigration experience—a factor that has also consistently been shown to be of importance in the migration process (Massey and Espinosa 1997; Singer and Massey 1998; Cerrutti and Massey 2001; Donato and Patterson 2004; Donato, Wagner, and Patterson 2008). Previous studies have found that as people accumulate migration-specific human capital they begin to rely less on network ties to cross the border and to integrate structurally into a receiving community (Singer and Massey 1998; Aguilera and Massey 2003; Donato and Patterson 2004; Donato, Wagner, and Patterson 2008). Rather than relying on family/friends or smugglers, more experienced migrants can draw on their own knowledge stores to minimize risk along the way. Further, as people gain firsthand migration experience, they become important social ties for future potential migrants. In terms of crossing modes, previous studies have consistently found that prior migration experience is associated with increased odds of crossing alone relative to with family/friends or coyotes (Singer and Massey 1998; Donato and Patterson 2004; Donato, Wagner, and Patterson 2008).

GENDER

Gender has been one of the most important demographic characteristics examined in connection with the migration phenomenon. Although women are now migrating at higher rates than in the past (Donato 1993; O'Leary 2009), unauthorized migration from Mexico continues to be a gendered social process. Research has found that Mexican men have a higher probability than women to cross without authorization and make subsequent trips (Donato 1993; Cerrutti and Massey 2001; Donato and Patterson 2004; Valdez-Suiter, Rosas-Lopez, and Pagaza 2007). Previous research has also identified notable differences between men and women relating to how they draw on network ties to facilitate migration attempts, with women relying on network ties much more so than men (Donato and Patterson 2004; Hagan 2008; Donato, Wagner, and Patterson 2008). Women are much more likely than men to cross with others than by themselves, and they tend to rely on family members with U.S. migration experience to facilitate a border crossing (Cerrutti and Massey 2001; Donato and Patterson 2004; Valdez-Suiter, Rosas-Lopez, and Pagaza 2007; Hagan 2008).

Though for different reasons, ranging from structural to biosocial, there appears to be consensus in the sociological literature that women tend to be more risk averse than men when it comes to physical forms of risk taking (Hagan, Simpson, and Gillis 1988; Roth and Kroll 2007; Collett and Lizardo 2009). The unauthorized crossing experience itself is a physically risky endeavor, which, along with prevailing gender norms throughout Mexico, helps explain why women are more likely to cross with others than by themselves when controlling for factors such as age and previous migration experience.

However, only a handful of quantitative studies exist examining the role of gender in crossing modes (Donato and Patterson 2004; Donato, Wagner, and Patterson 2008). Donato, Wagner, and Patterson (2008) find that "women entering the United States during the 1987–2004 period were significantly more likely than those entering earlier to cross using assistance from a paid smuggler (although they were no more likely to cross with family and friends)" and that men were less likely to use coyotes (349). The authors go on to suggest that "tougher immigration policies and enforcement activity after IRCA's passage insured that women's clandestine entry became more linked to assistance from paid smugglers than in the past" (Donato, Wagner, and Patterson 2008, 349). Women's lower levels of migration experience, economically marginalized status, higher risk of sexual abuse, and restricted access to social capital may also help explain these disparities (O'Leary 2012). Given these findings, a closer examination of gender differences in crossing modes in the contemporary era of increased border enforcement in southern Arizona deserves further attention.

COYOTAJE

Coyotaje can be described as the process of evading bureaucratic migration channels (Spener 2009, 91), and in the most parsimonious sense, it is synonymous with human smuggling (Izcara Palacios 2015). Nevertheless, *coyotaje* consists of extremely complex and dynamic processes (Spener 2009; Izcara Palacios 2015; Sanchez 2015). In this chapter I focus primarily on "*coyotes* as guides and facilitators" of unauthorized migration (Spener 2009, 93) in relation to different crossing modes (see Spener 2009 and Izcara Palacios 2015 for extensive discussions of *coyotaje*). As Lopez Castro (1998) notes, there exist at least three different types of coyotes whom undocumented migrants can rely on to facilitate a crossing: "local-interior" coyotes, "local and border" coyotes, and "border business" coyotes (966).

"Local-interior" coyotes typically operate from within sending communities and have a personal connection with the migrant. These coyotes travel to and across the border with the people they are guiding, live and work in the United States for a short period of time, and return to their sending community to repeat the process. "Local-interior" coyotes do not smuggle migrants on a full-time basis but rather do it to supplement their income or assist compatriots (Lopez Castro 1998, 967–68). Other studies have described these coyotes as *coyotes comunitarios* (O'Leary 2012, 149).

"Local and border" coyotes consist of people originally from a sending community who live along the border and generally do not personally know the migrants relying on their services. Rather, migrants are referred to them by family, friends, or acquaintances who have previously relied on their services in the past (Lopez Castro 1998, 967–68). Finally, "border business" coyotes are individuals who live near the border and smuggle people on a full-time basis. They do not personally know their clients, nor are they referred by previous clientele. "Border business" coyotes are more organized and consist of three main elements: recruiters, guides, and delivery persons (Lopez Castro 1998, 968).

Existing studies examining the facilitation of the undocumented crossing experience have furthered scholarship on the sociological mechanisms that contribute to a migrant's crossing modes. However, these studies have focused mainly on comparisons between crossing with family/friends or coyotes relative to crossing alone. Very little has been written comparing people who cross with family/friends to people who cross with coyotes, and few studies to date have included women in a quantitative analysis of crossing modes (for an exception see Donato and Patterson 2004; and Donato, Wagner, and Patterson 2008). Furthermore, as Spener (2009) points out, existing quantitative studies that have examined migrants' crossing modes have failed to differentiate between coyote types, were largely based on data collected before increased border enforcement, and focused on crossing attempts through Southern California. The failure to differentiate between specific types of coyotes in previous studies possibly confounds some of the true relationships between crossing modes, demographic characteristics, and different levels of various forms of capital. And while Spener (2009) has provided an exhaustive and detailed account of *coyote* types in an era of heightened border enforcement, his work is largely qualitative and focuses on *coyotaje* in South Texas. A systematic quantitative analysis of crossing modes that differentiates between coyote types can help provide a better understanding of whether or not recent increased enforcement efforts have changed the dynamics of unauthorized crossing attempts in a region such as southern Arizona.

In this chapter I focus on the variation between "border business" and "interior" coyotes because differentiating between the closely related "local and border" and "local-interior" coyote types proved difficult for the study's respondents. Nevertheless, distinguishing between these coyote types provides a significant contribution to the existing literature. Given a review of the literature, the formal hypotheses for the present analysis are as follows:

H1: Women are more likely to travel with family/friends and "interior" coyotes than with "border business" coyotes.

H2: Social capital (i.e., network ties) and migration-specific human capital (i.e., firsthand migration experience) are both negatively associated with reliance on "border business" coyotes.

H3: Social capital and migration-specific human capital are positively associated with the odds of crossing with family/friends.

DATA AND SAMPLE

This study examines migrants' crossing modes using survey data from the first wave of the MBCS (N = 415) (see chap. 1 of this volume). Probability weights are used when calculating the descriptive statistics but were not applied when conducting the inferential analyses. In situations where weights are a function of independent variables included in the inferential analyses, Winship and Radbill (1994) recommend using unweighted estimates because they are unbiased, consistent, and produce smaller standard errors. The methodology used to survey migrants in the MBCS as well as the generalizability of the sample and comparisons of demographic characteristics to estimates of the study population are discussed elsewhere (Martínez et al. 2017).

MEASUREMENT OF VARIABLES USED IN THE ANALYSIS

DEPENDENT VARIABLE

The existing literature identifies three ways in which a migrant can attempt an unauthorized crossing: alone, with family or friends (but not a coyote), or with a coyote. While I maintain these previously identified modes of crossing, the main objective of this study is to differentiate between coyote types. Among people who used a coyote, those who indicated that the coyote was from their hometown or that they had met the coyote through family or friends before arriving at the border were categorized as having traveled with an "interior" coyote. Conversely, people who crossed with a coyote they met for the first time near the border were coded as having traveled with a "border business" coyote. Table 7.1 provides the proportions for crossing modes examined in the

TABLE 7.1 Breakdown of crossing modes in southern Arizona

MODE OF CROSSING	PERCENT
"Border business" coyote	45
"Interior" coyote	30
Family or friends, but no coyote	17
Alone	8

Note: Dependent variable, multiply imputed data. m = 20; N = 395.
Source: Migrant Border Crossing Study, Wave I (weighted data).

analyses. Approximately 45 percent of the analytic sample relied on the services of "border business" coyotes, while 30 percent traveled with "interior" coyotes. Seventeen percent traveled with family/friends but not a coyote. Only 8 percent had attempted to cross the border completely alone.

INDEPENDENT VARIABLES

Table 7.2 illustrates descriptive statistics for independent variables used in the analysis. The independent variables are organized according to theoretically relevant conceptual groupings. Demographics characteristics include gender (female = 1; male = 0), age (in years since last birthday), formal educational attainment (in years), and the respondent's monthly household income before their most recent crossing attempt (in logged US$). Overall, respondents tended to be male (87%), to be near thirty-two years of age, to have seven years of formal education, and to report around US$490 in monthly household income.

"Migration-specific social capital" is captured through two variables: family in desired destination and friend in desired destination. The social capital variables used in this study vary when compared with those used in earlier studies and focus on the strength of ties to people residing in the respondent's desired destination at the time of the survey. The family variable measures the presence or absence of a strong familial tie in the respondent's desired U.S. destination. This variable includes some respondents with at least one friend in their desired destination. However, because familial ties represent stronger forms of social capital than ties to friends, the tie to a family member was of most interest. As noted in table 7.2, 57 percent of the analytic sample had at least one family member in their desired destination. On the other hand, the friend variable represents whether or not the respondent had at least one friend in their desired destination but not a family member. This tie is treated as a weaker tie when compared with a family member in the United States. Twenty-nine per cent of the sample had at least one friend in their desired destination but no family.

"Migration-specific human capital" is measured by whether or not a respondent's most recent crossing was their first border-crossing attempt, the number of times a respondent has attempted to cross the U.S.-Mexico border without authorization (including the most recent attempt), and the total number of years a person has spent living and working in the United States. Table 7.2 illustrates that 18 percent of respondents were first-time crossers. The typical respondent

TABLE 7.2 Descriptive statistics for key explanatory variables

	MEAN	SE
Demographics characteristics		
Female	.13	.033
Age	32.23	.771
Years of education	7.06	.239
Household income (in logged US$)	6.19	.095
Migration-specific social capital		
Family in desired destination	.57	.035
Friend in desired destination	.29	.031
Migration-specific human capital		
First crossing	.18	.029
Number of lifetime crossings	4.59	.365
Number of years lived in the United States	5.11	.594
Time of year of last crossing attempt		
March/April (peak migration months)	.24	.029
Summer crossing	.40	.036
Corridor of last crossing attempt		
Sasabe/Altar	.43	.036
Nogales	.27	.034
Naco/Cananea/Agua Prieta	.13	.027
Sonoyta	.12	.021
San Luis Rio Colorado	.05	.016
State-level controls		
Percent of homes with at least one person in the United States	4.61	.222
Marginalization index rank	13.96	.849
Monthly apprehensions from R's state	1395.65	71.849

Note: Multiply imputed data. $m = 20$; $N = 395$. SE = standard error.
Source: Migrant Border Crossing Study, Wave I (weighted data).

in the analytic sample had an average of 4.6 lifetime crossing attempts and had spent just over five years living and working in the United States.

"Time of year of last crossing attempt" consists of controls for the time during the calendar year that respondents had attempted their most recent crossing. Historically, U.S. Border Patrol (USBP) apprehensions have been highest during March and April of every year as migrants begin returning to the USA from holiday festivities in their hometowns. According to the USBP, 27 percent of all Tucson sector apprehensions during this study time period occurred in the months of March or April, which is consistent with the 24 percent of MBCS respondents who crossed in one of these months. This dichotomous variable accounts for whether or not a migrant's most recent crossing occurred during a month of peak unauthorized crossings. Summer crossing is a dichotomous variable that controls for whether or not the respondent's most recent border crossing occurred between the months of May and September. Unauthorized crossings through southern Arizona are most physically risky during summer months, when temperatures frequently exceed 100 degrees Fahrenheit in the Sonoran desert. The variable accounts for variation in crossing modes that may be attributed to crossing during a relatively hotter month. Approximately 40 percent of respondents in the sample crossed during a summer month (table 7.2).

"Corridor of last crossing attempt" controls for the specific geographical corridor where the respondent had attempted their most recent crossing. There are five primary crossing corridors along the Sonora-Arizona border, which were dichotomized for the purposes of this study. These corridors include Altar/Sasabe (43%), Nogales (27%), Naco/Agua Prieta/Cananea (13%), Sonoyta (12%), and San Luis Rio Colorado (5%). The Nogales corridor serves as the referent category in the analysis, as it historically tended to be the most frequent point of unauthorized crossings in Arizona before increased border enforcement efforts of the 1990s and 2000s.

"State-level controls" includes three important factors: percent of homes with migrants in the United States, marginalization index rank, and "monthly apprehension statistics. The percent of homes with migrants in the United States variable represents the percent of households in a respondent's home state with at least one member in the United States between 1995 and 2000 and serves as a proxy for migration prevalence at the state level. The data are estimates based on a 10 percent sample of the XII Censo General de Población y Vivienda 2000 as calculated by Mexico's Consejo Nacional de Población (CONAPO). Marginalization rank index measures varying levels of development within the country. Every five years CONAPO ranks each of Mexico's thirty-one states and Mexico City from lowest levels to highest levels of marginalization. The index was created using a principle components method and summarizes municipal and state levels of schooling, housing conditions, population density, and income characteristics (Anzaldo Gómez and Prado López 2005). This variable controls for variation in crossing modes associated with state-level marginalization. Monthly apprehensions from R's state consist of monthly USBP apprehensions from a respondent's state in the Tucson sector that occurred during the month of the survey. The variable accounts for monthly fluctuations in the unauthorized migration from each Mexican state, which may, in turn, alter the likelihood of a particular crossing mode.

METHODS

I utilized multinomial logistic regression to examine the relationships between crossing modes and the explanatory variables because the outcome variable of interest was coded as a categorical variable (Long 1997). This technique is more precise and exhaustive than binary logistic regression and allows comparisons to be made among specific modes of crossing rather than between one mode of crossing and all other modes, as would be the case with binary logistic regression.

RESULTS

Table 7.3 provides results of a multinomial logistic regression analysis examining the relationship between modes of crossing and predictor variables. The table provides coefficients, significance levels, and standard errors for each independent variable. Although not reported in the table, odds ratios can be derived by exponentiating the regression coefficient associated with each explanatory variable (Long 1997). Because of the low number of observations (about 8% of respondents), results for crossing "alone" are not the focus of this study and are therefore not reported in table 7.3, although they are included in the regression model. Moreover, because the factors contributing to crossing alone have been extensively examined by previous scholars (Singer and Massey 1998; Donato and Patterson 2004; Donato, Wagner, and Patterson 2008), the discussion of the empirical results focuses on differences between specific coyote types and crossing with family/friends.

GENDER AND MODE OF CROSSING

When controlling for all other factors, women had 82 percent lower odds of traveling with family/friends relative to "border business" coyotes (exp[−1.71] = 0.176). Women also had 85 percent lower odds of traveling with family/friends

TABLE 7.3 Multinomial logistic regression results for modes of crossing and explanatory variables

	FRIENDS/FAMILY VS. "BORDER BUSINESS" COYOTE	FRIENDS/FAMILY VS. "INTERIOR" COYOTE	"INTERIOR" COYOTE VS. "BORDER BUSINESS" COYOTE
Demographic characteristics			
Female	-1.71* (.786)	-1.92* (.799)	.21 (.380)
Age	-.01 (.018)	.02 (.020)	-.02 (.016)
Years of education	-.19 (.042)	-.06 (.048)	.05 (.038)
Household income (in logged US$)	.09 (.151)	.06 (.168)	.05 (.143)
Migration-specific social capital			
Family in desired destination	-.23 (.386)	-.55 (.447)	.32 (.368)
Friend in desired destination	-.32 (.440)	-1.10* (.493)	.78* (.394)
Migration-specific human capital			
First crossing	.55 (.388)	1.08* (.439)	-.53 (.353)
Number of lifetime crossings	.08* (.035)	.21*** (.063)	-.13** (.058)
Number of years lived in the United States	-.05 (.033)	-.04 (.039)	-.01 (.030)
Time of year of last crossing attempt			
March/April (peak migration)	-.45 (.392)	.31 (.437)	-.76* (.352)
Summer crossing	-.54 (.366)	-.14 (.399)	-.39 (.317)
Corridor of last crossing attempt			
Sasabe/Altar	-1.17** (.390)	-1.27** (.454)	.11 (.389)
Naco/Cananea/Agua Prieta	-.49 (.516)	-.71 (.587)	.23 (.504)
Sonoyta	-.22 (.503)	-.89 (.560)	.66 (.500)
San Luis Rio Colorado	1.51† (.891)	.68 (.923)	.82 (1.080)
State-level controls			
Percent of homes with at least one person in the United States	-.02 (.052)	-.03 (.058)	.01 (.045)
Marginalization index rank	-.01 (.018)	-.02 (.020)	.01 (.016)
Monthly apprehensions from R's state	-.00 (.000)	-.00† (.000)	.00 (.000)
McFadden's pseudo R^2	.156		

Note: Multiply imputed data. "Nogales" is the referent category for "Corridor of last crossing attempt." $m = 20$; $N = 395$. Values in parentheses are standard errors.

Source: Migrant Border Crossing Study, Wave I.

† $p < .10$, * $p < .05$, ** $p < .01$, *** $p < .001$

than with "interior" coyotes. However, there is not a statistically significant difference between specific coyote types among women. In other words, women are significantly more likely than men to travel with either coyote type than with family/friends. Not a single woman in the MBCS sample reported attempting to cross the border alone. This low prevalence of traveling alone among female MBCS respondents is consistent with previous studies that find women are more likely to cross with others rather than alone (Donato and Patterson 2004; Donato, Wagner, and Patterson 2008).

Given women's relatively recent migration experience in general as well as that women have tended to migrate for family reunification more so than men, it is likely that they and their family members prefer them to travel with a coyote than without one, regardless of the specific type. However, as the following case suggests, traveling with a coyote is not a sufficient condition to avoid abandonment or exploitation.[1] In this case, Julieta, a young female migrant with no crossing experience, relied on the services of a coyote coordinated by a friend in California rather than trying to cross with her group of friends:

> Julieta's family was bringing in about $2,000 a month before her crossing attempt, which is actually a decent income for that part of the country. Nevertheless, she has been unemployed for ten months and is trying to get to Fresno, California, where she has some friends from her hometown. She traveled to the border with a group of friends and met a "border business" *coyote* in Altar, Sonora, to whom she had been referred by a friend—the same friend who was also fronting the $1,500 smuggling fee. The group of seven, including the coyote, traveled east to Naco, Sonora, and began crossing the border. Julieta was mentally prepared for a three-day crossing, but three days turned into five after the guide abandoned Julieta and some of the group members. The remaining group of four was forced to turn themselves over to USBP. When asked if she would cross again, Julieta indicated she would not. The whole experience was just too difficult.[2]

This account is consistent with O'Leary's (2012) discussion regarding the relationships between women's border-crossing risk and vulnerability and people's growing reliance on coyotes stemming from increased border enforcement over the past two decades. As she emphasizes, increased border enforcement has created a context in which "border business" coyotes are not bound by communal bonds and trust as those found among *coyotes comunitarios* who protect migrants from abuse, exploitation, and abandonment (O'Leary 2012). Rather, "border business" coyotes are motivated primarily to compete with other entities for their share of human smuggling profits.

MIGRATION-SPECIFIC SOCIAL CAPITAL AND MODE OF CROSSING

Earlier studies have emphasized the importance of migration-specific social capital in the migration process. Interestingly, there do not appear to be significant relationships between strong ties and crossing modes. However, weak ties, or ties to friends in a migrant's desired destination, do help explain crossing modes. Specifically, people with weak ties in their desired destination (but no strong ties) have 67 percent lower odds of crossing with family/friends than "interior" coyotes. In a similar vein, migrants with friends in their destination have 2.2 times greater odds of traveling with "interior" coyotes than "border business" coyotes. In other words, controlling for all other factors, people with weak ties in their desired U.S. destinations have the greatest odds of traveling with "interior" *coyotes*, a point to which I return below.

MIGRATION-SPECIFIC HUMAN CAPITAL AND MODE OF CROSSING

Previous studies have noted the importance of firsthand migration experience in explicating how people facilitate unauthorized crossing attempts. Singer and Massey (1998) and Donato, Wagner, and Patterson (2008) found that as individuals gain migration-specific human capital (i.e., accumulate undocumented migration experience), the odds of crossing with a paid guide decrease. Thus, as migrants gain crossing experience, they rely less on the "assistance of others and more on abilities honed on earlier trips, thus substituting migration-specific human capital for general social capital" (Singer and Massey 1998, 564). Results from this study parallel these of earlier studies. The odds of traveling with family/friends rather than "interior" or "border business" coyotes increase with the accumulation of unauthorized crossing attempts. However, first-time crossers have nearly three times greater odds of crossing with family/friends than with "interior" coyotes. Thus, experienced migrants may forgo the services of a guide, opting instead to draw on their own border-crossing experiences to travel with family/friends. In some cases, migrants with more experience will serve as informal guides (i.e., free of charge) for first-time crossers from their communities of origin. The following vignette helps contextualize these results.

> Marcos is a thirty-one-year-old divorced male with three kids from the state of Durango. He never received any formal education, and before his last crossing attempt had been working in agriculture making about $200 a month. Marcos is an experienced migrant with thirty lifetime border crossings and thirteen years of experience in the United States. He was trying to get to Portales, New Mexico, near the border of the Texas panhandle, where his family lives. Marcos was planning on staying and working until whenever he would get caught.
>
> He last crossed the border in April 2008 through the Altar-Sasabe corridor, not with the assistance of a coyote but rather with five people he knew from his hometown. However, after five days of trekking through the desert, the group had split up, and Marcos and two others were apprehended by the USBP while walking. Despite his lengthy history of border-crossing attempts, he swears he is done trying without proper documentation.[3]

Here, rather than rely on the services of a coyote in an area known for being controlled by a drug-trafficking organization and frequented by *bajadores*, Marcos and his friends set out on their own, putting their border-crossing knowledge and skills to use. Although they managed to avoid trouble with drug mules and *bajadores*, they were not so fortunate when it came to U.S. authorities. Nevertheless, this particular case not only supports previous migration research that emphasizes the importance of prior experience in understanding modes of crossing (Singer and Massey 1998; Donato and Patterson 2004; Donato, Wagner, and Patterson 2008) but also the consensus in the literature noting that knowledge acquisition is associated with risk tolerance.

"INTERIOR" COYOTES VERSUS "BORDER BUSINESS" COYOTES

One of the main motivations for writing this chapter was to identify important sociological differences between people who rely on "interior" coyotes relative to "border business" coyotes. There are three important factors that help explain this difference: friends in one's destination, greater firsthand migration experience, and crossing during a month of peak migration.

As noted, when controlling for all other factors, migrants with weak ties in their destination have 2.2 times greater odds of crossing with "interior" coyotes relative to "border business" coyotes (column three of table 7.3). Because "interior" coyotes tend to be from migrants' hometowns or personally know migrants and their families, these social bonds likely serve as a source of reassurance that they will be looked after during the crossing attempt. Moreover, community and other social bonds between "interior" coyotes and their clients may act as important forms of informal social control that keep coyotes from overcharging, being abusive, or exploiting migrants during the journey. "Interior" coyotes also may not be operating in the same social contexts as "border business" coyotes, in which border enforcement efforts have led to increased competition between "border business" coyotes and other entities for a share of human smuggling fees. It is precisely this social context that has decreased the relative importance of social capital—manifested as trust and communal bonds—between migrants and "border business" coyotes relative to "interior" coyotes (O'Leary 2012).

Firsthand migration experience, operationalized as respondents' number of lifetime crossing attempts, also helps explain differences between traveling with "interior" coyotes and "border business" coyotes. For example, greater migration experience is associated with lower odds of crossing with an "interior" coyote. It is likely that seasoned migrants are particularly comfortable with traveling to the border on their own and contracting the services of a coyote near the border.

Finally, there do appear to be important differences between modes of crossing and seasonality along the Arizona-Sonora border. People whose last crossing attempt was during a peak migration month (i.e., March or April) had 53 percent lower odds of crossing with "interior" coyotes in favor of "border business" coyotes. "Border business" coyotes tend to live and work near the border and will take on clients all year as long as the financial compensation is sufficient. Therefore, migrants wishing to cross during months of peak migration may have to rely on the services of "border business" coyotes if there is a shortage of "interior" coyotes available to guide people across the border.

CONCLUSION

Increased border enforcement efforts over the past two decades have made southern Arizona one of the most important unauthorized crossing corridors along the entire U.S.-Mexico border. Yet relatively little quantitative research exists focusing exclusively on this area, especially when it comes to examining the mechanisms that play a role in facilitating unauthorized crossing attempts in this region. Previous quantitative studies on crossing modes have relied on data largely consisting of migrants who crossed through Southern California before the border buildup in the mid-1990s. Those studies highlighted the importance of demographic characteristics and various forms of capital in the migration process. This study supports some of those results, does not support others, and offers new insightful findings.

First, and consistent with earlier studies, migration-specific social capital influences modes of crossing in southern Arizona. However, it is weak ties, in the form of friends in one's desired destination, rather than strong ties that influence this process. Respondents with weak ties to their destination have lower odds of crossing with family/friends relative to "interior" coyotes but have higher odds of traveling with "interior" coyotes than "border business" coyotes.

Second, and as illustrated in earlier research, firsthand migration experience (migration-specific human capital) appears to be the single most important predictor of crossing modes. Findings show that more experienced migrants tend to travel with family/friends rather than with either coyote type. In other words, as people gain more migration experience they rely more on their own honed experiences and less on the services of guides. However, first-time crossers have higher odds of traveling with family/friends than "interior" coyotes relative to people with at least one previous crossing before their most recent attempt.

Third, results also illustrate that, even when controlling for prior migration experience, women are much more likely to travel with either type of coyote than with family/friends and that not a single female MBCS respondent traveled alone during their most recent crossing. Several intersecting sociological factors shed light on this finding. Women in general tend to have less cumulative migration experience and are more likely to be recent migrants, while the migration process in the Mexican context remains highly gendered. More broadly, sociological research suggests women are more risk averse than men when it comes to physical risk taking, and as the immigration literature illustrates, hiring a coyote is one way migrants attempt to mitigate risk. Collectively, these findings illustrate that unauthorized migration continues to be largely a social process. Findings from this study do, however, refute results from previous work. For instance, previous work finds age to be a strong predictor of crossing modes, particularly crossing alone rather than with a coyote. However, this study found no statistically significant relationship between age and crossing mode.

One important contribution of this study is that I examined the relationship between various factors and the use of specific coyote types, something that had not been done in extant quantitative studies examining the migration experience. Results from this study suggest that people with weak ties in their desired U.S. destination have higher odds of traveling with an "interior" coyote. Moreover, migrants with more cumulative migration experiences are more likely to travel with "border business" coyotes rather than "interior" coyotes, as are people who crossed during a month of peak migration.

There are two interrelated points of departure for future research based on findings from this study. The first relates to a geographical and contextual analysis of where migrants chose to cross, which may be predicated on the increasing geographic overlap between *coyotaje*, drug-trafficking organizations, and *bajadores* along the Arizona-Sonora border. Although I am unable to explicitly identify the causal relationship between crossing corridor and crossing mode, I did find an association between these factors. Respondents who crossed through the Altar/Sasabe corridor of northern Mexico have higher odds of traveling with either coyote type than with family members/friends when compared with people who crossed near Nogales, Sonora. These important differences may be a result of the emerging hierarchical and standardized nature of *coyotaje* in southern Arizona as competition between drug cartels, coyotes, and border bandits has increased in this contested region, especially in the Sasabe/Altar corridor. This complex relationship deserves further systematic research. The other possible point of departure for future research relates to gender and crossing modes. My analysis suggests women are more likely to travel with either coyote type than with family members/friends or alone. But to what extent does traveling with coyotes protect women from abuse and exploitation during the journey? This, too, warrants closer examination.

Implications of this research extend beyond the U.S.-Mexico border. Systems of unauthorized migration are prevalent throughout the world as globalization continues unabated. In the present era of increased neoliberalism, capital moves relatively freely while the movement of marginalized people has become more restricted in the name of increased securitization. Aspiring migrants, especially women, are increasingly turning to human smugglers to facilitate unauthorized border-crossing attempts between regions such as Northern Africa and the European Union, East Asia and the United States, or Southeast Asia and Australia, often with deadly results (Brian and Laczko 2014; Donnelly and Hagan 2014). Findings from this research suggest that social capital continues to play an important role in unauthorized migrants' crossing modes. I find that aspiring migrants are able to draw on social ties to secure passage with "interior" coyotes that may ultimately be more socially motivated to protect their clients from exploitation, abuse, abandonment, or death. Future research should examine the relative importance of social capital in other border-crossing contexts to determine whether these types of ties serve as protective factors in other regions of the world.

NOTES

Originally published as D. E. Martínez, "Coyote Use in an Era of Heightened Border Enforcement: New Evidence from the Arizona-Sonora Border." *Journal of Ethnic and Migration Studies* 42 (1): 103–19. Adapted and reprinted by permission.

1. All vignettes were constructed using data collected from closed-ended and open-ended responses in the survey as well as researcher field notes. Direct quotes from the respondents are noted when applicable. All names used are pseudonyms.
2. Case ID 4082009650.
3. Case ID 04070820079.

REFERENCES

Aguilera, Michael B., and Douglas S. Massey. 2003. "Social Capital and the Wages of Mexican Migrants: New Hypotheses and Tests." *Social Forces* 82 (2): 671–701.

Allison, Paul D. 2002. *Missing Data.* Thousand Oaks, Calif.: Sage.

Andreas, Peter. 2009. *Border Games: Policing the U.S.-Mexico Divide.* Ithaca, N.Y.: Cornell University Press.

Anzaldo Gómez, Carlos, and Minerva Prado López. 2005. *Indices de marginación, 2005.* Mexico City: Consejo Nacional de Población. http://www.conapo.gob.mx/en/CONAPO/Indices_de_marginacion_2005.

Bailey, Thomas, and Roger Waldinger. 1991. "Primary, Secondary, and Enclave Labor Markets: A Training Systems Approach." *American Sociological Review* 56: 432–45.

Brian, Tara, and Frank Laczko. 2014. *Fatal Journeys: Tracking Lives Lost During Migration.* Geneva: International Organization for Migration.

Cerrutti, Marcela, and Douglas S. Massey. 2001. "On the Auspices of Female Migration from Mexico to the United States." *Demography* 38 (2): 187–200.

Collett, Jessica L., and Omar Lizardo. 2009. "A Power-Control Theory of Gender and Religiosity." *Journal for the Scientific Study of Religion* 48 (2): 213–31.

Cornelius, Wayne A. 2001. "Death at the Border: Efficacy and Unintended Consequences of US Immigration Control Policy." *Population and Development Review* 27 (4): 661–85.

Donato, Katherine M. 1993. "Current Trends and Patterns of Female Migration: Evidence from Mexico." *International Migration Review* 27 (4): 748–71.

Donato, Katherine M., and Evelyn Patterson. 2004. "Women and Men on the Move: Undocumented Border Crossing." In *Crossing the Border: Research from the Mexican*

Migration Project, edited by Jorge Durand and Douglas S. Massey, 111–30. New York: Russell Sage Foundation.

Donato, Katherine M., Brandon Wagner, and Evelyn Patterson. 2008. "The Cat and Mouse Game at the Mexico-U.S. Border: Gendered Patterns and Recent Shifts." *International Migration Review* 42 (2): 330–59.

Donnelly, Robert, and Jacqueline Hagan. 2014. "Dangerous Journeys." In *Hidden Lives and Human Rights: Understanding the Controversies and Tragedies in Undocumented Immigration*, edited by Lois Ann Lorentzen, 71–105. Santa Barbara, Calif.: Praeger.

Eschbach, Karl, Jacqueline Hagan, Nestor Rodriguez, Rubén Hernández-León, and Stanley Bailey. 1999. "Death at the Border." *International Migration Review* 33 (2): 430–54.

Espinosa, Kristin, and Douglas S. Massey. 1997. "Undocumented Migration and the Quantity and Quality of Social Capital." *Soziale Welt* 12: 141–62.

Felbab-Brown, Vanda. 2009. *The Violent Drug Market in Mexico and Lessons from Colombia*. Washington, D.C.: Brookings Institution.

Fuentes, Jezmine, Henry L'Esperance, Raul Perez, and Caitlin White. 2007. "Impacts of U.S. Immigration Policies on Migration Behavior." In *Impact of Border Enforcement on Mexican Migration*, edited by Wayne A. Cornelius and Jessa M. Lewis, 53–73. San Diego, Calif.: Center for Comparative Immigration Studies.

Graham, John W., Allison E. Olchowski, and Tamika D. Gilreath. 2007. "How Many Imputations Are Really Needed? Some Practical Clarifications of Multiple Imputation Theory." *Prevention Science* 8 (3): 206–13.

Grasmuck, Sherri, and Patricia R. Pessar. 1991. *Between Two Islands: Dominican International Migration*. Berkeley: University of California Press.

Hagan, Jacqueline, Ruben Hernández-León, and Jean-Luc Demonsant. 2015. *Skills of the "Unskilled": Work and Mobility Among Mexican Migrants*. Berkeley: University of California Press.

Hagan, Jacqueline Maria. 1998. "Social Networks, Gender, and Immigrant Incorporation: Resources and Constraints." *American Sociological Review* 63 (1): 55–67.

———. 2008. *Migration Miracle: Faith, Hope, and Meaning on the Undocumented Journey*. Cambridge, Mass.: Harvard University Press.

Hagan, John, John Simpson, and A. R. Gillis. 1988. "Feminist Scholarship, Relational and Instrumental Control, and a Power-Control Theory of Gender and Delinquency." *British Journal of Sociology* 39: 301–36.

Hicken, Jonathan, Mollie Cohen, and Jorge Narvaez. 2010. "Double Jeopardy: How U.S. Enforcement Policies Shape Tunkaseño Migration." In *Mexican Migration and the U.S. Economic Crisis: A Transnational Perspective*, edited by Wayne A. Cornelius, David Fitzgerald, Pedro Lewin Fischer, and Leah Muse-Orlinoff, 47–92. San Diego, Calif.: Center for Comparative Immigration Studies.

Izcara Palacios, Simón Pedro. 2015. "Coyotaje and Drugs: Two Different Businesses." *Bulletin of Latin American Research* 34 (3): 324–39.

Kimball, Ann, Yesenia Acosta, and Rebecca Dames. 2007. "Impacts of U.S. Immigration Policies on Migration Behavior." In *Mayan Journeys: The New Migration from Yucatan to the United States*, edited by Wayne Cornelius, David Fitzgerald, and Pedro Lewin Fischer, 91–114. San Diego, Calif.: Center for Comparative Immigration Studies.

Long, J. Scott. 1997. *Regression Models for Categorical and Limited Dependent Variables.* Thousand Oaks, Calif.: Sage.

Lopez Castro, Gustavo. 1998. "Coyotes and Alien Smuggling." In *Binational Study: Migration Between Mexico and the United States.* Vol. 3, *Research Reports and Background Materials*, 965–74. Mexico City: Mexican Ministry of Foreign Affairs; Washington, D.C.: U.S. Commission on Immigration Reform. http://www.utexas.edu/lbj/uscir/binpapers/v3a6lopez.pdf.

Martínez, Daniel E., Kraig Beyerlein, Jeremy Slack, Prescott Vandervoet, Kristin Klingman, Paola Molina, and Shiras Manning et al. 2017. "The Migrant Border Crossing Study: A Methodological Overview of Research Along the Sonora-Arizona Border." *Population Studies* 71 (2): 249–64.

Martínez, Daniel E., Robin C. Reineke, Raquel Rubio-Goldsmith, and Bruce O. Parks. 2014. "Structural Violence and Migrant Deaths in Southern Arizona: Data from the Pima County Office of the Medical Examiner, 1990–2013." *Journal on Migration and Human Security* 2 (4): 257–86.

Massey, Douglas S., Joaquin Arango, Graeme Hugo, Ali Kouaouci, Adela Pellegrino, and J. Edward Taylor. 1993. "Theories of International Migration: A Review and Appraisal." *Population and Development Review* 19 (3): 431–66.

Massey, Douglas S., and Felipe García España. 1987. "The Social Process of International Migration." *Science* 237 (4816): 733–38.

Massey, Douglas S., and Kristen E. Espinosa. 1997. "What's Driving Mexico-U.S. Migration? A Theoretical, Empirical, and Policy Analysis." *American Journal of Sociology* 102 (4): 939–99.

O'Leary, Anna Ochoa. 2009. "The ABCs of Migration Costs: Assembling, Bajadores, and Coyotes." *Migration Letters* 6 (1): 27–35.

———. 2012. "Of Coyotes, Crossings, and Cooperation: Social Capital and Women's Migration at the Margins of the State." In *Political Economy, Neoliberalism, and the Prehistoric Economies of Latin America*, edited by Ty Matejowsky and Donald C. Wood, 133–60. Bingley: Emerald.

Parks, Kristen, Gabriel Lozada, Miguel Mendoza, and Lourdes Garcia Santos. 2009. "Strategies for Success: Border Crossing in an Era of Heightened Security." In *Migration from the Mexican Mixteca: A Transnational Community in Oaxaca and California*, edited by Wayne A. Cornelius, David Fitzgerald, Jorge Hernández-Díaz, and Scott Borger, 31–61. San Diego, Calif.: Center for Comparative Immigration Studies.

Portes, Alejandro. 1998. "Social Capital: Its Origins and Applications in Modern Sociology." *Annual Review of Sociology* 24: 1–24.

Portes, Alejandro, and Julia Sensenbrenner. 1993. "Embeddedness and Immigration: Notes on the Social Determinants of Economic Action." *American Journal of Sociology* 98 (6): 1320–50.

Roth, Louise Marie, and Jeffrey C. Kroll. 2007. "Risky Business: Assessing Risk-Preference Explanations for Gender Differences in Religiosity." *American Sociological Review* 72 (2): 205–20.

Royston, Patrick. 2009. "Multiple Imputation of Missing Values: Further Update of ICE, with an Emphasis on Categorical Variables." *Stata Journal* 9: 466–77.

Rubin, Donald B. 1987. *Multiple Imputation for Nonresponse in Surveys*. New York: Wiley.

Rubio-Goldsmith, Raquel, M. Melissa McCormick, Daniel Martínez, and Inez Magdalena Duarte. 2006. *The "Funnel Effect" and Recovered Bodies of Unauthorized Migrants Processed by the Pima County Office of the Medical Examiner, 1990–2005*. Tucson, Ariz.: Binational Migration Institute.

Sanchez, Gabriella. 2015. *Human Smuggling and Border Crossings*. New York: Routledge.

Singer, Audrey, and Douglas S. Massey. 1998. "The Social Process of Undocumented Border Crossing Among Mexican Migrants." *International Migration Review* 32 (3): 561–92.

Spener, David. 2009. *Clandestine Crossings: Migrants and Coyotes on the Texas-Mexico Border*. Ithaca, N.Y.: Cornell University Press.

Valdez-Suiter, Elisabeth, Nancy Rosas-Lopez, and Nayeli Pagaza. 2007. "Gender Differences." In *Impacts of Border Enforcement on Mexican Immigration: The View from Sending Communities*, edited by Wayne A. Cornelius and Jess M. Lewis, 97–114. San Diego, Calif.: Center for Comparative Immigration Studies.

von Hippel, Paul T. 2007. "Regression with Missing Y's: An Improved Strategy for Analyzing Multiply Imputed Data." *Sociological Methodology* 37 (1): 83–117.

Williams, Allan M., and Vladimir Baláž. 2011. "Migration, Risk, and Uncertainty: Theoretical Perspectives." *Population, Space and Place* 18 (2): 167–80.

Winship, Christopher, and Larry Radbill. 1994. "Sampling Weights and Regression Analysis." *Sociological Methods and Research* 23 (2): 230–57.

8

ON *NARCO-COYOTAJE*

Illicit Regimes and Their Impacts on the U.S.-Mexico Border

JEREMY SLACK AND HOWARD CAMPBELL

INTRODUCTION

"They [the Sinaloa Cartel] kidnapped our group and tortured the guide for *calentando el terreno*—attracting too much attention. They tortured the guides by tying them up and hanging them upside down while hitting them with cactus pads for having crossed at the wrong time and without permission," explained Jose.[1] (He and his group had been held on a ranch where drugs and guns were being stored.) "There were about three hundred captives in all. The men told me: 'We have the right to kill you.'"[2]

During this incident, which was collected by Slack during field research in Nogales, Sonora, the kidnappers raped the women and held everyone at gunpoint but did not ask for any money, suggesting that their interest in the captives had more to do with territorial control than extortion. The potential border crossers were let go after three days and nights without further discussion of why they had been held. This story illustrates that the relationship between human smugglers known as coyotes and drug traffickers has powerful conse-quences for both smugglers and migrants.

The mass media, advocates, and scholars have raised numerous questions about the nature of human smuggling (Comisión Interamericana de Derechos Humanos 2013; Francis 2008; O'Leary 2009). Are coyotes responsible for large-scale gruesome murders along the U.S.-Mexico border? Are coyotes the same as the cartel leaders so frequently discussed on the evening news? To these empirical questions the answer, of course, is no. However, this type of question highlights the conceptual ambiguity concerning the relationships among illicit practices, organizations, and even drug cartels. While scholars have previously tried to address the question of whether coyotes are categorically involved or are separate from drug cartels, they have generally concluded that they are distinct businesses (Izcara Palacios 2012, 2015; Sanchez 2014). However, all of this research, especially by Izcara Palacios (2015), notes that drug trafficking and other types of organized crime have certainly had an effect on migration and human smuggling such as the prevalence of kidnapping. Therefore, asking whether these are separate businesses or not obscures the complex interactions between one form of clandestine activity and another. We prefer to ask how human smuggling and drug trafficking relate to one another as well as what effects this relationship has produced, which helps us better understand illicit industries and the future of criminal organizations along the U.S.-Mexico border.

For this chapter, our goal is to help define questions regarding human smuggling, drug trafficking, and the interrelationships among different criminal activities more broadly. This paper is driven by an inversion of the questions that have been asked by other scholars of *coyotaje* as well as border and immigration scholars more broadly. Instead of simply asking whether coyotes are involved with drug trafficking, we ask, are coyotes being influenced by drug trafficking, and if so, how does this affect them and the migrants they help? This takes us to the core of the issue; what do the relationships between different types of extralegal activities mean for the migrants who are attempting to cross through these clandestine spaces as well as border residents in general?

Such questions lead into broader levels of inquiry—namely, how should we understand, conceptualize, and interrogate the illicit world? We must break from crude binaries generated by law enforcement (legal/illegal, innocent/criminal, good guy/bad guy). Such approaches are firmly grounded in a Manichean, juridical, state perspective that simplifies complex realities. Academics should push these boundaries to examine what illicit identities mean, how they function, and what this can tell us about the interconnections between individuals and groups participating in extralegal activities such as human smuggling or drug trafficking (Andreas 2000; Andreas and Nadelmann 2006; Banister, Boyce, and Slack 2015; Boyce, Banister, and Slack 2015; Campbell and Heyman 2007; Heyman and Smart 1999). Our larger goal is to develop a theoretical understanding of how multiple illicit industries work in shared spaces at the margins of the state.

We argue that there is a de facto hierarchy based on the power and profitability of specific clandestine activities (in this case drug trafficking is the dominant criminal activity). This leads to an illicit regime of narco-governmentality, one that functions in opposition to or in collusion with the law and whose basis is survival, profitability, and evading arrest. Illicit geographies separate themselves from the state but constantly establish their own rules and power structure, mimicking the state's activities in many ways. Indeed, our case studies suggest that in settings where powerful illicit regimes exist, such as the U.S.-Mexico border region, the state is not the sole actor in these configurations of power.

This is not to ignore the role of the state nor to negate the power of the much discussed border enforcement apparatus on the U.S. side (Nevins 2002). Rather, our goal is to highlight products of this unique configuration that give rise to other powerful actors. While thinking of criminal organizations as a form of parallel governance is not new (Leeds 1996), our concern is how different types of criminal activities overlap, interact, and self-govern. This will draw us away from categorical questions about whether or not coyotes and narcos make up the same organizations and allow us to develop an understanding about how these illicit systems actually work vis-à-vis one another.

We begin this chapter with a brief methodological note followed by dis-cussion of our theoretical orientation and the relevant literature on *coyotaje* and drug trafficking. Then we present our cases: a historical perspective on the evolution of human smuggling in the 1990s in Baja California and Southern California, the current context of the Sonora-Arizona crossing, and the most extreme example of control and oppression by an illicit regime in Tamaulipas. These three sites, detailing different time periods, represent unique formations of illicit power and also focus specifically on time periods in which each area was the most highly crossed region along the border. It is important to note that the border is a complex and dynamic region. However, most of the previous work on *coyotaje* and much of the empirical work on drug trafficking has occurred in singular field sites because of the obvious challenges of researching these topics (Baird and van Liempt 2016).

RESEARCH METHODOLOGY

The research for this article is based on a complex series of projects and eth-nographic engagements spanning many years of work along the U.S.-Mexico border. For the purpose of clarity it will be broken down into several distinct periods of fieldwork. Research on migration was conducted in Sonora mostly between 2007 and 2013 by Slack, who interviewed migrants staying in shelters in Nogales, Sonora, and to a limited extent Altar, Sonora. Research in Nuevo Laredo, Tamaulipas, occurred mostly in the fall of 2013 and focused on the effect of insecurity on deportees in the northeast of Mexico. Campbell conducted additional work on drug trafficking and other forms of smuggling in the El Paso/Ciudad Juárez area for the last ten years.

We also draw on descriptive statistics from the Migrant Border Crossing Study (MBCS, Wave II). These data, collected in 2011 and 2012, focus explicitly on forms of violence experienced by migrants.

UNDERSTANDING ILLICIT ORGANIZATIONS: RESISTANCE OR HIERARCHY, SMOOTH OR STRIATED?

Illegal activity is a complex issue that has still not been thoroughly theorized (see Campbell and Heyman 2007; Heyman and Smart 1999; Naim 2010; Van Schendel and Abraham 2005). In order to understand the issue of *narco-coyotaje* and the evolution of drug trafficking and human smuggling, we need to discuss how we conceive of illicit activity. Our goal is to understand how illicit regimes are formed and maintained and what impacts they have on other clandestine activities and those around them.

Scholars have highlighted illegal activity as a form of resistance and even an escape from the controls of the oppressive state apparatus (Scott 2009; Truett 2008). Researchers have devoted considerable attention to studying and theorizing the unique ways that states operate at their borders. This is particularly pronounced in terms of scholarship regarding the buildup of border enforcement (Andreas 2000; Brown 2010; Dunn 1996, 2009; Miller 2014; Nevins and Aizeki 2008) and its impact on migrants (De León 2015; Eschbach et al. 1999; Nevins and Aizeki 2008). The state is central in migration and border scholarship, and scholars have examined such issues as how states have governed sexuality through immigration law (Coleman 2008), the deterritorialization of access to asylum protections (Hyndman and Mountz 2007), state controls over their own diasporas (Délano and Gamlen 2014), and the neoliberal management of travel and trade (Sparke 2006). In this chapter we break with the state-centered analysis of many other scholars and use the state and state practices as the backdrop for a host of other actions. To borrow from Deleuze and Guattari (1977), our analysis conceives of the state, or states (Mexico and the United States) in this case, as the "body without organs," the plane on which desires and conflicts play out. Because of the great volume of literature on this topic, we do not feel the need to retheorize the state. Instead we complicate existing narratives of illegality and border enforcement by arguing that while illicit organizations do act in opposition to the state, among each other they replicate similar structures of hierarchy, control, and oppression.

We use the concept of illicit regimes to explore the unwritten rules, norms, and power structures that govern drug trafficking and human smuggling.[3] This comparison is apposite and contributes to the migration literature and burgeoning research on drug smuggling because both smugglers and guides are part of relatively high volume and lucrative industries, both are *mala prohibita* (bad because it is prohibited as opposed to bad by nature), and both rely on the border region and its unique topography. Because the clandestine space of the border is highly contested, surveilled, and policed (De Genova 2002; Dunn 1996; Inda 2006), illicit groups respond accordingly.

In trying to understand how the illicit world functions as a nonstate or parastate space, the nature of enforcement and legal prohibitions guides efforts to evade the law, which produces a hierarchy that reinforces the most lucrative activities (i.e., narcotics trafficking). The opening vignette shows this hierarchy. By crossing without permission or at a time that attracted unwanted attention from nearby law enforcement agents, the coyotes were punished and made an example of by drug traffickers. There are specific rules set by the most powerful actors, who try to create a bountiful equilibrium by allowing other illicit businesses to function, profiting off other types of criminal activity by exacting a toll known as the *derecho de piso*, but making sure that these other businesses do not affect their own core income-generating activities. Although we will not examine the other industries that make up illicit regimes, activities include extortions on businesses and wealthy individuals, the sale of pirated merchandise (CDs, DVDs, clothes, handbags, etc.), robbery, police bribery, and control of prostitution, bars, and brothels. Extralegal taxes, also called *cuotas*, have become ubiquitous along the border; human smugglers are charged a fee to cross through a specific territory or to operate at all, and they must never do anything to disturb other activities such as drug trafficking, as the guides from the opening vignette likely did (Izcara Palacios 2012). Because illicit regimes operate outside the law, there will never be written rules, so the tool of violence becomes particularly important for regulation and control.

Understanding how actions are controlled, through illicit and licit forms, has been central to migration research for some time, drawing extensively from the Foucauldian concept of governmentality (Foucault 2008). The gaze of the state, enacted through the border industrial security complex, has been thoroughly analyzed and critiqued (De Genova and Ramos-Zayas 2003; Inda 2006; Lugo 2008), but we must recognize that there is also a decidedly nonstate aspect of control that is communicated and internalized through the illicit practices of criminal organizations.[4] These illicit regimes represent a particular form of governmentality that is enacted without the typical mechanisms of power that we associate with Foucault's (2007) genealogical approach to understanding state power—namely, the written word codified into law and enacted into a practice that becomes the state. For Foucault, the increased sophistication of power—as enacted through the law, technology, research (especially social science), and the medical profession—was a hallmark of Western governance emerging with growth of population and decline in sovereign power. This generates power that has no clear origin; it is exercised on us unknowingly without the need to use overt force. Illicit regimes, on the other hand, derive power through direct relationships—through threats, interpersonal connections, acts of violence, and, essentially, their ability to escape or negate the written law (for more on the law, see Benjamin 1978).

However, some scholars have contested Foucault's conception of power, which has a tendency to become all encompassing and totally inescapable. James Scott (2009) explores the ability of the hill tribes in Southeast Asia to escape the trap of the state. Building on the concept of resistance in his previous work (Scott 2008), he discusses how people in this region draw from natural and physical surroundings to escape governance. By utilizing oral traditions and eschewing mathematics and the written word, these groups avoid leaving records and being counted, and therefore they avoid being subsumed by the state. This argument is similar to Deleuze and Guattari's (1987) work on smooth and striated spaces, whereupon the state is an apparatus of capture, a machine working to codify, count, measure, and thereby control. On the other hand, there is the war machine, operating in smooth space and constantly warding off the stratification of state forces. Deleuze and Guattari use the analogy of the desert as smooth space versus the steppes as striation; one allows for continuity and change while the other is broken, complex, and compartmentalized. Similar arguments have been made about the U.S.-Mexico border because of its remoteness and inaccessibility, profitability for smugglers, and distance from the power centers of the state (Díaz 2015; Truett 2008). Moreover, Deleuze and Guattari (1987) reject binaries, deploying them strategically, only to assert that concepts such as the war machine and the state are two poles on a spectrum oscillating back and forth between anarchic/chaotic and codified/controlled.

While illicit regimes are decidedly nonstate formations of power in that they work counter to official state doctrine, the relationship between the state and these regimes is coconstitutive, intimate, and mutually dependent. We do not want to create a binary model of state and nonstate governance; rather, we suggest a situation of two poles tied to one another and shaped by each other. State and nonstate actors, practices, and performativity are linked (Boyce, Banister, and Slack 2015). However, rather than simply leave this discussion with the conclusion that there are multiple linkages, crossovers, and relationships between the illicit world and the state creating a kind of "narco-assemblage" (Zigon 2015), we feel it is important to trace these linkages and determine how specific types of state formation actually create different, hierarchical illicit regimes. This, in turn, affects people who live within or pass through these systems in drastically different ways. Namely, the type of governmentality that originates in the state also creates the type of illicit regime, in this case a kind of narco-governmentality. For example, Mexico's patronage system, centralized governance, and emphasis on strong personalities who exert control over territorial units (Knight 2006) are mirrored by the structure of illicit activity. Combine this with the United States' highly militarized border, as well as its large consumer base, and a more sophisticated form of criminal governance arises.

THE MEXICAN STATE AND ILLICIT REGIME FORMATION

The particular formation of the Mexican state has allowed powerful individuals to control vast sectors of the state and its resources (Gil 1992; Lomnitz 1977; Lomnitz, Elena, and Adler 2010). The Mexican state's clientelist populism created the conditions for violence to erupt as soon as the one-party system was broken (Astorga 2005; Astorga and Shirk 2010). Without the linear, top-down chain of command within the Partido Revolucionario Institucional (PRI) that ended with the 2000 election of Vicente Fox, bribes and corruption did not function as efficiently. However, we are expanding on this analysis by understanding not just how corruption works but how illicit organizations react to, mimic, and insert themselves into the state (and vice versa as state actors insert themselves into illicit businesses), creating their own complex sets of rules and hierarchies that in turn influence how they interact with one another.

With the explosion of illicit activity in Mexico during the 1980s and 1990s, local bosses developed mutually beneficial relationships with the illicit world that mirrored the structure of the state. Eventually, strong drug lords, or *capos* (albeit never as strong as state actors), overpowered local political bosses and controlled how illicit businesses were conducted (Grillo 2011). Further, as the so-called drug war erupted in 2006–2007, these criminal organizations responded to the top-down approach taken by the Calderón administration by fragmenting further, decentralizing their power structures into regional organizations. This ability to shift territory and build a cell structure, protecting the most powerful actors, also highlights the ability to de- and reterritorialize much faster than the state and the ability of illicit regimes to transfer from a smooth to a relatively striated geography.

RESISTING THE STATE?

As mentioned, Foucault's understanding of state power as deriving from legibility and Deleuze and Guattari's characterization of the state as a striation machine conflict vis-à-vis the illicit world. Namely, the clandestine world has the ability to change, hide, and react much faster than even the most sophisticated bureaucracy, giving a distinct advantage to illicit regimes over their more powerful but also constrained opponents. This works in a number of ways that are important to acknowledge.

First, identities and groups must be considered emergent, not static and clearly labeled, as is common when "thinking like a state" (Scott 1998). This is important to remember when we discuss coyotes, low-level drug smugglers known as *burreros,* or even their bosses, the *capos*. They all have multiple identities. In Gabriela Sanchez's (2014) study of coyotes, she notes how her informants did not want to be identified as coyotes, *polleros,* or even human smugglers. Therefore she uses the term *facilitators*. This is precisely because these types of identities become codified only when they come into contact with the state, in the form of criminal charges and convictions. The same is true of drug smugglers. Many of the drug smugglers we have interviewed over the course of this research were actually seasonal agricultural workers in Sonora, occasional industrial workers in Chihuahua, or similarly sparsely employed in informal urban economies. Moreover, many coyotes easily switch back and forth between the identity of migrant or drug smuggler or drug dealer depending on when it becomes advantageous or dangerous.

For example, many of the coyotes we interviewed were staying at migrant shelters after being deported. Later, they revealed specific circumstances of their arrests, or how they arrange groups of migrants to cross. We should be wary of statements such as "real coyotes don't traffic drugs, don't leave people behind," and so forth, through which smugglers and scholars define the image of the coyote and what is and is not considered part of their economic activity (Izcara Palacios 2012). Indeed, the same performance of interior/exterior boundaries, as defined by those most likely to face punitive consequences, is precisely the power of the illicit—evading definition and adapting to threats.

DRUG CARTELS: POWER, STRUCTURE, AND HIERARCHY

An obstacle to determining how *coyotaje* and drug trafficking relate to one another has been an existing essentialist understanding of both. While there are different levels of individual involvement in each activity, we have to be clear about what we mean when we use the terms *drug cartel* or *organized criminal organization*. The scholarship on this issue has helped problematize popular conceptions of cartels as highly organized, top-down structures (Blancornelas 2004; Campbell 2009, 2014). Within different drug-trafficking organizations and at different periods of time, the degree of vertical control has varied, usually in relationship to the politics surrounding enforcement and prosecution of traffickers and the extent of intra- and intercartel conflict. Some scholars reject the term *cartel* because no one group has ever fully been able to control and set the price of drugs as per the classical economic definition of a cartel (Payan and Staudt 2013).[5] Instead the acronyms DTO (drug-trafficking organization) and TCO (transnational criminal organization) are frequently employed. The former has lost ground to the latter because, with increasing frequency, a panoply of activities, not just drugs, are being employed to earn illicit cash within these organizations. This is in fact one of our objects of critique. Because activities such as *coyotaje* or extortion occur within the geographical confines of more powerful and violent regional criminal organizations, what does this relationship entail? We argue that criminal organizations involve loosely structured activities. These diverse activities are tied together in the form of taxation (*cuotas*) and regulation or punishments that mimic state governance.

This is particularly true of paramilitary-oriented groups such as the Zetas and the Familia Michoacana / Knights Templar who have long employed tactics such as charging protection to local (licit and illicit) businesses and, in a particularly lucrative move, mines (Grayson 2010; Maldonado Aranda 2012). However, all of these terms tend to imply that there is central, hierarchical control over an organization, some essential essence and structure, rather than a fragmented, regional cell structure.

Campbell (2009) states that these organizations are far less structured than is often assumed, with people sometimes working together, sometimes not, and many not knowing explicitly which organization they work for. Often, the only unifying characteristic is that the group of people successfully sells drugs in or moves drugs through a particular *plaza*, paying appropriate tolls to more powerful individuals. If we can define this as an organized criminal group, is it any different when coyotes pay a toll for using a particular geographical area? Understanding drug cartels and human smuggling groups as far looser organizations also necessitates acknowledging how fluid the roles of the participants must be. Some authors suggest that hitmen, known as *sicarios*, are not actually *narcos*, blurring the inside/outside dichotomy of participation in drug-related activities (Muehlmann 2013).

While the lack of hard boundaries and firm binaries is an important point to constantly remember, pursuing exactly what role people play related to an illicit activity has material consequences. *Sicarios* (assassins), for example, come in different forms, from high-level professional killers (often former police or military hitmen such as the original Zetas) to the more common "hitboys" who get paid much smaller amounts to kill people on a regular basis. In the former case, the *sicarios* may be fairly well integrated into the cartel or loosely connected. In the latter case, the hitboys are fairly loosely connected but not necessarily any more so than, for example, subcontracted transborder car drivers carrying loads of drugs. However, no one suggests that the death and destruction created by sicarios and other armed enforcers is somehow not drug or crime related. Rather, these fluid relationships frequently generate internal conflicts that are worked out through acts of violence. Combine this with the increasingly diversified repertoire of these loose criminal networks, and it becomes less and less productive to assert who is and who is not a part of a drug cartel.

Similarly, if we try to connect coyotes generically to specific criminal organizations, then we may end up creating a caricature of that criminal organization. Instead, it is much more productive to focus on how the norms, procedures, and unwritten rules of the clandestine world affect people who are directly and indirectly involved. Before exploring data from interviews with migrants, drug traffickers, and human smugglers, we will briefly review the extant literature on *coyotaje*.

COYOTAJE AND DRUGS: ARE WE ASKING THE WRONG QUESTIONS?

Recent scholars studying *coyotaje* have pushed against the grain of negative stereotypes about coyotes that exist despite, or perhaps because of, the abundant journalism and academic literature concerned with undocumented migration between Mexico and the United States. Baird and van Liempt (2016) have outlined the various approaches to studying human smugglers as coming from a particular genre: smuggling as a crime, smuggling as a business, smuggling through networks, smuggling as part of the global political economy, and smuggling and human rights. We are most interested in scholarship about the U.S.-Mexico border that has challenged work from the "smuggling as crime" perspective. While resisting "straw man" characterizations of smugglers as criminals is a worthy endeavor, there is a danger when attempting to create a counternarrative: overcompensation. Namely, we may end up negating the moments when coyotes and migrants have distinctly different goals (profit vs. successful immigration) and when the practices of the U.S. Border Patrol have actively driven wedges between these groups.

Of particular interest is David Spener's (2009) research on *coyotaje* in South Texas that takes an ethnographic perspective, interviewing and interacting with coyotes on both sides of the border. He concludes that discourse around coyotes as abusers and villains is largely a myth, since most coyotes rely on a word-of-mouth business, and mistreatment of migrants would limit future business and referrals. Spener (2009) asserts that strong contacts and referrals by friends or family to a particular coyote are likely to improve treatment since the word-of-mouth business model is so prevalent among his interviewees. This would mean that coyotes who work directly at the border are less likely to be trustworthy.

However, we suggest that the power structures of illicit regimes actually work significantly to dampen this word-of-mouth effect, making it harder for coyotes with limited ties to more powerful criminal groups to attract the large number of migrants who arrive at the border without a preset guide. In chapter 7 of this volume, Martínez asserts that 45 percent of migrants crossing through Sonora/Arizona traveled with a border business coyote as opposed to 30 percent who used a smuggler from the interior of Mexico, suggesting that the primacy of local networks in locating and choosing a coyote has been seriously compromised. No longer do the majority travel with a coyote from their hometowns; rather, in order to cross, they rely heavily on guides who live directly on the border.

One important facet of this complexity is Spener's (2009) classification of "aberrant forms of coyotaje." This includes people who do not actually intend to give passage to migrants but rather to extort them and leave them stranded (false *coyotaje*) as well as those whose real goal is to transport drugs and not people. While it is important to understand that these may represent real differences between groups of people, one legitimately offering services while the other is simply pretending, sorting through this from the perspective of a migrant (or a researcher for that matter) is an enormous task. From the migrant perspective, the goal is to find a guide who will not kidnap, abandon, or abuse them, making negligible questions about whether or not the people who extort or kidnap migrants are actually "coyotes" in that they actually do facilitate moving people across borders. Empirically testing whether people actually engage in both extortion and facilitate successful migration is an impossible task. Izcara Palacios (2015) notes that most coyotes assert that once recruited by drug cartels, they no longer take people across the border but only aid in kidnapping people for ransom; however, aside from the assertions of coyotes, how could we test this?

Any group that has been vilified or arrested will often construct self-defensive narratives (see, e.g., the narratives in Bourgois 2003; Bourgois and Schonberg 2009). There is a particularly apt comparison with members of organized crime who attempt to claim the moral high ground, such as Pablo Escobar, who boasted that he supported the Colombian poor through philanthropy, or Rafael Caro Quintero, who famously—although apocryphally—offered to pay off the Mexican national debt with marijuana sales (Enciso 2013).[6] Moreover, drawing a stark line between participation in human smuggling and drug trafficking can also vilify those involved with drugs. However, it is the scholar's job to interpret these narratives rather than accepting them as gospel. What stands out through all this discussion is the fact that there are dangers present that were not as prevalent before the consolidation of illicit power that has taken place in recent years. In the next sections we explore different aspects of this cooptation of the migratory experience at the intersections of drug trafficking and *coyotaje*. What follows is not a "tour" of different locales in the borderlands but diverse examples from specific border sites that illustrate the dialectical relationship between the illicit organizations and the state.

A HISTORICAL PERSPECTIVE ON SMUGGLING

While human smugglers, guides, or "migration facilitators" have clearly existed for decades (Sanchez 2014), scholars have widely agreed that migration after the 1990s became much more expensive and dangerous with the advent of more organized coyotes (Massey, Durand, and Malone 2002). Much of the narrative about changes to human smuggling is centered on the enforcement strategy pioneered in the El Paso sector, whereupon the border patrol concentrated their efforts in urban centers, pushing people into more remote and challenging desert terrain (Dunn 2009; Nevins 2002). "Everything changed because of Silvestre Reyes," exclaimed Jack Lowery.[7] Lowery, an experienced smuggler who freely shared his knowledge with the researchers, had begun working as a coyote in Southern California in the early 1980s, picking up migrants from hotels in San Ysidro, California, and driving them through the San Clemente checkpoints several hours to the north. This narrative is meant to be an example of how changes in enforcement and state practices affected the power structures of human smuggling. It is by no means a definitive case, although it does align with other scholarship from the region (Bustamante 2000; Cornelius 2001). Lowery became very successful and continued his illegal activities, even after being caught in the mid-1980s, until 1991, when he switched from human smuggling to drug trafficking. After he was arrested for human smuggling, Lowery began informing on his fellow smugglers to the Alien Smuggling Unit (ASU), a now defunct unit in the border patrol, while continuing to engage in the "alien business," as he calls it. In his words,

> The biggest difference between 1980 and 1990 . . . was [that] the alien business was basically a group of families—mamas, papas, family-oriented businesses, taxi drivers, the people in hotels . . . they would buy and sell the aliens . . . like a swap meet, because the alien had value. . . . The price [the amount he would pay to pick up an individual] in 1981 was $250; by 1990 it was $300. When I say it was a lot more peaceful, then they didn't use guns to control them, they [the "aliens"] were clients, . . . the hotels in Tijuana lived off the aliens crossing the border. . . . Business was done on a handshake. . . . [After the early 1990s hyper-militarization of the border,] all of the families that had been in the business and the taxi drivers went back to legitimate businesses. As the business became more dangerous, people began using guns. Now they steal the aliens. They would steal the aliens because they are like gold. The attitude of the ASU—they didn't give a fuck. The ASU said

"goddamn this El Paso shit." The ASU opposed it [Reyes's Operation Blockade / Hold the Line policy], they just wanted to get paid, not work hard, and retire.[8]

Lowery also engages in the same defensive authenticity narrative present in other studies of *coyotaje*, asserting that his treatment of migrants is exemplary and somehow different from current standards.

Lowery,[9] a cogent observer of and participant in the human smuggling and drug businesses, provided intricate information about smuggling tactics, practices, and the hierarchy, including the names of the top families involved in human smuggling in Tijuana. "They were just a regular local family in charge at that time," he explained. All that changed quickly, according to his account.

After Operation Gatekeeper came to San Diego, local families were no longer in control, and smuggling became more and more professional, violent, and tied to drug trafficking. So much so that Lowery was approached by the Drug Enforcement Administration (DEA) to inform on drug trafficking in the region. The same tactics and knowledge of how checkpoints worked that Lowery used in the human smuggling business served him well when he began transporting drugs. It is revealing that Lowery's two clandestine careers occurred during separate periods and that his account (the most evocative of many we have collected that point to the same outcome) demonstrates the greater criminalization of the two businesses over time as they became more similar and began to overlap.

It should be noted that Operation Gatekeeper served to push the migrant stream away from Southern California and into southern Arizona, with the number of apprehensions in the Tucson sector skyrocketing in the early 2000s (Martínez et al. 2014). Lowery blames the rise in drug trafficking by coyotes instead of human smuggling on the decrease in migrants who had hitherto provided the coyotes' livelihood. Because it became increasingly difficult for migrants to cross through Southern California, drugs became a more important and valuable criminal enterprise for former human smugglers. This, among other factors, changed the dynamics of the criminal organizations in the region and helped create the hierarchical illicit regime we are exploring in this article.

ALTAR: TRANSITION FROM A MIGRANT CROSSING TO DRUG SMUGGLING CORRIDOR

Altar, Sonora, became synonymous with undocumented migration at the turn of the twenty-first century. In 2000, the U.S. Border Patrol in the Tucson sector reported 616,386 apprehensions, and a majority of these migrants started their transborder journey in this small desert town about an hour's drive south of the border (U.S. Customs and Border Protection 2015b). With the influx of migrants came increasingly sophisticated services and products, such as locally produced water bottles that were made of thick black plastic that are resistant to cactus needles (De León 2012). The plaza in front of the local church often looked like a festival, with hundreds of people milling about every day, buying supplies and trying to find a guide with whom to attempt the difficult border crossing (Magaña 2013). However, as the number of USBP agents grew to over four thousand in 2014 (U.S. Customs and Border Protection 2015a), the challenges for migrants also began to change.

While the plaza in Altar still contained the shops and their tailored migration paraphernalia, by the late 2000s much of the negotiations had moved inside. *Casas de huespedes*, or guest houses, began popping up. Migrants arriving in town were almost immediately shuttled into these establishments, where they would wait for the signal to cross. During fieldwork in 2008 at a number of different *casas de huespedes*, it was obvious that they varied widely in quality. Some were similar to low-cost hotels, while others packed people in, dozens to a bunk, renting each scrap of padding and cloth for an additional charge. Moving people indoors, into these controlled environments, allowed individuals to regulate which guides were taking people across the border. According to a key informant, this helped remove opportunities for guides without local ties. The spatial regimes of potential border crossing at Altar changed in response to this increased enforcement as well as to the increased value and scarcity of crossers. Pushing migrants behind closed doors, into controlled environments, also increased the potential for abuse by would-be guides. This spatial seclusion has become an increasingly dangerous aspect of migration through the Sonoran corridor.

One migrant named Esmeralda was held at a *casa de huespedes* for two days before being transferred to an even more remote location outside of Altar, known as the *ladrillera* (brick factory). The guides demanded money, so she gave one man 8,000 pesos, about US$800 at the time, but they demanded more. She described the coyotes' behavior as follows: "The first one, the one that tells you things and arranges travel, is always nice, but the ones that walk with people are *groseros* [rude, uncouth]. They are on drugs, so they can keep walking," she explained.[10]

Another important factor uncovered during research was frequent reports that groups of migrants from Sonora to Arizona were being coordinated so as to provide cover for drug trafficking. This became apparent only when people were separated from their groups or tried to turn back. The following field data demonstrate this: "After being robbed by *bajadores* [rip crews or bandits] and losing all his money, and even food and water, Horacio and his group turned around and headed back toward Mexico. Soon, they ran into a group of narcos. The backpackers [*burreros*] were carrying AR-15s, which they pointed at Horacio and his group, instructing them that they had to keep walking into the US. Horacio said that they were using the migrants as a shield so the *burreros* can cross with marijuana. '¡Si regresas, te mato!' [If you go back, I'll kill you!], said one narco."[11]

Migrants in Altar were consistently being sent in staggered groups of ten or twenty each half hour with a group of *burreros* behind the last group as a way to distract the border patrol. Horacio's story demonstrates that there is a relationship between the people guiding migrants across the border and those tasked with taking drugs. However, one cannot accurately assert categorically whether coyotes participate in this arrangement willingly, for monetary gain, rather than under duress. Another facet of the border-crossing experience sheds light on how these arrangements are established.

In 2008 and 2009, robberies such as the one mentioned here were also rampant. The thieves, called *bajadores*—a local idiomatic expression derived from *te bajan todo* (they take everything off you)—were extorting and robbing migrants as well as stealing drug shipments all along the Sonora-Arizona border. Previous research with recent migrants found that one in three were accosted by bandits in their last crossing attempt (Martínez 2013; Slack and Whiteford 2011). However, on the morning of April 24, 2009, a man was found murdered in the border city of Nogales, Sonora, with a message, commonly referred to as a *narcomanta*, attached to the body. It read: "This will happen to all *bajadores*, or *ratas* as well as the people that help them by letting them use their ranches; we know where and who they are, you are screwed."[12] In the following three months, the same newspaper noted thirty similar killings in the area. These killings led to a drastic reduction in robbery reported by migrants. In 2011, MBCS survey data found the number reporting contact with *bajadores* or thieves dropped to 12 percent ($N = 1,109$).

This coincided with a toll set up just outside the city on the sand road for people traveling from Altar to the border. The checkpoint, manned by armed men not in uniform, charged migrants about 500 pesos at first, but the toll steadily rose and soon people were paying an average of 1,500 pesos (about US$150) for the opportunity to get near the border. By 2014, this price had continued to rise to a reported 6,000 pesos (US$429).[13] This was followed by a reduction of migrants and a rise in drug trafficking. "That young guy at the check-point is the top *sicario* [assassin] around here—*te mata*—boom," explained a local informant, pointing his fingers in the shape of a gun.[14] The increase in marijuana smuggling and the decrease in migration through Altar precipitated a shift in the illicit regime, one that has become particularly repressive; however, it is not as violent as the region that currently experiences the most migration.

TAMAULIPAS: STATE DETERIORATION AND ILLICIT REGIME CONTROL

In September 2011, several brutal murders changed the narrative of domination and control by drug cartels. On September 13, two bodies were found hanging from a bridge in Nuevo Laredo with a message declaring that this will happen to all the people on the Internet posting anonymous information about crime to multiple social media sites. About a week later, a prominent local (also anonymous) blogger and journalist named Marisol Macías Castañeda, known as "La Nena de Laredo" was murdered in a brutal fashion (Valor por Tamaulipas 2012). These events showed a heightened level of illicit control, one that deeply affected research with migrants and coyotes. The Zetas—the ex-military, former enforcers for the Gulf Cartel—had broken off to form their own drug cartel using the highly valuable border town of Nuevo Laredo as their home base (Osorno 2012). This zone, one of the most oppressive in the country, along with Coahuila, shows an extreme example of the strength and power of illicit regimes. The operation of all economic activities here runs into the power of the illicit world through extortion, kidnapping threats, and "protection" rackets. As the illicit regime grows in power, there is greater emphasis on information and mobility, and the spatial regimes dictating the mobility of outsiders become more oppressive.

> "Es que quiero irme de aqui"—"It's just that I want to get out of here," Cristian said, his eyes red with tears. Despite his banging loudly on the mirrored glass doors, it took five minutes for someone with keys to come and open the migrant shelter. "You should have walked with the rest of them to the plaza when it was safe," scolded the shelter worker. Cristian was shaking, his normal youthful bravado gone, replaced by fear. "Are they after you?" I asked. He shrugged and shook his head in an unconvincing "no." He asked if we could call him a taxi. I ducked inside and made a call from the office to one of the taxis I used. They showed up quickly and he jumped inside.[15]

Scenes like this were not uncommon in the migrant shelter where Slack did fieldwork, particularly the admonishment of people that did not "follow the rules." Slack witnessed one group being kidnapped by men in a van because they were hanging out in front of the shelter during the day. People frequently returned to the migrant shelter beaten and bloody. Those caught trying to cross the river without an approved guide—meaning someone who had paid the requisite tolls—as well as those who wandered outside approved areas for migrants (select plazas and streets where they could be monitored), would be beaten with a wooden board with nails in it or holes drilled in it (known as *el tablazo*). One day, a coyote who was staying at the shelter while looking for clients came back with his eye severely swollen, limping from the beating given to his backside. He said they caught him "somewhere he should not have been."[16] The importance of territorial control and the lack of official affiliation with the dominant illicit organization helps us understand why this type of violence is so prevalent.

Migrants were frequently approached by individuals recruiting them to "guard the river," sometimes with promises of money and women, other times with threats of violence. Guarding the river is a key aspect of the geographical control necessary for an illicit regime to maintain the plaza. Ensuring that independent coyotes or drug smugglers cannot operate in this area without paying a toll demonstrates the power of organized crime. Tamaulipas is an extreme example, one that shows how illicit regimes can themselves become so oppressive and controlling that they mimic the very state they are in contention with. To borrow once more from Deleuze and Guattari (1987), the co-opted war machine of the drug cartels itself becomes striated, operating like the oppressive, controlling, and prohibitionist state that it once resisted.

CONCLUSIONS

The debate concerning how *coyotaje*, human smuggling processes on the U.S.-Mexico border, relates to drug cartels is merely a starting point for a larger, more complicated question about the nature of illicit industries. We argue that rather than representing a release from the control of the state (Scott 2009; Truett 2008), these industries create a mimetic but distorted image, one that copies the attempts from law enforcement to curtail illicit activity. By acting as both tax collector in the form of payments for the *derecho de piso* and enforcer by dealing out violent forms of justice, illicit regimes have essentially co-opted some of the essential functions of the state (see Weber 1965). The result is a criminal hierarchy prioritizing the most powerful and profitable clandestine activity, in this case, drug trafficking. By demonstrating that the relationships between various clandestine activities do in fact change the actual experience of migration, we illustrate the weakness of a perspective that analytically isolates *coyotaje* and drug trafficking, thus failing to capture the complexity of the situation.

The relationship between drugs and human smuggling within the shared geography of the border is productive of an especially violent and dangerous situation. Research on illicit activity could benefit from this methodological approach, one that interrogates relationships between illicit organizations rather than taking them as one ubiquitous set of processes engaged only with the state or viewing specific criminalized acts as sui generis, entirely separate from other illicit endeavors.

While we have deliberately eschewed an extensive theorization of the state (or states in this case), future research could help define the diverse sets of relationships produced through illicit regimes and their legal counterparts. This will help expand a growing literature concerned with illicit geographies and the role of the state in creating, promoting, or curtailing violence and human insecurity (Chatterjee 2009; Garmany 2011; Gregory and Pred 2007) as well as literature on the myriad forms of illicit agency vis-à-vis states and their margins. By refocusing literature about coyotes and drug trafficking onto how the current security situation is affecting, changing, and rewriting the migratory experience, we can better understand the threats to people living, working on, and crossing the border. This line of questioning helps us understand the hierarchical relationships among criminal activities and organizations and has many possibilities for broader theoretical and practical insights beyond the simple question of the involvement of coyotes in drug trafficking. Sadly, border residents and migrants must cope with the violence of the state and the illicit regime, creating a situation of double jeopardy that bifurcates the expectations, regulations, and day-to-day realities of life in the borderlands into two oppressive systems in collusion and conflict with each other.

NOTES

Originally published as J. Slack and H. Campbell, "On Narco-Coyotaje: Illicit Regimes and Their Impacts on the US-Mexico Border." *Antipode* 48, no. 5 (2016): 1380–99. Adapted and reprinted by permission.

1.   This and all other names are pseudonyms.
2.   Personal communication, July 19, 2011.

3. We use the term *illicit* to note that these regimes rely on the explicit use of violence as a regulatory mechanism. As scholars have noted, the term *illicit* denotes a social ill rather than something that is illegal, which is merely against the law (Van Schendel and Abraham 2005).

4. We use *nonstate* in an official sense. Regardless of whether or not the actors doing the extortion are working for the state (as many members of the police and military also work for drug cartels and enforce their mandates), these forms of control do not originate in the legal apparatus of the state.

5. We prefer the term *cartel* because it has cultural significance. It is a signifier of a particular type of power, violence, and danger that people are aware of and live with on a daily basis.

6. This quote originated as a satire of his postapprehension interview; however, it has stuck in the popular imaginary of narcos in Mexico (Enciso 2013).

7. Scholars have debated the true impact of Silvestre Reyes and his Operation Blockade on increased immigration enforcement measures in the 1990s (Hernandez 2010; Dunn 2009); however, this quote reinforces its centrality for those involved with smuggling during the period.

8. Interview, July 16, 2015.

9. A search of legal records confirmed Lowery's participation as an informant in several large cases involving drug trafficking and human smuggling.

10. Personal communication, Nogales, Sonora, April 29, 2011.

11. Personal communication, Nogales, Sonora, February 4, 2010.

12. *El Diario*, April 24, 2009.

13. Personal communication, May 27, 2014.

14. Personal communication, May 26, 2014.

15. Personal communication, Nuevo Laredo, Tamaulipas, December 11, 2013.

16. Personal communication, November 5, 2013.

REFERENCES

Andreas, P. 2000. *Border Games: Policing the US-Mexico Divide*. Ithaca, N.Y.: Cornell University Press.

Andreas, P., and E. A. Nadelmann. 2006. *Policing the Globe: Criminalization and Crime Control in International Relations*. Oxford: Oxford University Press.

Astorga, L. 2005. *El siglo de las drogas: El narcotráfico, del porfiriato al nuevo milenio*. Mexico City: Plaza y Janés.

Astorga, L., and D. A. Shirk. 2010. "Drug Trafficking Organizations and Counter-Drug Strategies in the U.S.-Mexican Context." Working paper, Center for U.S.-Mexican Studies, University of California, San Diego. http://escholarship.org/uc/item/8j647429.

Baird, T., and I. van Liempt. 2016. "Scrutinising the Double Disadvantage: Knowledge Production in the Messy Field of Migrant Smuggling." *Journal of Ethnic and Migration Studies* 42 (3): 400–417.

Banister, J. M., G. A. Boyce, and J. Slack. 2015. "Illicit Economies and Stateless. Geographies: The Politics of Illegality." *Territory, Politics, Governance* 3:365–68.

Benjamin, W. 1978. "Critique of Violence." In *Reflections*, edited by P. Demetz, 277–300. New York: Harcourt Brace Jovanovich.

Blancornelas, J. 2004. *El cartel: Los Arellano Felix, la mafia mas poderosa en la historia de America Latina*. Mexico City: Debolsillo.

Bourgois, P. 2003. *In Search of Respect: Selling Crack in El Barrio*. Cambridge: Cambridge University Press.

Bourgois, P., and J. Schonberg. 2009. *Righteous Dopefiend*. Berkeley: University of California Press.

Boyce, G. A., J. M. Banister, and J. Slack. 2015. "You and What Army? Violence, the State, and Mexico's War on Drugs." *Territory, Politics, Governance* 3 (4): 446–68.

Brown, W. 2010. *Walled States, Waning Sovereignty*. Cambridge, Mass.: MIT Press.

Bustamante, J. A. 2000. "Migración irregular de México a Estados Unidos: Diez años de investigación del Proyecto Cañón Zapata." *Frontera Norte* 12 (23): 7–49.

Campbell, H. 2009. *Drug War Zone: Frontline Dispatches from the Streets of El Paso and Juárez*. Austin: University of Texas Press.

———. 2014. "Narco-propaganda in the Mexican 'Drug War': An Anthropological Perspective." *Latin American Perspectives* 41 (2): 60–77.

Campbell, H., and J. Heyman. 2007. "Slantwise: Beyond Domination and Resistance on the Border." *Journal of Contemporary Ethnography* 36 (1): 3–30.

Chatterjee, I. 2009. "Violent Morphologies: Landscape, Border, and Scale in Ahmedabad Conflict." *Geoforum* 40: 1003–13.

Coleman, M. 2008. "US Immigration Law and Its Geographies of Social Control: Lessons from Homosexual Exclusion During the Cold War." *Environment and Planning D* 26: 1096–114.

Comisión Interamericana de Derechos Humanos. 2013. "Derechos Humanos de los migrantes y otras personas en el contexto de movilidad humana en México." Comisión Interamericana de Derechos Humanos, Organización de los Estados Americanos. http://www.oas.org/es/cidh/migrantes/docs/pdf/informe-migrantes-mexico -2013.pdf.

Cornelius, W. A. 2001. "Death at the Border: Efficacy and Unintended Consequences of US Immigration Control Policy." *Population and Development Review* 27 (4): 661–85.

De Genova, N. 2002. "Migrant 'Illegality' and Deportability in Everyday Life." *Annual Review of Anthropology* 31: 419–47.

De Genova, N., and A. Y. Ramos-Zayas 2003. *Latino Crossings: Mexicans, Puerto Ricans, and the Politics of Race and Citizenship*. New York: Psychology Press.

Délano, A., and A. Gamlen. 2014. "Comparing and Theorizing State-Diaspora Relations." *Political Geography* 41: 43–53.

De León, J. 2012. "'Better to Be Hot Than Caught': Excavating the Conflicting Roles of Migrant Material Culture." *American Anthropologist* 114: 477–95.

———. 2015. *The Land of Open Graves: Living and Dying on the Migrant Trail*. Berkeley: University of California Press.

Deleuze, G., and F. Guattari. 1977. *Anti-Oedipus*. New York: Viking.

———. 1987. *A Thousand Plateaus*. Minneapolis: University of Minnesota Press.

Díaz, G. T. 2015. *Border Contraband: A History of Smuggling Across the Rio Grande*. Austin: University of Texas Press.

Dunn, T. J. 1996. *The Militarization of the US-Mexico Border, 1978–1992: Low-Intensity Conflict Doctrine Comes Home*. Austin: University of Texas Press.

———. 2009. *Blockading the Border and Human Rights: The El Paso Operation That Remade Immigration Enforcement*. Austin: University of Texas Press.

Enciso, F. 2013. "Mito, ofrecimiento de Caro Quintero para pagar deuda esterna." *El Universal*, August 11. http://www.redpolitica.mx/nacion/un-mito-caro-quintero-nunca -ofrecio-pagar-la-deuda-externa.

Eschbach, K., J. Hagan, N. Rodriguez, R. Hernandez-Leon, and S. Bailey. 1999. "Death at the Border." *International Migration Review* 33: 430–54.

Foucault, M. 2007. *Security, Territory, Population: Lectures at the College de France, 1977– 1978*. New York: Palgrave Macmillan.

———. 2008. *The Birth of Biopolitics: Lectures at the College de France, 1978–1979*. New York: Palgrave Macmillan.

Francis, D. 2008. "Mexican Drug Cartels Move into Human Smuggling." *San Francisco Chronicle*, March 31. http://www.sfgate.com/news/article/Mexican-drug-cartels -move-into-human-smuggling-3221740.php.

Garmany, J. 2011. "Drugs, Violence, Fear, and Death: The Necro- and Narco-geographies of Contemporary Urban Space." *Urban Geography* 32: 1148–66.

Gil, C. B. 1992. *Hope and Frustration: Interviews with Leaders of Mexico's Political Opposition*. Wilmington, Del.: Scholarly Resources.

Grayson, G. W. 2010. "La Familia Drug Cartel: Implications for US-Mexican Security." Strategic Studies Institute, US Army War College. http://ssi.armywarcollege.edu /pdffiles/pub1033.pdf.

Gregory, D., and A. Pred, eds. 2007. *Violent Geographies: Fear, Terror, and Political Violence*. New York: Routledge.

Grillo, I. 2011. *El Narco: Inside Mexico's Criminal Insurgency*. New York: Bloomsbury

Hernández, Kelly Lytle. 2010. *Migra! A History of the U.S. Border Patrol*. Berkeley: University of California Press.

Heyman, J. M., and A. Smart. 1999. *States and Illegal Practices*. Oxford: Berg.

Hyndman, J., and A. Mountz. 2007. "Refuge or Refusal." In *Violent Geographies: Fear, Terror, and Political Violence*, edited by D. Gregory and A. Pred, 77–92. New York: Routledge.

Inda, J. X. 2006. *Targeting Immigrants: Government, Technology, and Ethics*. Malden, Mass.: Blackwell.

Izcara Palacios, S. P. 2012. "Coyotaje y grupos delictivos en Tamaulipas." *Latin American Research Review* 47: 41–61.

———. 2015. "Coyotaje and Drugs: Two Different Businesses." *Bulletin of Latin American Research* 34 (3): 324–39.

Knight, A. 2006. "Patterns and Prescriptions in Mexican Historiography." *Bulletin of Latin American Research* 25: 340–66.

Leeds, E. 1996. "Cocaine and Parallel Polities in the Brazilian Urban Periphery: Constraints on Local-Level Democratization." *Latin American Research Review* 31 (3): 47–84.

Lomnitz, L. A. 1977. *Networks and Marginality: Life in a Mexican Shantytown.* New York: Academic Press.

Lomnitz, L. A., R. S. Elena, and I. Adler. 2010. *Symbolism and Ritual in a One-Party Regime: Unveiling Mexico's Political Culture.* Tucson: University of Arizona Press.

Lugo, A. 2008. *Fragmented Lives, Assembled Parts: Culture, Capitalism, and Conquest at the US-Mexico Border.* Austin: University of Texas Press.

Magaña, R. 2013. "On Shifting Ground." In *Uncharted Terrains: New Directions in Border Research Methodology, Ethics, and Practice,* edited by A. O. O'Leary, C. M. Deeds, and S. Whiteford, 83–100. Tucson: University of Arizona Press.

Maldonado Aranda, S. 2012. "Drogas, violencia y militarización en el México rural: El caso de Michoacán." *Revista Mexicana de Sociología* 74: 5–39.

Martínez, D. E. 2013. "The Crossing Experience: Unauthorized Migration Along the Arizona-Sonora Border." PhD diss., University of Arizona. http://arizona.open repository.com/arizona/handle/10150/293415.

———. 2016. "Coyote Use in an Era of Heightened Border Enforcement: New Evidence from the Arizona-Sonora Border." *Journal of Ethnic and Migration Studies* 42 (1): 103–19.

Martínez, D. E., R. C. Reineke, R. Rubio-Goldsmith, and B. O. Parks. 2014. "Structural Violence and Migrant Deaths in Southern Arizona: Data from the Pima County Office of the Medical Examiner, 1990–2013." *Journal on Migration and Human Security* 2: 257–86.

Massey, D. S., J. Durand, and N. J. Malone. 2002. *Beyond Smoke and Mirrors: Mexican Immigration in an Era of Economic Integration.* New York: Russell Sage Foundation.

Miller, T. 2014. *Border Patrol Nation: Dispatches from the Front Lines of Homeland Security.* San Francisco: City Lights.

Muehlmann, S. 2013. *When I Wear My Alligator Boots: Narco-Culture in the US-Mexico Borderlands.* Berkeley: University of California Press.

Naim, M. 2010. *Illicit: How Smugglers, Traffickers and Copycats Are Hijacking the Global Economy.* New York: Random House.

Nevins, J. 2002. *Operation Gatekeeper: The Rise of the "Illegal Alien" and the Making of the US-Mexico Boundary.* New York: Routledge.

Nevins, J., and Aizeki, M. 2008. *Dying to Live: A Story of US Immigration in an Age of Global Apartheid.* San Francisco: City Lights.

O'Leary, A. O. 2009. "The ABCs of Migration Costs: Assembling, Bajadores, and Coyotes." *Migration Letters* 6: 27–35.

Osorno, D. E. 2012. *La guerra de los Zetas.* Mexico City: Grijalbo.

Payan, T., and K. Staudt, eds. 2013. *A War That Can't Be Won? Binational Perspectives on the War on Drugs.* Tucson: University of Arizona Press.

Sanchez, G. 2014. *Human Smuggling and Border Crossings.* New York: Routledge.

Scott, J. C. 1998. *Seeing Like a State.* New Haven, Conn.: Yale University Press.

————. 2008. *Weapons of the Weak*. New Haven, Conn.: Yale University Press.

————. 2009. *The Art of Not Being Governed*. New Haven, Conn.: Yale University Press.

Slack J., D. E. Martínez, S. Whiteford, and E. Peiffer 2015. "In Harm's Way: Family Separation, Immigration Enforcement Programs, and Security on the US-Mexico Border." *Journal on Migration and Human Security* 3: 109–28.

Slack, J., and S. Whiteford. 2011. "Violence and Migration on the Arizona Sonora Border." *Human Organization* 70: 11–21.

Sparke, M. 2006. "A Neoliberal Nexus: Economy, Security, and the Biopolitics of Citizenship on the Border." *Political Geography* 25: 151–80.

Spener, D. 2009. *Clandestine Crossings: Migrants and Coyotes on the Texas-Mexico Border*. Ithaca, N.Y.: Cornell University Press.

Truett, S. 2008. *Fugitive Landscapes: The Forgotten History of the US-Mexico Borderlands*. New Haven, Conn.: Yale University Press.

U.S. Customs and Border Protection. 2015a. "United States Border Patrol: Sector Profile—Fiscal Year 2014." U.S. Customs and Border Protection. https://www.cbp.gov/sites/default/files/documents/USBP%20Stats%20FY2014%20sector%20profile.pdf.

————. 2015b. "United States Border Patrol–Southwest Border Sectors–Total Illegal Alien Apprehensions By Fiscal Year." U.S. Customs and Border Protection (accessed February 23, 2016; no longer posted). https://www.cbp.gov/sites/default/files/documents/BP%20Southwest%20Border%20Sector%20Apps%20FY1960%20-%20FY2015.pdf.

Valor por Tamaulipas. 2012. "El día que los Zetas decapitaron a 'La Nena de Laredo.'" *Valor por Tamaulipas*, June 12. http://www.valorportamaulipas.info/2015/06/el-dia-que-los-zetas-decapitaron-la.html.

Van Schendel, W., and I. Abraham. 2005. *Illicit Flows and Criminal Things: States, Borders, and the Other Side of Globalization*. Bloomington: Indiana University Press.

Weber, M. 1965. *Politics as a Vocation*. Philadelphia: Fortress Press.

Zigon, J. 2015. "What Is a Situation? An Assemblic Ethnography of the Drug War." *Cultural Anthropology* 30: 501–24.

9

CAPTIVE BODIES

Migrant Kidnapping and Deportation in Mexico

JEREMY SLACK

INTRODUCTION[1]

"I WOKE UP ON the floor in my own blood and excrement. I don't know how long I was out, but I couldn't handle the electric shocks. *No sé porque no aguante* [I don't know why I couldn't handle it]," said Juanito in a low voice, fighting back tears.[2] "My right arm was dislocated, and my wrists were bloody from the handcuffs they were hanging me by. My eye was swollen shut and my lip was split open. I was missing four fingernails and six toenails and my testicles were swollen and burned from where they put the cables." "They pulled out your fingernails after you passed out?" I asked. "I don't know," he said, showing me his shiny, freshly regrown nails, "I think they exploded when they shocked me."

Juanito, twenty-one, originally from Chihuahua, recounted in gruesome detail the psychological, physical, and sexual abuse enacted by the Zetas in San Fernando, Tamaulipas.[3] The most brutal torture occurred daily within the first month as they collected information on his family and demanded US$5,000 ransom, which was paid immediately. After the first month, he was put to work processing marijuana bound for the United States. This continued for five months until they sent him with a group carrying backpacks of marijuana and, luckily, he was arrested.

This chapter relies on data taken from interviews and surveys about deportees' experiences being kidnapped or held against their will. Migrant kidnapping has increased in quantity and brutality during recent years, leaving policy makers, activists, and academics struggling to answer why. I examine the role of place and space in explaining why people in motion or "bodies out of place" have become the prime targets. Those engaged in clandestine border crossing have become the perfect victims not because of their wealth but because of their relationship to the border. Juanito explained that focusing on bodies in movement is a way to avoid the backlash from locals who might stand up and fight if their loved ones and relatives were taken but are less willing to risk death for strangers.

By exploring the border as topological, we can create a clearer picture of why certain people can be kidnapped because they are either undocumented Central Americans headed through Mexico or deportees dropped off on the streets of an unfamiliar border city. The movement through this contested space opens up a specific type of subjectivity whereupon they can be taken, held, tortured, and exploited in a variety of ways without repercussions. This leads us to questions about the utility of kidnapping relatively impoverished people. Is it just about ransom, or are there other motives and utilities to taking possession of people's bodies?

BACKGROUND: HIDDEN SECRETS OF DEPORTATION

Juanito was kidnapped along with eighty other people in Chihuahua City after being deported from the United States to Piedras Negras, Coahuila, Mexico. The kidnappers identified themselves as Grupos Beta agents, a government organization created to help migrants.

The world was shocked and outraged by the August 2010 massacre of seventy-two would-be migrants in San Fernando, Tamaulipas. Photographs of their bodies adorned the front pages of international newspapers, drastically changing the imaginary of Central American migration and the war on drugs in Mexico. Reports by Mexico's Comisión Nacional de los Derechos Humanos (CNDH) estimated that about ten thousand kidnappings occurred during two six-month periods in 2009 and 2010 (Comisión Nacional de los Derechos Humanos 2009, 2011).[4] By Juanito's own estimate, more than seven hundred people were being held on that one ranch at a given time, and more than two hundred people were executed during the five months he spent in captivity. While it is still difficult to know how prevalent kidnappings similar to Juanito's are, the simple facts of his account are cause enough for alarm.

The accused drug cartel, Los Zetas, has diversified their criminal enterprise by extorting businesses, trafficking humans, and of course kidnapping migrants. Deserters from Mexico's U.S.-trained special forces formed this paramilitary enforcement wing for the Gulf Cartel in 1997 (Garzon 2008). Their brutal tactics and training in counterterrorism has changed the face of the drug war in what has been described as the zetafication of Mexico. In 2010 they broke away from the Gulf Cartel (Grillo 2011; Osorno 2012) and began their own organization, which has quickly spread through Mexico and Central America (Osorno 2012).

Deportees have an intimate relationship with the heightened violence of the border, which is at the center of the drug conflict that has cost more than 150,000 lives in Mexico between 2006 and 2016. The nearly four hundred thousand people deported annually (Instituto Nacional de Migracion 2013) are highly visible on the streets. Many wear dark clothing to aid in the crossing or are dressed in prison-issue clothing (blue slip-on shoes, gray sweaters, baggy khaki pants), and they often carry bags reading "Department of Homeland Security." They also face discrimination and abuse because of the racial and ethnic differences between southern and northern Mexico. Moreover, about one in five deportees arrive between 10 p.m. and 5 a.m. (Slack et al. 2013; also see chap. 4 of this volume). This visibility, combined with the knowledge that people engaged in international migration have contacts in the United States who can supply several thousand dollars in ransom quickly, makes them prime targets for kidnapping and extortion. I begin this chapter with a theoretical outline and literature review, giving background and context to scholarly work on kidnapping and drug violence.

FEMINIST GEOPOLITICS AND A TOPOLOGY OF VIOLENCE

In this article I expand on the burgeoning literature exploring how place and space shape and are shaped by violent events (Gregory and Pred 2007; Garmany 2011; Chatterjee 2009). Some have engaged with the politics of fear either through how it shapes people's day-to-day interactions (Pain 2001; Garmany 2011; Green 1999) or their perceptions of the state and their role within it (Garmany 2011; Green 1999; Pain 2001; Oslender 2007; Secor 2007; Wright 2011, 2013), the role of violence in subject formation (Wright 2011), and urban revitalization projects (Wright 2013). However, these scholars have not explored explicitly the notion of topological spaces of violence, which helps us further nuance how specific people live violence based on who they are in relation to where they are. "Topology deals with surfaces and their properties, their boundedness, orientability, decomposition, and connectivity—that is, sets of properties that retain their relationships under processes of transformation" (Blum and Secor 2011, 1034).

Juanito's experience as a deportee marks his relationship to the border, which in turn renders a specific type of vulnerability—namely, that he can be taken, extorted, enslaved, and ultimately disappeared. While in movement through the clandestine spaces of the border, that contested relationship became the defining characteristic he shared with the other victims.

Jorge Bustamante (2002, 2011) has explored the explicit nature of vulnerability and migration, whereupon a person's vulnerability increases by leaving their place of origin. This critique expands on previous assertions that increased enforcement has resulted in an escalation of the cost of crossing the border (Durand and Massey 2004) as well as exacerbating human rights violations (Nevins and Aizeki 2008). Violence and vulnerability are inherent to the clandestine movement of people. The current rash of migrant kidnappings and disappearances can be largely attributed to the higher cost of migration, the militarization of the U.S.-Mexico border (Dunn 1996), increasingly severe penalties for immigration violations (Martínez and Slack 2013; Coleman 2007), and the general turmoil created in areas such as northeastern Mexico.

However, Bustamante's analysis centers on a linear relationship, making distance the most important factor with the added caveat that international and national distance are quite different. Moreover, the framework for analysis falls squarely within the highly normative realm of international human rights (Bustamante 2002). By viewing space as topological, we can take the argument one step further and also interrogate how and why these relationships are created.

A feminist geopolitical framework, however, allows us to study macrolevel geopolitical struggles, in this case the war on drugs and undocumented migration, with an emphasis on embodied practices firmly rooted in place (Hyndman 2007; Williams and Massaro 2013). This approach provides an important counternarrative to mainstream analysis of drug violence, which relies on geopolitical narratives that reduce a complex conflict to the machinations of disembodied nation-states (Shirk 2011), the all-too-frequent discussions of a failed state (Grayson 2010; Morton 2012), or alarmist calls for military action (Longmire 2011).

While critical geopolitics has focused on how power flows through geopolitical struggles and colonial projects (Dalby and Tuathail 2002), feminist geopolitics takes it a step further "by noting the need for a more grounded critique of geopolitics—one that . . . attends to the gendered, racialized, classed, sexualized, and otherwise differentiated everyday spaces previously ignored in geopolitical analysis" (Massaro and Williams 2013, 569–70). I focus on kidnapping because it is the moment of capture whereupon migrants cease to be fully recognizable state subjects and become instead bodies without state attachment. Kidnapping therefore can lead to a whole array of exploitative practices such as human trafficking and organ harvesting.

KIDNAPPING

While there are tomes of first- and secondhand accounts of kidnapping by victims and journalists (Betancourt and Anderson 2010; Scherer Garcia and Editorial 2009; Braun 1994; Planeta Colombiana Editorial 1994; Echeverria Gavilanes 1988; Campos Azuara 2003), there is very little academic work. The few exceptions have analyzed the economic logic of kidnapping insurance (Lobo-Guerrero 2007), the connection of neoliberalism and other social factors to the increase in kidnapping (Campos Azuara 2003), or a broader discussion of why clandestine migration attracts violence (Casillas 2011; Slack and Whiteford 2011; Boehm 2011). Other authors have chronicled their experience as ransom negotiators for insurance companies (Bles and Low 1987; Wright 2009). Despite this quantity of work, authors have not attempted to theorize the existence of kidnapping nor its patterns. It is important to interrogate the utility of taking possession of bodies beyond the simple ransom-profit narrative.

PROJECT OVERVIEW AND METHODS

The quantitative data for this article come from Wave II of the MBCS. While I will use some descriptive and bivariate statistics about these experiences, this paper draws more on my ethnographic field notes and nineteen in-depth interviews I conducted. I decided to make Juanito's in-depth story the central narrative of this article because of the extraordinary detail and length of his captivity. At the time this was written, we were in close contact and had discussed the writing of this article in detail. I conducted two official interview sessions, each more than three hours long, and have had many more follow-up conversations by phone. While his story is not typical of our interviewees, it sheds light on many aspects of kidnapping by organized crime that are only partially explained in our survey.

FINDINGS: KIDNAPPING AND MIGRATION

Eighty-three participants (about 7% of MBCS respondents) reported having been kidnapped or held against their will during a migration experience. Kidnappings are generally considered extremely rare events, usually measured by number per five hundred thousand inhabitants, so to have a measurable percentage of a population reporting a similar event is shocking. Table 9.1 shows some descriptive statistics about deportees' experiences of kidnapping.

Since kidnapping exists in many forms, it is hard to encompass in one discussion. Sometimes people are simply released. Of the eighty-three respondents, thirteen reported simply being let go, usually because they did not have any international contacts or a way to get money. Another ten people were able to

TABLE 9.1 Kidnapping victims

VARIABLE	PERCENT (MEAN)
Male	88 (73)
Female	12 (10)
Age (years)	33
Kidnapped by coyote/guide	51 (42)
Kidnapped by gang/bandits	36 (30)
Time in captivity (days)	6
Number of people held simultaneously	20
Ransom demanded	69 (57)
Ransom demanded (US$)	2,800
Ransom paid (of people asked)	58 (33)
Ransom paid (US$)	2,149
Reported physical abuse	27 (22)
Reported verbal abuse	72 (57)
Threatened with a weapon	55 (44)
Report physical abuse of others	49 (38)

Note: $N = 83$.
Source: Migrant Border Crossing Study, Wave II.

escape. About 29 percent of respondents reported being interrogated, but no one ever demanded ransom on their behalf (N = 24). Kidnapping has also become a form of recruitment. Juanito paid but was not let go, and as he unequivocally stated, people pay and then work until they can no longer do so. "Then what?" I asked. "Well, they kill them."

Gender plays a role in how this happens. Captured men may be asked to kill someone to prove their loyalty to the criminal organization, while women must work as prostitutes or informants in order to gain their freedom. This is not limited to people kidnapped by the Zetas. Both of these forms of "payment" further bind individuals to their captors, allowing them to leave the spaces of captivity but only if they participate in the violence around them. Those who can pay may escape with their scars, while those who choose work tie their fate to the kidnappers. Kidnapping therefore is not purely about using the body to access accumulated capital, as one traditionally conceives of elite kidnapping, but also a way to harness the intrinsic functions of the body such as labor and sex. This breaks the dominant narrative about kidnapping that focuses only on punishment and pays little attention to the underlying causes of kidnapping. Mexico has reacted to kidnapping by increasing prison sentences from twenty to forty years to forty to eighty years for kidnappers (Notimex 2014), which has led some to believe that these penalties are leading to a greater number of captives being killed rather than released. Feminist geopolitics helps to deconstruct the binary of victim and kidnapper and address deeper, structural causes related to class and race. Those doing the kidnapping are often former migrants displaced by lack of work and land, or former victims of kidnapping themselves. To address this problem, one must try to change the structural factors that push people to migrate in the first place.

According to the data, there is no subgroup that seems to be particularly at risk among deportees. They are about the same age as the general population, and the same gender breakdown, and they hail from the same states in Mexico. The important conclusion is that kidnapping occurs simply because one is a migrant: migrant kidnapping is provoked by the shared precariousness of traveling in these clandestine spaces coupled with the fact that their family connections in the United States could quickly come up with a few thousand dollars.

Juanito described the role of deportation in his own kidnapping as well as some eighty others taken simultaneously. He arrived in Coahuila and went home to Chihuahua for a few days, but when his brother sent him the money for a bus ticket to go to work in Tijuana, he headed to the city to get a bus. At the station there were agents claiming to be from Grupos Beta, dressed in their orange uniforms. They were asking whether people had been deported and were offering half-price bus tickets. He told them that he had been deported about a week ago, but they signed him up anyway. "They told us that the bus wasn't leaving for a few hours, so they would take us to dinner first. I don't know why I went with them. I had the money," he said staring off blankly. "They stopped a few minutes after we got in the car and men dressed in black came into the vans. They had machine guns, *cuernos de chivo*, and handed everyone a black hood. We put the hoods on ourselves and then they handcuffed us together. They pulled a drawstring tight around our necks," he stated. A study of Mexico's immigration services found widespread corruption, lack of accountability, and ties to organized crime (Insyde 2013). The very fact that migrant kidnappings, particularly of Central Americans, have occurred in such large numbers and with such broad public knowledge points to a great deal of collusion or at least tacit approval and impunity by state actors.

Not surprisingly, there are significant differences between the experiences of people kidnapped by human smugglers, known as coyotes, and those kidnapped by gangs (see table 9.2). Forty-two people reported being held by coyotes or people acting as a guide, thirty by gangs or cartels, and five people explicitly stated they were kidnapped by members of the Zetas, although we did not ask people to identify specific groups for safety reasons. We noted that there is a

TABLE 9.2 Comparison between people kidnapped by their coyote or guide and those kidnapped by gangs

VARIABLE	KIDNAPPED BY COYOTE (N = 42)	KIDNAPPED BY GANGS (N = 30)	DIFFERENCE
Held in the United States (%)	64	25	39**
Number of people held	17	26	9***
Drugs present at safe house (%)	32	57	25*
Ransom paid (US$)	1,893	2,534	641**
Report physical abuse (%)	17	33	16
Report verbal abuse (%)	59	92	33**
Threatened with weapon (%)	30	87	57***

Note: N = 72 (includes only those who were able to identify their kidnappers).
Source: Migrant Border Crossing Study, Wave II.
$^{*}p < .05$, $^{**}p < .01$, $^{***}p < .001$

significant difference in the nature of the kidnapping when people identified their captors as gangs versus guides. Coyotes sometimes hold people captive to assure payment or extract extra money in addition to the preagreed price for crossing. While these experiences are certainly horrible in their own right, they pale in comparison to the treatment and complexity of gang kidnappings, a fact that dominant security narratives in Mexico have not taken into account when establishing sentences.

Descriptions of torture from our surveys and interviews corroborate Juanito's story. Juanito describes the same board with nails, called the *tablazo*. They used it to hit people on the back, chest and feet. "I stayed alive by being submissive," he explained, trying somehow to rationalize his own survival. "They didn't think I was strong so they didn't care what I did and kept me around. . . . The men that fought back got killed instantly. They dissolved the bodies in a vat in the back of the complex and spread what was left on the fields. It was white like fertilizer."

SEXUALITY, MASCULINITY, AND TORTURE

Highlighting the importance of feminist geopolitics, torture becomes a tool of subjugation constructed to demasculinize. If we view torture as a technology of control, as per Foucault (1977), then the processes of breaking people down by inflicting physical, emotional, and sexual abuse was being used by the Zetas to create its own subjects. There is a large literature on torture; however, a particularly relevant subset examines sexuality, masculinity, and homosexuality in state-sanctioned torture in the Middle East (Puar 2005a, 2005b; Butler 2008). The Zetas originated as U.S.-trained special forces. The tactics of humiliation, homophobic sexualization, and degradation mimic carefully planned practices developed by states. The Zetas and other groups frequently publish videos online of executions that include castration. Juanito explained, "They're recruiting people. After they eliminate weakness in them, they make them strong and give them guns and send them to different parts of the Mexican Republic to try and take territory from other organizations." This process of degradation and subjugation was different for Juanito as a gay man. For his torturers he was always already passive, never a threat.

His identity within that space had a profound impact on how he was treated and how he eventually survived something that few live to talk about. He was raped and beaten like many others, but not pressured to join the Zetas or to execute his fellow captives. His sexuality allowed him to pass unnoticed and escape from that particular topology of violence, leaving behind his captors. Juanito instead worked as slave labor, cloning marijuana, packing it for transport, and even assisting in organ harvesting.

For Juanito, this is his biggest challenge as he attempts to deal with the psychological trauma of his ordeal. At the end of our four-hour interview he said, "I want to be clear about one thing. There were kids there. They were between six and nine years old. They smothered them with plastic bags and immediately cut out their livers, kidneys, and heart. They made me help six times." He explained that they put the organs in coolers with dry ice that were quickly taken away. Juanito began weeping and said, "I wish I hadn't done it. I should have let them kill me. That would have been easier." From 2008 to 2010 there were thirty-six cases of organ trafficking brought to the prosecutor's office resulting in four prosecutions (Vega 2011). Furthermore, arrests in March 2014 found strong evidence of a child kidnapping and organ harvesting ring by the Knights Templar in Michoacán, whose practices mirror the Zetas (Bacchi 2014).

CONCLUSIONS

The National Security Archive uncovered documents from the U.S. embassy in Mexico detailing concerns about the state of affairs in northeastern Mexico, linking state officials to organized crime before the August 2010 massacre (Evans and Franzblau 2013). Cables after the massacre describe the efforts of the government to distance itself from and minimize the size of the tragedy. Despite these assertions, why has the United States continued to escalate the number of people being deported into this region?

Simple things could be done to make people safer. Deportation practices contribute to people's vulnerability. We found that 18 percent of people are deported between the hours of 10 p.m. and 5 a.m. One in four people had their Mexican identification taken and not returned, an essential document for receiving government services and money transfers (Slack et al. 2013, also see chap. 4 of this volume). Moreover, lateral repatriations, known as the Alien Transfer and Exit Program, move people from one area of the border to another (León 2013). Tamaulipas now receives more deportations than any other state in Mexico, about seventy thousand more in 2013 than the number of Mexican nationals apprehended in the area. These facts leave us questioning the role of the U.S. immigration system in promulgating these types of disasters not only indirectly, by creating the highly militarized border and criminalizing the migration experience, but by funneling a never-ending supply of vulnerable people into these geographies of violence. Through a feminist geopolitical lens of immigration enforcement, we clearly see that the result of these policies is not security but rather placing people in situations so horrible that they will not come back, and we can understand how kidnapping fits with this scheme. To return to the agenda set forth by feminist geopolitics, "a focus on human security, rather than national security provides a way to attend to the lived realities of individuals as they are shaped by and influence geopolitical processes" (Massaro and Williams 2013, 507).

Migrants are uniquely situated among the casualties of the war on drugs. They are already dislocated from their families and social networks. Some have access to cash, some do not. Some pass through the border unharmed, others disappear forever. Looking for the disappeared is nearly impossible. It is difficult even in the United States, where scholars and activists have tirelessly documented migrant remains (Martínez et al. 2013). This does not compare with the communal graves and lack of forensic records in Mexico as typified by the botched investigation of the San Fernando massacres (Evans and Franzblau 2013). Impunity and collusion by the state during the drug war has raised alarms but on the whole has not affected the exponential increase in the size and power of the military and police.

At the time of authorship, Juanito had been deported to Mexico and is currently living in his hometown. He was subsequently kidnapped by a different criminal organization and accused of working with the Zetas but let go after one week. He continues to want to tell his story.

NOTES

Originally published as J. Slack, "Captive Bodies: Migrant Kidnapping and Deportation in Mexico," *Area* 48 (3): 271–77. Reprinted by permission.

1.   This article contains graphic firsthand accounts of torture and murder. I tried to be as faithful as possible to the wishes of the individual whose story makes up the central focal point of the story. We worked together closely to decide which details to publish and which to hide. It is therefore designed to be difficult to read and hopefully accurately conveys the realities of a widespread humanitarian disaster.

2.   Juanito is a pseudonym used to protect the identity of the individual who has experienced the events described in this paper.

3. He was not 100 percent sure he was being held in San Fernando. He questioned whether it might have been called San Vicente but was adamant about the fact that it was the same ranch where the August 2010 massacre took place.

4. The reports cite that about 10 percent of the interviews were with Mexicans, but the whole report is still framed in terms of Central Americans. Moreover, there are significant methodological problems with these assertions since this number is derived from victim reports to authorities about the number of people being held simultaneously. This provides the possibility of an overcount in the event of double reporting or an undercount because we know that the vast majority of victims do not report the crimes committed against them, particularly undocumented Central American migrants.

REFERENCES

Bacchi, U. 2014. "Mexico: Knights Templar Drug Cartel Made Recruits Eat Children's Hearts in Initiation Rite." *International Business Times*, March 21.

Betancourt, I., and A. Anderson. 2010. *Even Silence Has an End: My Six Years of Captivity in the Colombian Jungle*. New York: Penguin.

Bles, M., and R. Low. 1987. *The Kidnap Business*. London: Pelham Books.

Blum, V., and A. Secor. 2011. "Psychotopologies: Closing the Circuit Between Psychic and Material Space." *Environment and Planning D: Society and Space* 29: 1030–47.

Boehm, D. A. 2011. "US–Mexico Mixed Migration in an Age of Deportation: An Inquiry into the Transnational Circulation of Violence." *Refugee Survey Quarterly* 30: 1–21.

Braun, H. 1994. *Our Guerrillas, Our Sidewalks: A Journey into the Violence of Colombia*. Boulder: University Press of Colorado.

Bustamante, J. A. 2002. "Immigrants' Vulnerability as Subjects of Human Rights." *International Migration Review* 36: 333–54.

———. 2011. "Extreme Vulnerability of Migrants: The Cases of the United States and Mexico/La vulnerabilidad extrema de los migrantes: Los casos de Estados Unidos y Mexico." *Migraciones Internacionales* 97: 6.

Butler, J. 2008. "Sexual Politics, Torture, and Secular Time." *British Journal of Sociology* 59: 1–23.

Campos Azuara, A. J. 2003. *El secuestro economico: La nueva forma de criminalidad en el Mexico neoliberal: 1980–1999*. Puebla, Mexico: Benemerita Universidad Autonoma de Puebla.

Casillas, R. 2011. "The Dark Side of Globalized Migration: The Rise and Peak of Criminal Networks; The Case of Central Americans in Mexico." *Globalizations* 8: 295–310.

Chatterjee, I. 2009. "Violent Morphologies: Landscape, Border and Scale in Ahmedabad Conflict." *Geoforum* 40: 1003–13.

Coleman, M. 2007. "Immigration Geopolitics Beyond the Mexico-US Border." *Antipode* 39: 54–76.

Comisión Nacional de los Derechos Humanos. 2009. "Todos saben, nadie sabe: Tres anos de muerte de migrantes." Annual Report. Mexico City: Comisión Nacional de los Derechos Humanos.

————. 2011. "Informe especial sobre el secuestro de migrantes en Mexico." Annual Report. Mexico City: Comisión Nacional de los Derechos Humanos.

Dalby, S., and G. O. Tuathail. 2002. *Rethinking Geopolitics.* New York: Routledge.

Dunn, T. J. 1996. *The Militarization of the US-Mexico Border, 1978–1992: Low-Intensity Conflict Doctrine Comes Home.* Austin: CMAS Books, University of Texas at Austin.

Durand, J., and D. S. Massey, eds. 2004. *Crossing the Border: Research from the Mexican Migration Project.* New York: Russell Sage Foundation.

Echeverria Gavilanes, E. 1988. *Secuestro.* Quito: Editorial El Conejo.

Evans, M., and J. Franzblau. 2013. "Mexico's San Fernando Massacres: A Declassified History." *Migration Declassified.* National Security Archive, November 6. http://nsarchive2.gwu.edu/NSAEBB/NSAEBB445/.

Foucault, M. 1977. *Discipline and Punish: The Birth of the Prison.* New York: Pantheon Books.

Garmany, J. 2011. "Drugs, Violence, Fear, and Death: The Necro- and Narco-geographies of Contemporary Urban Space." *Urban Geography* 32: 1148–66.

Garzon, J. C. 2008. *Mafia and Co: The Criminal Networks in Mexico, Brazil, and Colombia.* Washington, D.C.: Woodrow Wilson International Center for Scholars.

Grayson, G. W. 2010. *Mexico: Narco-violence and a Failed State?* New Brunswick, N.J.: Transaction.

Green, L. B. 1999. *Fear as a Way of Life: Mayan Widows in Rural Guatemala.* New York: Columbia University Press.

Gregory, D., and A. Pred, eds. 2007. *Violent Geographies: Fear, Terror, and Political Violence.* London: Routledge.

Grillo, I. 2011. *El Narco: Inside Mexico's Criminal Insurgency* New York: Bloomsbury Press.

Hyndman, J. 2007. "Feminist Geopolitics Revisited: Body Counts in Iraq." *Professional Geographer* 59: 35–46.

Instituto Nacional de Migracion. 2013. *Estadistica migratoria: Sintesis 2012.* Mexico City: Instituto Nacional de Migracion.

Insyde. 2013. *Diagnostico del Instituto Nacional de Migración: Hacia un Sistema de Rendición de Cuentas en Pro de los Derechos de la Personas Migrantes en México.* Mexico City: Instituto para la Seguridad y Democracia. http://insyde.org.mx/wp-content/uploads/2013/09/R_E_Diagn%C3%B3stico_INM_final.pdf.

León, J. 2013. "The Efficacy and Impact of the Alien Transfer Exit Programme: Migrant Perspectives from Nogales, Sonora, Mexico." *IMIG International Migration* 51: 10–23.

Lobo-Guerrero, L. 2007. "Biopolitics of Specialized Risk: An Analysis of Kidnap and Ransom Insurance." *Security Dialogue* 38: 315–34.

Longmire, S. 2011. *Cartel: The Coming Invasion of Mexico's Drug Wars.* New York: Palgrave Macmillan.

Martínez, D., R. Reineke, R. Rubio-Goldsmith, B. Anderson, and G. H. B. Parks. 2013. *A Continued Humanitarian Crisis on the Border: Undocumented Border Crossers Deaths Recorded by the Pima County Office of the Medical Examiner, 1990–2012.* Tucson, Ariz.: Bi-National Migration Institute, University of Arizona.

Martínez, D., and J. Slack. 2013. "What Part of 'Illegal' Don't You Understand? The Social Consequences of Criminalizing Unauthorized Mexican Migrants in the United States." *Social and Legal Studies* 22 (4): 535–51.

Massaro, V. A., and J. Williams. 2013. "Feminist Geopolitics." *Geography Compass* 7: 567–77.

Morton, A. D. 2012. "The War on Drugs in Mexico: A Failed State?" *Third World Quarterly* 33: 1631–45.

Nevins, J., and M. Aizeki. 2008. *Dying to Live: A Story of US Immigration in an Age of Global Apartheid.* San Francisco: City Lights.

Notimex. 2014. "Duplican sentencias para secuestradores en México." *24 Horas*, June 3. http://www.24-horas.mx/duplican-sentencias-para-secuestradores-en-mexico/.

Oslender, U. 2007. "Spaces of Terror and Fear on Colombia's Pacific Coast." In *Violent Geographies: Fear, Terror and Political Violence*, edited by D. Gregory and A. Pred, 111–12. New York: Routledge.

Osorno, D. E. 2012. *La guerra de los Zetas: Viaje por la frontera de la necropolítica.* Mexico City: Grijalbo.

Pain, R. 2001. "Gender, Race, Age and Fear in the City." *Urban Studies* 38: 899–913.

Planeta Colombiana Editorial. 1994. *Rostros del secuestro.* Santa Fe, Bogotá: Planeta Colombiana Editorial.

Puar, J. K. 2005a. "On Torture: Abu Ghraib." *Radical History Review* 93: 13–38.

———. 2005b. "Queer Times, Queer Assemblages." *Social Text* 23: 121–39.

Scherer Garcia, J., and G. Editorial. 2009. *Secuestrados.* Mexico City: Grijalbo.

Secor, A. 2007. "An Unrecognizable Condition Has Arrived." In *Violent Geographies: Fear, Terror and Political Violence,* edited by D. Gregory and A. Pred. New York: Routledge.

Shirk, D. 2011. *The Drug War in Mexico: Confronting a Shared Threat.* New York: Council on Foreign Relations, Center for Preventive Action.

Slack, Jeremy, Daniel Martínez, Scott Whiteford, and Emily Peiffer. 2013. "In the Shadow of the Wall: Family Separation, Immigration Enforcement and Security." Report, Center for Latin American Studies, Tucson: University of Arizona. https://las.arizona.edu/sites/las.arizona.edu/files/UA_Immigration_Report2013web.pdf.

Slack, J., and S. Whiteford. 2011. "Violence and Migration on the Arizona-Sonora Border." *Human Organization* 70: 11–21.

Vega, A. 2011. "Confirma la PGR cuatro casos de tráfico de órganos." *Excelsior*, May 31.

Williams, J., and V. Massaro. 2013. "Feminist Geopolitics: Unpacking (In)security, Animating Social Change." *Geopolitics* 18: 751–58.

Wright, M. W. 2011. "Necropolitics, Narcopolitics, and Femicide: Gendered Violence on the Mexico-US Border." *Signs* 36: 707–31.

———. 2013. "Feminicidio, Narcoviolence, and Gentrification in Ciudad Juarez: The Feminist Fight." *Environment and Planning D: Society and Space* 31: 830–45.

Wright, R. P. 2009. *Kidnap for Ransom: Resolving the Unthinkable.* Boca Raton, Fla.: CRC Press.

10

KNOW YOUR ENEMY

How Repatriated Unauthorized Migrants Learn
About and Perceive Anti-Immigrant Mobilization
in the United States

MATTHEW WARD AND DANIEL E. MARTÍNEZ

INTRODUCTION

GRASSROOTS MOBILIZATION IN opposition to unauthorized immigration into the United States has been on the rise recently (Chavez 2008; Doty 2009; Navarro 2009; Ward 2014). Of particular note are minutemen organizations, which are not only fervently anti-immigrant but also observe and patrol the U.S.-Mexico border (and interior regions) to report unauthorized migrants to the authorities. In some cases, minutemen have attempted apprehension and detainment of migrants.

Media outlets and scholars have dissected the minutemen's motives, ideology, and goals (for review of these, see Cabrera and Glavac 2010; Doty 2009; Dove 2010; Shapira 2013). However, the absence of rigorously collected data on unauthorized migrants' perspectives leaves a void in this discussion. To fill this gap, we address three unanswered questions: Among repatriated unauthorized migrants who have heard of minutemen, from where do they get their information? What qualities or characteristics do repatriated unauthorized migrants ascribe to minutemen? And how closely do these perceptions align with common tropes about minutemen? In what follows, we draw on original data from Wave I of the Migrant Border Crossing Study (MBCS) to answer these questions.

Repatriated migrants relied heavily on media outlets in the United States and Mexico and—to a lesser extent—family members and friends in Mexico and the United States as well as the migration process itself to obtain information about nativist mobilization or social movement activity supposedly geared toward preserving and protecting the interests of nonimmigrant Americans. Interestingly, repatriated unauthorized migrants were also mixed in their perceptions of exactly who minutemen were, and migrants varied greatly in their use of dominant tropes to identify minutemen. These findings reveal the composition of repatriated unauthorized migrants' knowledge networks and the role these played in diffusing knowledge about minutemen as well as give voice to the important, yet largely silenced, population that U.S. nativists target. The findings also illuminate differences in the qualitative content of the minuteman-related information repatriated unauthorized migrants received. We conclude with implications and directions for future research.

ANTI-IMMIGRANT VIGILANTISM

Despite increased border enforcement from the 1990s onward, the growth of the unauthorized population generated the perception of a poorly secured border among a portion of the general U.S. public, thereby facilitating—along with other factors—anti-immigrant vigilantism during the mid- to late 2000s, especially in southern Arizona. Nevertheless, earlier studies suggest that anti-immigrant vigilante efforts actually precede the growth of the unauthorized population and date to just after the implementation of the Immigration Reform and Control Act (IRCA) in 1986 (Doty 2009). IRCA ultimately allowed millions of racialized immigrants to step out of the shadows and into public life, which largely led to the misconception that the United States was being overrun by unauthorized immigrants, further contributing to anti-immigrant fervor and discourse (Chavez 2008).

Anti-immigrant vigilantism along the U.S.-Mexico border has a long history. Here we briefly describe the emergence and evolution of contemporary minuteman organizations (for a more extensive discussion, see Doty 2009). Beginning with the U.S. government's "prevention through deterrence" strategy and the Operation Gatekeeper complex in the late 1980s and early 1990s (Vina, Nynez-Neto, and Weir 2006), U.S. residents began embracing vigilante border patrol as a viable tactic (Doty 2009). An early instantiation took place in 1989 in San Diego. Dubbed the "Light Up the Border" campaign, residents drove to the San Diego–Tijuana border to patrol and petition for effective barriers.

Groups like Border Solution Task Force, U.S. Citizen Patrol, Voices of Citizens Together, American Border Patrol, Ranch Rescue, and Civil Homeland Defense cropped up over the following two decades.

Contemporary manifestations, notably the Minuteman Project (MMP) and the Minuteman Civil Defense Corps (MCDC), brought with them the same anti-immigrant concerns but succeeded where their predecessors had failed—not in stopping unauthorized immigration but in generating substantial national attention for their anti-immigrant cause. After their inaugural border muster in Arizona in 2005, minutemen were a topic of national conversation (Chavez 2008). Subsequent years saw these organizations expand into nearly every state by 2010, totaling upward of three hundred chapters during the time in which data from the first wave of the MBCS (2007–2009) were collected (Beirich 2011).

During this time, minutemen also targeted employers and migrants in the workplace and increased their efforts to reform local and state policies. By the mid-2000s the anti-immigrant agenda had been largely normalized, as numerous locales considered or passed restrictive housing ordinances and legislation foreshadowing Arizona's SB 1070 and Alabama's HB 56. However, increased interior enforcement and greater attention to legislative reform did not translate into a complete absence of civilian border patrols (diminishing it only relative to earlier levels). Patrols in Arizona, for instance, continued well into 2009 and even 2010 (Shapira 2013; Neiwert 2013). Yet by 2011—well after Wave I data were collected (2007–2009)—minuteman mobilization had waned in part because the nativist agenda had been transformed from fringe to mainstream. The emergence of the Tea Party accelerated this decline by offering a more legitimate, institutionalized space in which residents could harbor anti-immigrant sentiments behind the veneer of traditional conservative ideals (Skocpol and Williamson 2013). By 2013 the kind of anti-immigrant border vigilantism of the early to mid-2000s was being replaced by smaller, radical splinter cell organizations (Neiwert 2013).

DATA, SAMPLING, AND SURVEY MODULES

We use data from the first wave of the MBCS (N = 415) to answer the following questions: Among repatriated unauthorized migrants who have heard of minutemen, from where do they get their information? What qualities or characteristics do they ascribe to minutemen? And, finally, how closely do these descriptions align with dominant tropes about minutemen? Doing so provides insight into repatriated unauthorized migrants' networks and the information they diffuse as well as reveals differences in the qualitative content of the information that gets diffused. To our knowledge, no researchers have studied these issues with the same rigor the MBCS affords us. Moreover, because these data were collected at the height of nativist mobilization in the United States (Beirich 2012)—in what at the time was the single most traversed crossing corridor along the U.S.-Mexico border and the epicenter for anti-immigrant vigilantism—the data are uniquely suited to address our questions. The MBCS Wave I included a module on repatriated migrants' perceptions toward anti-immigrant activism, something that was not addressed in the second wave of the study. This makes the first wave the ideal (and only) data set available to shed light on our questions.

ANALYSIS

WHERE DO REPATRIATED UNAUTHORIZED MIGRANTS GET THEIR KNOWLEDGE ABOUT MINUTEMEN?

Approximately 43 percent of Wave I respondents indicated they had previously heard of minutemen. In light of all the hurdles migrants must account for during the unauthorized crossing experience, it is interesting to note that, nonetheless, a substantial proportion of respondents were aware of nativist mobilization at the border. That nearly half of our respondents were aware of minuteman organizations suggests that nativist mobilization was garnering the attention of not only the media and politicians but also the very population minutemen sought to deter.

After asking repatriated unauthorized migrants if they had ever heard of minutemen, we followed up by asking (among those who said they had heard of them) *from where* they had received their information. Table 10.1 provides descriptive statistics for the different sources of this information. Because the data provided in the table were compiled using open-ended responses from our respondents, we must note that multiple mentions were accepted, and the categories are not mutually exclusive. Therefore the reported means sum to over 100%.

Generally speaking, respondents report three primary ways in which they gained their information about the minutemen: from "media outlets," "during

TABLE 10.1 Descriptive statistics of repatriated migrant characteristics, MBCS I

CHARACTERISTICS	SURVEY QUESTION	MEAN/PERCENT	N
Male	Is the respondent male	86.4%	415
Age	How old are you	32.1 years	415
Household income (in log dollars)	What was your monthly household income before your last crossing attempt	$6.1	361
Education	How many years of formal education have you completed	7.1 years	406
Indigenous-language speaker	Do you speak an indigenous language	19.6%	413
Employed (in United States or Mexico)	Were you employed before your most recent crossing	68.8%	408
North	Is the respondent from the "north" region of Mexico	15.2%	411
West-central ("traditional")	Is the respondent from the "west-central" region of Mexico	23.5%	411
Central	Is the respondent from the "central" region of Mexico	30.7%	411
South	Is the respondent from the "south" region of Mexico	30.5%	411
Family in U.S. destination	Do you have family members currently living your desired destination in the United States	57.2%	415
Friends in U.S. destination	Do you have friends currently living your desired destination in the United States	56.7%	415

First crossing	Was your last crossing attempt your first	18.1%	415
Number of lifetime crossings	How many times have you attempted to cross the border, including your most recent crossing	4.7 times	415
Number of lifetime apprehensions	How many times have you been apprehended by any U.S. authority, including your most recent apprehension	4.3 times	415
Current home in United States	Is your current home located in the United States	16.4%	343
Used a coyote or guide	Did you use a *coyote* or guide during your last crossing attempt	71.4%	411
Group size	How many people were you traveling with when you first crossed the border	11.9 people	404
Days traveled	How many days did you spend traveling in the desert before being apprehended or picked up to proceed to the next leg of the journey	2.4 days	413
Plan to cross again	Do you plan on crossing the border again without papers		415
Yes		41.3%	
No		48.9%	
Don't know		9.8%	

Source: Migrant Border Crossing Study I, weighted data.

the migration process," or "family members, friends, or acquaintances." We also provide subcategories in table 10.2 for each of these mention types to differentiate where exactly respondents received their information. Further, we provide a net macrogrouping for each category as to not double count multiple mentions within the same category. For instance, a respondent may have indicated that he or she heard about minutemen from "family members in Mexico" as well as "friends in the United States." In these cases, each individual response was recorded within the "family, friends, or acquaintances" subcategories but was counted only once in the "net family, friends, or acquaintances" macrogrouping.

As noted in table 10.2, the majority (63%) of respondents who had previously heard of minutemen indicated they had done so through media outlets, with nearly 30 percent noting that they heard about the group through U.S. media sources (e.g., "I was in Houston and saw them on the news") and 10 percent mentioning media in Mexico as the source of the information (e.g., "I heard about them through news in Agua Prieta"). Twenty-five percent of respondents noted a media outlet without mentioning the specific country (e.g., "I heard

TABLE 10.2 Where did you hear about the minutemen?

	MEAN	SE
Net media	.63	.055
Media in the United States	.29	.056
Media, unspecified	.25	.051
Media in Mexico	.09	.026
Net during the migration process	.21	.048
From other migrants while crossing	.10	.033
In Mexico, unspecified	.10	.040
While in immigration detention in United States	.01	.006
Saw minutemen while crossing	.01	.006
Net family, friends, or acquaintances	.15	.033
Family, friends, or acquaintances in the United States	.07	.019
Family, friends, or acquaintances, unspecified	.05	.017
Family, friends, or acquaintances in Mexico	.04	.016
In the United States, unspecified	.07	.027
In Mexico, unspecified	.02	.009
Other	.02	.008

Note: N = 154. SE = standard error. Among people who have heard of the minutemen, includes multiple mentions.
Source: Migrant Border Crossing Study I, weighted data.

about them on television"). One in five respondents who had previously heard of the minutemen said they became aware of them during the migration process, including during the actual crossing attempt (10%) and/or while migrating but still in Mexico (10%). One respondent indicated that he heard of the minutemen while in an immigration detention facility in the United States, and one other person indicated that he actually encountered minutemen while crossing the U.S.-Mexico border. This respondent informed us that he was stopped and was held against his will, having his wrists placed in plastic ties behind his back and held in a van until border patrol agents arrived. Previous research has found that networks of families and friends play a key role in transmitting information about unauthorized crossing and even employment opportunities (Singer and Massey 1998; Massey and Espinoza 1997). While our findings do not undermine such conclusions, they do suggest that when it came to the transmission of information about anti-immigrant activism to repatriated migrants, the media (especially U.S. media) played a critical role.

HOW DO REPATRIATED UNAUTHORIZED MIGRANTS DESCRIBE MINUTEMEN?

We followed up with respondents (again, who had previously heard of minutemen) by asking them to describe in detail who or what they believed the minutemen to be. A range of responses was collected. Table 10.3 provides the dominant tropes respondents used to describe minutemen. Similar to the information provided in table 10.2, responses in table 10.3 came from open-ended responses and included multiple mentions as well as net macrogroupings associated with each script.

Overall, we identified three broad labeling strategies mentioned by our respondents. Approximately 48 percent of respondents described minutemen as individuals that hold "anti-immigrant or anti-Mexican beliefs." For example, some respondents suggested minutemen were "all racist people who don't like Mexicans," were "racist people that don't want people to enter their country," or were "the ones that don't like immigrants. They are racists, and sometimes they kill immigrants." Next, roughly 41 percent cited a "specific role or duty" when discussing who minutemen were. Such answers described minutemen as, for example, "officials," "part of the border patrol," "a group of ranchers," "ranchers that shoot people," or "militia helping out the Border Patrol . . . catching and turning in migrants." Finally, 19 percent of migrants mentioned nationality or ethnicity while describing minutemen. In these instances, minutemen were

TABLE 10.3 In your opinion, who are the minutemen?

	MEAN	SE
Net anti-immigrant	.48	.057
Racists, don't understand Mexicans or Mexican culture	.35	.052
Against migrants crossing the border	.15	.043
Bad, cruel people	.02	.011
Net mention of a specific role or duty	.41	.058
Keep migrants from crossing, catch migrants, guard border	.14	.040
Try to attack, harm, hurt, kill, or hunt migrants	.10	.040
Ranchers	.06	.024
Doing a job that is not theirs, no right to do what they do	.04	.038
To help migrants	.04	.024
Volunteers, group, organization	.04	.016
To help U.S. Border Patrol	.03	.014
Retired, old people	.02	.013
Net nationality / ethnic group	.19	.047
Non-Hispanic white Americans	.08	.031
Latinos / Mexican Americans / Chicanos	.07	.038
U.S. citizens, unspecified	.05	.016
Don't know	.15	.035
Other	.06	.019

Note: N = 152. SE = standard error. Among people who have heard of the minutemen, includes multiple mentions.
Source: Migrant Border Crossing Study I, weighted data.

understood not as racists or individuals carrying out specific duties or occupying particular roles but rather, first and foremost, as "*gringos*" and "Americans," or surprisingly even as "Chicanos" and "Mexicans." Interestingly, the frequencies in each of these nationality/ethnicity categories are virtually the same. An additional 15 percent of respondents who had previously heard of minutemen reported having no real idea who the minutemen were or what they did.

HOW CLOSELY DO REPATRIATED UNAUTHORIZED MIGRANTS' DESCRIPTIONS ALIGN WITH COMMON TROPES ABOUT MINUTEMEN?

After assessing each open-ended response describing respondents' perceptions of minutemen, we determined whether or not these migrants' descriptions of minutemen closely aligned with dominant tropes about the nativist group.

Doing so provided an opportunity to assess differences in the qualitative content of the information available to repatriated unauthorized migrants. Some descriptions closely aligned with dominant tropes about minutemen. Others did not. As noted in table 10.4, 26 percent of all responses aligned closely with dominant tropes about minutemen. Seventeen percent had heard of the group but failed to describe minutemen by drawing on dominant tropes. An additional 57 percent had never heard of the group. However, if we limit the sample to those migrants who had previously heard of the minutemen, 61 percent described minutemen by drawing on dominant tropes.

To demonstrate that the qualitative content of migrants' descriptions about minutemen varied significantly, we assessed how closely migrants' descriptions of minutemen aligned with two tropes that were commonly found in both scholarly and media accounts of minutemen. Because the overwhelming majority of migrants received their information through media outlets, it is appropriate to use the dominant tropes migrants would have been most likely to encounter from these sources as a means of differentiating among and cataloging migrants' multiple subjectively positioned views about the minutemen. First, minutemen are routinely identified by reference to their unique and controversial *actions*. For instance, minutemen are typically described as individuals that engage in border patrol, catch migrants, keep migrants from crossing, and help border patrol (e.g., Cabrera and Glavac 2010; Doty 2009; Dove 2010; Shapira 2013; Ward 2014). Second, minutemen are also frequently portrayed as individuals harboring nativist, anti-Mexican and/or racist attitudes (e.g., Beirich 2011; Chavez 2008; Doty 2009; Ward 2014).

TABLE 10.4 Did the respondent describe the minutemen using dominant tropes?

	MEAN	SE
Among all respondents[a]		
Yes	.26	.032
No	.17	.030
Had not previously heard of the minutemen	.57	.036
Among those who had heard of the minutemen[b]		
Yes	.61	.057
No	.39	.057

Source: Migrant Border Crossing Study I, weighted data.
[a]$N = 410$.
[b]$N = 157$.

In our survey, responses closely aligned with either of these two dominant narratives were distinguished from responses vaguely suggesting minutemen were "citizens" or "volunteers" or even "bad or cruel people," as the latter did not closely conform to the aforementioned dominant tropes. This is not to suggest that these migrants' perceptions are wrong. Yet it became clear from our analyses that sharp disparities existed both in the amount of information some migrants had relative to others as well as in the qualitative content of that information and how well it aligned with dominant tropes about minutemen.[1]

As noted above, minutemen are typically identified by reference to either their unique actions or their fervently anti-immigrant attitudes. Given the different possibilities as to *how* repatriated unauthorized migrants might identify minutemen, we believed it would be interesting to further partition the responses and ask what attributes (either attitudes or actions) are such migrants most often relying on to identify minutemen when they do, in fact, utilize the aforementioned dominant tropes. Among the respondents who employed a dominant trope to identify minutemen, 65 percent did so by referencing only negative beliefs about immigrants or Mexicans. On the other hand, roughly 35 percent referenced a specific role or activity aimed at preventing migrants from crossing the border. It thus appears that minutemen are, relatively speaking, more well known—among repatriated migrants—for their anti-immigrant attitudes than for their activities.[2]

CONCLUSION

Budding scholarship on contemporary nativist mobilization in the United States provides insight into factors fueling anti-immigrant activism as well as how politicians and the broader public view nativists' efforts. Yet no systematic approach has been taken to study the perceptions of the unauthorized migrants that nativists are organizing against. Orienting the analysis toward repatriated unauthorized migrants' perspectives allows us to address a number of as yet unanswered questions: From where are repatriated unauthorized migrants getting their information? How do such migrants perceive minutemen? And how closely do these perceptions align with dominant tropes about minutemen? Results suggest migrants attempting a clandestine crossing (and that are ultimately repatriated) will not have equal access to information about minutemen, nor will they have access to the same kind of information.

The data presented here provide insight into the specific sources from which many repatriated unauthorized migrants obtain their information about emerging threats embodied in U.S. resident–led, anti-immigrant mobilization. While it may be the case, as previous studies have found, that networks of families and friends are critical in transmitting information about modes of unauthorized crossing as well as for securing employment and higher wages in receiving communities (Singer and Massey 1998; Massey and Espinoza 1997), we find that media outlets—specifically, those in the United States—most often supplied information about nativist mobilization to repatriated unauthorized migrants. Information from the migration process itself or from friends and family served as less used, yet still important, alternative streams of information. The centrality of media—rather than established social networks—in transmitting crucial information about nativist mobilization may reflect the relative newness of minuteman organizations, which did not come to prominence until 2005. Future research will need to examine the generalizability of this finding by exploring the intersection between organizational age and the particular mode through which information is disseminated. The marginal importance of the migration process in transmitting information about minutemen may also reflect minutemen's relatively small numbers (compared to U.S. authorities, such as border patrol) and the lower relative likelihood that migrants will come into contact with them or need to alter travel plans to move around them.

Patterns in our data support these inferences and also suggest another important issue for future consideration. For certain kinds of information— namely, information about potential nonenvironmental, nongovernmental security and infrastructure obstacles to clandestine migration—we found that particular modes of transmission came into play more frequently than others. As such, it may not be enough for scholars to simply acknowledge that social ties or media "matter" for the transmission of information about the clandestine migration process. Rather, we should also consider how the specific information being transmitted (i.e., information about vigilantes, coyotes, how to dress, what supplies to bring, etc.) and the mode of transmission (i.e., networks of close friends or family, media, acquaintances, guides, etc.) interact in complex ways. This raises a new line of inquiry: Are particular modes of transmission (commonly used in the clandestine migration process) better equipped (or more likely) to diffuse certain kinds of information about that process?

Furthermore, our data reveal how these sources of information can, collectively, shape repatriated unauthorized migrants' perceptions of anti-immigrant

activists in the United States. Such repatriated migrants largely describe minutemen either by reference to racial/ethnic or nationality categories (and, surprisingly, frequencies are rather evenly distributed among categories of "Non-
Hispanic, White Americans," "Latino/Mexican/Chicano," and "U.S. Citizen"),
by reference to specific roles or duties (notably, "keeping migrants from crossing
the border"), or by reference to a constellation of negative attitudes toward
migrants and Mexicans (notably, constructing minutemen as "racists").

Yet simply because repatriated unauthorized migrants are aware that minutemen exist does not guarantee they all think and feel similarly about minutemen. In fact, our data suggest that significant differences exist in the qualitative
character of the information to which repatriated migrants have access. This
finding opens up additional lines of inquiry for future research, as scholars
will need to examine why these differences exist, how they are produced, and
any effects they may yield with respect to repatriated migrants' likelihood of
attempting future clandestine border crossings. It may be the case that access
to information makes some migrants more or less susceptible to a variety of
border-crossing deterrents. This is because more or less access to information
may alter the perceived risks and costs migrants associate with each deterrent.
This may be especially true when the deterrent is relatively new—as is the case
with nativist mobilization at the U.S.-Mexico border (Doty 2009)—because
newness is likely to generate uncertainty.

NOTES

Originally published as M. Ward and D. E. Martínez, "Know Your Enemy: How
Repatriated Unauthorized Migrants Learn About and Perceive Anti-immigrant
Mobilization in the United States," *Migration Letters* 12 (2): 137 (http://www.tp
london.com/journal/index.php/ml/article/view/398).

1.   We readily acknowledge that minutemen are more complex than these two dom-
     inant narratives indicate. While minutemen may also be strongly motivated by
     a desire for camaraderie, a need to find meaning, and a longing for an idealized
     way of life that is quickly falling by the wayside (Shapira 2013), such dominant
     narratives are not readily available to the overwhelming majority of migrants.
     Indeed, none of our 415 respondents described minutemen in these terms, which
     is not surprising given that the overwhelming majority of our respondents received
     their information about minutemen from either the media or during the crossing
     experience itself. Therefore, given the one-sided media portrayal of minutemen as
     well as their own efforts at image crafting (see, e.g., Gilchrist and Corsi 2006), we
     would not expect migrants to describe them in ways that stray significantly from
     the two aforementioned tropes. Moreover, while it is not incorrect to state that

minutemen are volunteers or citizens, such descriptions—again—do not conform to dominant, readily available tropes associated with minutemen.

2.   Responses that cited a "specific action" in addition to a "belief" were coded as a "specific action" only. We recoded these responses in this manner because a specific "action" taken to prevent migrants from crossing the border arguably constitutes a higher-order subset of a "belief system." In other words, people who actively patrol the border searching for unauthorized migrants probably hold anti–unauthorized immigrant or anti-Mexican beliefs, but what separates them from others who harbor negative feelings about unauthorized migrants is that they have become mobilized.

REFERENCES

Beirich, H. 2011. "The Year in Nativism." *Intelligence Report of the Southern Poverty Law Center* (Spring): 137.

———. 2012. "Nativist Movement Collapses amid Infighting." *Intelligence Report of the Southern Poverty Law Center* (Spring): 145.

Cabrera, L., and S. Glavac. 2010. "Minutemen and Desert Samaritans: Mapping the Attitudes of Activists on the United States' Immigration Front Lines." *Journal of Ethnic and Migration Studies* 36 (4): 673–95.

Chavez, L. R. 2008. *The Latino Threat: Constructing Immigrants, Citizens, and the Nation.* Stanford, Calif.: Stanford University Press.

Cornelius, W. A. 2001. "Deaths at the Border: Efficacy and Unintended Consequences of US Immigration Control Policy." *Population and Development Review* 27 (4): 661–85.

Doty, R. L. 2009. *The Law into Their Own Hands: Immigration and the Politics of Exceptionalism.* Tucson: University of Arizona Press.

Dove, A. L. 2010. "Framing Illegal Immigration at the U.S.-Mexican Border: Anti-illegal Immigration Groups and the Importance of Place in Framing." In *Research in Social Movements, Conflicts and Change*, vol. 30, edited by Patrick C. Coy, 199–237. Bingley: Emerald.

Eschbach, K., J. Hagan, and N. Rodriguez. 2003. "Deaths During Unauthorized Migration: Trends and Policy Implications in the Era of Homeland Security." *In Defense of the Alien* 26: 37–52.

Fuentes, J., H. L'Esperance, R. Perez, and C. White 2007. "Impacts of U.S. Immigration Policies on Migration Behavior." In *Impact of Border Enforcement on Mexican Migration*, edited by W. A. Cornelius and J. M. Lewis, 53–73. San Diego, Calif.: Center for Comparative Immigration Studies.

Gathmann, C. 2008. "Effects of Enforcement on Illegal Markets: Evidence from Migrant Smuggling Along the Southwestern Border." *Journal of Public Economics* 92 (10/11): 1926–41.

Gilchrist, J., and J. Corsi. 2006. *Minutemen: The Battle to Secure America's Borders.* Los Angeles, Calif.: World Ahead.

Martínez, D. E., Reineke, R. C., and R. Rubio-Goldsmith. 2014. "Structural Violence and Migrant Deaths in Southern Arizona: Data from the Pima County Office of the Medical Examiner, 1990–2013." *Journal on Migration and Human Security* 2 (4): 257–86.

Martínez, D. E., et al. 2015. "The Migrant Border Crossing Study: A Methodological Overview and Theoretical Contributions." Unpublished working paper.

Massey, D. S., J. Durand, and N. Malone. 2003. *Beyond Smoke and Mirrors: Mexican Migration in an Era of Economic Integration.* New York: Russell Sage Foundation.

Massey, D. S., and K. E. Espinoza. 1997. "What's Driving Mexico-U.S. Migration? A Theoretical, Empirical, and Policy Analysis." *American Journal of Sociology* 102 (4): 939–99.

Navarro, Armando. 2009. *The Immigration Crisis: Nativism, Armed Vigilantism, and the Rise of a Countervailing Movement.* Lanham, Md.: AltaMira.

Neiwert, D. 2013. "Smaller, More Radical Border Militias Patrolling Arizona Desert." Southern Poverty Law Center, September 30. http://www.splcenter.org/blog/2013/09/30/smaller-more-radical-border-militias-patrolling-arizona-desert/.

Parks, K., G. Lozada, M. Mendoza, and L. G. Santos. 2009. "Strategies for Success: Border Crossing in an Era of Heightened Security." In *Migration from the Mexican Mixteca: A Transnational Community in Oaxaca and California,* edited by W. A. Cornelius, D. Fitzgerald, J. Hernandez-Dias, and S. Borger. San Diego, Calif.: Center for Comparative Immigration Studies.

Passel, J. S., D. Cohn, and A. Gonzalez-Barrera. 2013. "Population Decline of Unauthorized Immigrants Stalls, May Have Reversed." Pew Research Hispanic Trends Project, September 23. http://www.pewhispanic.org/2013/09/23/population-decline-of-unauthorized-immigrants-stalls-may-have-reversed/.

Rubio-Goldsmith, R., M. M. McCormick, D. Martínez, and I. M. Duarte. 2006. "The 'Funnel Effect' and Recovered Bodies of Unauthorized Migrants Processed by the Pima County Office of the Medical Examiner, 1990–2005." Binational Migration Institute, Report, October. Tucson: Binational Migration Institute, Mexican American Studies and Research Center, University of Arizona. http://www.derechoshumanosaz.net/images/pdfs/bmi%20report.pdf.

Shapira, H. 2013. *Waiting for José.* Princeton, N.J.: Princeton University Press.

Singer, A., and D. S. Massey. 1998. "The Social Process of Undocumented Border Crossing Among Mexican Migrants." *International Migration Review* 32 (3): 561–92.

Skocpol, T., and V. Williamson. 2013. *The Tea Party and the Remaking of Republican Conservatism.* Oxford: Oxford University Press.

Slack, Jeremy, Daniel Martínez, Scott Whiteford, and Emily Peiffer. 2013. "In the Shadow of the Wall: Family Separation, Immigration Enforcement and Security." Report, Center for Latin American Studies, Tucson: University of Arizona. https://las.arizona.edu/sites/las.arizona.edu/files/UA_Immigration_Report2013web.pdf.

Vina, S. R., B. Nunez-Neto, and A. B. Weir. 2006. *Civilian Patrols Along the Border: Legal and Policy Issues.* Congressional Research Service Report for Congress, RL33353. Washington, D.C.: Congressional Research Service, Library of Congress.

U.S. Customs and Border Protection. 2014a. "U.S. Border Patrol Fiscal Year Apprehension Statistics." https://www.cbp.gov/sites/default/files/assets/documents/2016-Oct/BP%20Southwest%20Border%20Sector%20Apps%20FY1960%20-%20FY2016.pdf.

U.S. Customs and Border Protection. 2014b. "U.S. Border Patrol Fiscal Year Budget Statistics." https://www.cbp.gov/sites/default/files/assets/documents/2016-Oct/BP%20Budget%20History%201990-2016.pdf.

Ward, M. 2014. "They Say Bad Things Come in Threes: How Economic, Political and Cultural Shifts Facilitated Contemporary Anti-immigration Activism in the United States." *Journal of Historical Sociology* 27 (2): 263–92.

CONCLUSION

Where Do We Go from Here?

SCOTT WHITEFORD, JEREMY SLACK,
AND DANIEL E. MARTÍNEZ

THE RESEARCH FOR THIS book stems from a deep concern with the human tragedy of various forms of violence—including death—experienced by vulnerable people. Moreover, the disturbing lack of data and understanding of the challenges related to immigration reform have allowed a misportrayal by the national media and woefully uniformed and dangerous policy decisions by lawmakers. We grappled with whether carefully designed and implemented research could document the structures and processes transforming people's lives crossing the borderlands. We asked if this, in turn, could lead to greater public awareness and support for a more comprehensive and humanitarian immigration policy. The original question still looms large: Does empirical research even matter in the quest to change the state's approach to immigration? This question has become even more relevant recently as "alternative facts" and "posttruth" understandings of society have gained traction with those on the political right. As scholars, we must question the primal hatred or fear of people from "somewhere else" and yet continue to push forward despite the primacy of the xenophobic agenda that currently grips American politics. We contend that social scientists can affect the public understanding of immigration by generating data helpful to lawyers, policy makers, and NGOs working for social change. While there have been seminal cases in which academic research has contributed to policy change, such cases are not the norm. All too often, academic research is lost on library shelves or in the remote corners of the Internet.

We must try to do better as a field and push into the murky waters of public policy, media messaging, and advocacy based on our findings.

We decided on a research strategy—described in the methods chapter—that included a binational interdisciplinary research team that carried out quantitative and qualitative research in multiple locations across the U.S.-Mexico border. The binational nature of the research was important for us because of the diverse perspectives generated by the team and the importance of publishing in Spanish as well as English. Carrying out research at diverse locations on the border was important, as each region of the border is significantly different from other regions. Once the data were gathered and analyzed, we faced the challenge of how and when to have the findings reviewed by experts in the field as well as how to get the information out to the public and policy makers in a timely manner. Would publication of the research findings in peer-reviewed journals provide validation of the findings, and was critical review necessary before sharing the research with the public? Even more perplexing for us was how to share the research findings in a meaningful way that would reach a broad public. We were fortunate to reach both a large print and television audience, but sharing finds with the public continues to be an ongoing challenge for our research team as well as for other scholars. We have worked hard to communicate our major finding: "Mexican deportees have strong social connections to the United States, and despite increasingly harsh penalties for migration, many intend to return."

Our findings illustrate the punitive basis of the current enforcement strategy, one that is directed against repeat border crossers, utilizing the full force of the carceral state. We have shown how violence, originating both in the state apparatus and from criminal organizations, has become an integral part of the migratory experience. However, there is unevenness as the actions, even of federal law enforcement officers, appear to vary greatly across space. Migrant Border Crossing Study data have provided a unique perspective by which to understand contemporary migratory experiences and violence along the U.S.-Mexico border. We hope that more scholars embrace a postdeportation methodology in order to more fully understand the devastating consequences of mass removal.

The chapters in this volume specifically and the Migrant Border Crossing Study more broadly must be placed in a broader context of increasing interconnectedness of societies across the world. While the work in this volume is focused directly on the U.S.-Mexico context, the approach we outline methodologically and theoretically is relevant worldwide. Globalization has simultaneously enhanced human mobility for some while restricting the mobility of others. Increased human mobility, facilitated by "time-space compression," has been liberating for some while also casting shadows of suspicion on others. Globalization has also led to great economic prosperity and human development for countless but has also resulted in tragedy and violence for others. As this book goes to press, war and terror have spawned a humanitarian crisis across broad swaths of the Middle East, Europe, Asia, Africa, and Latin America, threatening to transform nation-states and undermine political order. In countries receiving migrants, the currents of change are creating divisive political debates and anti-immigrant movements. At the same time, international and domestic organizations have responded with medical support, food, and shelter, but sadly not enough to ameliorate human suffering. Because of the unprecedented scale of suffering, aid organizations are unable to keep up with the challenge.

In the Americas, violence and poverty are pushing people across national borders into neighboring countries and beyond. Central Americans fleeing a history of authoritarian, racist, and repressive government regimes as well as gang violence have moved north. Colombians have been displaced internally or have fled to Ecuador in search of peaceful lives, and Ecuadorians have moved to Spain looking for work. Bolivian migration has transformed northern Argentina, while Brazil continues to receive Latin American migrants in large numbers. The U.S.-Mexico border is one of the most volatile and most militarized in the continent. The U.S. government's response to migrants crossing the border, including unaccompanied children from Central America and Mexican families separated by the border and through mass deportation, as documented in our study, has spawned an increasingly hostile public reaction and a massive state security apparatus philosophically guided by the Consequence Delivery System. Equally important, NGOs and other citizen organizations have mobilized to help desperate undocumented families and children. Opposition to massive detention and deportation has become a social movement for social justice and human rights.

President Obama, whose administration deported more people than any other administration, earning him the title of "Deporter in Chief," attempted through executive authority to lessen the threat of deportation through Deferred Action for Parents of Americans (DAPA) for the millions of immigrants with U.S.-citizen children. In June of 2016, a four to four split in the Supreme Court stalled his effort to provide relief for an estimated five million parents of U.S. citizens and legal permanent residents. As a result, after eight years of Obama in office, there has been almost no progress on badly needed immigration reform. Congress played a major role in blocking reform efforts. Despite the Obama administration's generally harsh treatment of migrants and asylum seekers, President Donald Trump has managed to stir the pot of xenophobia to new heights. In an era of historically low migration, his promises of a border wall as well as other draconian anti-immigrant measures swept him into the White House. Despite losing the popular vote by a wide margin, Trump still garnered wide-reaching support and nearly sixty-three million votes with anti-immigration measures as his major campaign policy. At the time of writing, his agenda has brought about little substantial change over the years of heavy enforcement in the Obama administration, although promises to stop asylum and to prosecute parents for smuggling their children across the border represent real threats to the undocumented (or those with tenuous legal status in the United States).

Social and economic changes have provoked varied reactions in Europe and the United States, including nationalist and anti-immigration movements. In the Americas, NAFTA and other trade agreements have generated economic growth for some but have increased inequality and displacement for thousands of others who sadly lack social safety nets. Postglobalization inequality, poverty, and violence are driving new migration, forcing millions of people to search for a better life for their families. Because of the ubiquitous spread of and access to the media, including various forms of social media, people are exposed to advertisements and images of a better life in the global north. Through the media and firsthand accounts of community members living elsewhere, people in rural Mexico and Central America are aware of greater opportunities to enhance their family's future, especially in the United States. Families from Mexico and Central America have fled the desperate conditions to start new lives.

In the United States, fears of potential terrorist attacks have led to a sense of ontological insecurity and nativism among a segment of the population who view migrants as a threat to the established order. This, in turn, has mobilized ever-increasing demands for greater border security measures and harsher treatment of migrants. Given the underlying racism, class privilege, and power alignment in the country, the United States is increasingly divided, challenging leaders and the public to search for solutions that can move the country forward with greater social justice. Debates about how to enhance security without undermining human rights and basic individual freedoms surface in the media and Congress. However, restricting migration of noncitizens has become a key characteristic of the contemporary political rhetoric and discourse.

In 2016, debates in the European Union recast definitions of international borders and citizenship, questioning the ways borders are enforced to stem migration and to protect special interests and trade. At the core of Brexit is a strong anti-immigrant reaction. With Australia's prohibition on asylum seekers arriving by boat and the subsequent tragic deaths of Rohingya refugees (Brough et. al 2012) and the EU's tepid, uneven response to Syrian refugees causing thousands to die at sea (Fargues and Bonfanti 2014), it is easy to see this as a worldwide trend. Even for those people and nations still accepting immigrants and refugees, the outrage over thousands of deaths each year, all stemming from an international obsession with keeping people out, has largely been absent. Among those concerned for migrant rights, there is still a general consensus that "securing the border" is an acceptable, commonsense policy when in fact it is this very process that has made migration so deadly around the world.

As chapters in this book document, the militarization of the border, all in the name of "security," has cost thousands of lives while having relatively little impact on the illicit trade of drugs, guns, or money flowing across the border. As we turn our attention to the future, there are many questions facing policy makers and citizens about the meaning of security, how it is achieved, and at what human cost. Does the criminalization of migrants from our neighboring countries for illegal entry or reentry ensure security, or are there other less punitive ways to reduce insecurity and ensure prosperity? Our view is that alternative strategies need to be pursued before the damage is too great to be irrevocable.

The chapters in this book tell the stories of migrants and the dangerous journey north to work and to reunite with their families. The stories are told in multiple ways—quantitatively and qualitatively. Together, the narratives capture the remarkable struggles and sacrifice people endure and the dangerous obstacles they face in an attempt to improve their lives. The volume documents how people learn about the challenges of the dangerous journeys, how they calculate risks, and why they are willing to face dying in the desert or spending years in detention separated from their families. It documents the stripping of people's personal belongings by U.S. authorities—including medications, cell phones, identification, family photos, and clothing—before they are deported back to Mexico, where they face threats of gang violence without government protection. We question the logic and justice of lateral repatriation and the demeaning and dangerous system of nighttime deportation.

Violence in its many forms has been a force driving people to risk migrating to the United States. Wars in Central America and the internal conflicts in

Mexico stemming from drug-trafficking organization activity have extracted a disastrous toll and forced people to flee their homes. Networks trafficking in arms, money, and drugs traverse national borders, enriching some while destroying the lives of many. Chapters 8 and 9 examine organized crime and its impact on citizens as well as migrants. Despite the militarization of the border, kidnappings and violence have increased alongside massive increases in trade and selected prosperity. Border violence, in its many forms, must be reduced. Binational collaboration and cooperation can replace walls and do away with increased punitive immigration policies and enforcement for a more holistic security that will increase the health, happiness, and fulfillment of everyone.

Mexico and the United States share much more than a border and continent: they are coupled economically, historically, and socially. Linked by booming trade in agricultural products, manufactured goods, and increasing research, the futures of Mexico and the United States are deeply intertwined. The borderlands are blessed with a growing population of bilingual and bicultural people who celebrate the cultures of both countries while providing skilled labor. Together, the United States and Mexican governments have addressed complex problems of their shared environmental resources ranging from issues of water rights to preserving biodiversity. They have designed elaborate protocols for trade. The future of both countries increasingly depends on continued economic and political cooperation; this includes the treatment of each other's citizens with dignity, protection, and respect.

The wall along the U.S.-Mexico border casts a long shadow. It reaches beyond the physical space it occupies by rupturing families, killing those searching for what remains of the American Dream, and colonizing the minds of people with little knowledge of the culturally vibrant border region. It is a specter, constantly haunting the dreams and nightmares of terrified individuals throughout the United States. Families that have been split apart by the wall are a reminder of racist policies and the continuous exclusion of people whose blood ties simply are not enough to bring them together. For those who fear change, who hide their notions of racial purity and xenophobia behind loosely formulated ideas of security, it represents the perfect symbol of separation. The wall is both a metaphor and a physical manifestation of the segregation between "us" and "them." It is simple, brutal, radical, and useless. With undocumented migration at a thirty-year low, we ask why walls and barriers continue to grab the attention of millions of Americans. The only possible answer is the durability of xenophobia and racism. While politicians and certain media outlets are blamed for stoking these fears, the racist anxiety surrounding the foreign other has remarkable staying power, causing us to question whether or not this is truly an innate characteristic of our society. How can these issues be addressed when people consistently revert to base paranoia?

For starters, we must demystify migration and call attention to the human costs of these tragedies. Deportees are not simply strangers attempting to come to our land. Rather, they are mothers, fathers, sisters, and brothers of U.S. citizens. They are people who have spent decades living and working in the United States. Their removal creates ripples of violence and trauma that affect millions. We must wholeheartedly reject the narrative that the border is "already secure," because this portrays the current state of affairs as acceptable, when in reality it is a violent and destructive precedent that should worry everyone in the United States. We must push for a reform that allows people whose home is already the United States to be here and participate fully in our democracy. We must create humane immigration policies that will account for future flows of people through increased protections for asylum seekers and simultaneously provide access for people whose main goal is to work. Obviously, each of these policies is not without challenges, and we need rational, informed policy debates about migration that rise above xenophobic fearmongering. We need to refocus on the human costs of enforcement and the consequences for everyone if we continue down the path of fear and racism.

REFERENCES

Brough, Mark, Robert Schweitzer, Jane Shakespeare-Finch, Lyn Vromans, and Julie King. 2012. "Unpacking the Micro-Macro Nexus: Narratives of Suffering and Hope Among Refugees from Burma Recently Settled in Australia." *Journal of Refugee Studies* 26 (2): 207–25.

Fargues, Philippe, and Sara Bonfanti. 2014. "When the Best Option Is a Leaky Boat: Why Migrants Risk Their Lives Crossing the Mediterranean and What Europe Is Doing About It." Policy Brief. Migration Policy Centre. http://cadmus.eui.eu /bitstream/handle/1814/33271/MPC_PB_2014-05.pdf.

APPENDIX
A Note on Migrant Shelters

JEREMY SLACK

WHILE THE MBCS is explicitly *not* a study of shelters in Mexico, we wanted to discuss the important dynamics of these spaces and the possible confusion about who comes to these institutions and how. We deliberately avoided research questions about the practices and procedures of shelters as a way of diffusing the local tensions and anxieties about which shelters should receive the most funding, donations, and recognition. This is always a point of conflict along migrant routes. Local debates rage about who is serving the "real" migrants, often accusing other organizations of catering to homeless people and drug addicts or alcoholics. While none of these categories are mutually exclusive, the contention in and of itself is a slippery one. What, if anything, constitutes a real migrant? Deportation? Intent to cross? How recent must those experiences have been before people become residents of the border? Because of the complexity of these questions as well as the important role shelters play in shaping the politics of migrant treatment along the border, we wanted to devote a short section to these complex spaces. We deliberately will not name any of the eleven shelters we worked in in an effort to maintain anonymity, making these simply general observations and tendencies we have observed during this project.

Shelters tend to be located in poor, often slightly dangerous neighborhoods. This serves a number of purposes. First, it is cheap to buy and own land there. Sometimes local governments or the church have even donated these plots.

However, perhaps most importantly, this fits with the "not in my backyard" approach to migration prevalent in border towns. Migrants are often celebrated in the abstract as "hard-working family members" who are sacrificing to send money back home, but they are generally viewed as a nuisance locally, begging for money, work, clothing, or food. By placing shelters in areas with relatively poor, working-class populations, the political clout of those who would complain and shut down the shelters is limited. Nevertheless, maintaining good relationships with neighbors is paramount, as any such problems can quickly spiral out of control, jeopardizing the existence of a migrant shelter.

For their day-to-day operations, they tend to vary in terms of what services are offered. While there are some shelters whose sole purpose is to give food, we exclusively work in shelters that provide overnight lodging. Shelters that maintained formal relationships with the local or federal government would often receive some form of payment from the government or discounts on electricity and water, food donations, or other local privileges. This often causes tension, as levels of funding vary drastically. Some provide three nights maximum, others a week, but very rarely do individuals stay longer. Most deportees leave the next day, as soon as they have been able to procure passage to their hometowns in Mexico or cross back to the United States. Generally, those that stay the maximum nights have difficulty making their next move. Some have been in the United States so long that they have limited connections in Mexico, or they did not send money back and subsequently were "burned" (*quemado*) in their hometowns, making it difficult or impossible to ask for support. Others are dead set on returning to the United States but lack the money for the crossing.

Some shelters will charge a nominal fee after people have surpassed the allowed number of days, but this is rarely advertised. There are countless informal "shelters" that resemble flop houses and that charge a few bucks a night for people to stay in shoddy rooms or on shared bunk beds. While we do not want to engage in the "real versus fake migrants" debate, it was important for us to clarify that we were interested in interviewing only recent deportees. Anyone with more than thirty days since removal was excluded by our selection criteria. This was simply an effort to make sure that everyone had an experience with the current immigration enforcement apparatus but it leaves us grappling with the question: At what point do people simply become border residents who have a history of migration?

Some shelters provide basic goods (toothbrushes, clothes, soap, razors), but this is rare. Very few have the infrastructure to provide psychological or legal services, and those that have tried have run into problems with the government and with organized crime after reporting human rights abuses. However, members of the Comision Nacional de Derechos Humanos, a government organization interested in human rights, often visit shelters. Whether or not they address these abuses is a difficult question to answer. In our experience they often take photos of the migrants and leave.

The majority of the shelters we worked in have some sort of religious affiliation. This can be unofficial, such as privately run shelters with religious names that hold mass regularly or those run directly by the church. This accompanies some challenging social practices that are often difficult for the casual observer to endorse. Gender norms are strictly followed, separating men and women. Sometimes there are family areas, but in our experience, these are rarely used, as shelter workers tend to simply send the children with the women. For the few transgendered women we have encountered in our research, they have always been placed with the men.

Strict rules on the consumption of alcohol or drugs, sexual relationships, and often the use of cell phones have become the norm. We have witnessed dozens of people thrown out into the street over the course of this research. Despite the sometimes harsh treatment, it is important to note that were such strict rules not observed, it would be a challenge to maintain a functioning, safe environment. There is a very realistic fear that one group of criminal actors would infiltrate and control a shelter. Since so many shelters have been under threat over the past few years and a number of them have had incursions by armed men who take migrants out, maintaining diligence is of the utmost importance. For example, if one criminal group came to control (or even if they were perceived to control) a shelter, it would make them a target for rival groups. Multiple rehabilitation shelters were attacked over the past decade. One attack in Ciudad Juárez in 2009 left seventeen dead. These events weighed heavily on people's minds while operating a shelter. An attack could be triggered by something as simple as one group of coyotes consistently operating out of a shelter. When the power structure changes, tolls could be raised or someone else could decide they want access to the lucrative captive audience of potential migrants, and it could easily become violent. Shelters have frequently had to fire people who have participated in the process of *enganchando*, literally hooking, or recruiting migrants for coyotes.

This vigilance is important, not because coyotes are some great evil but because a separation between the for-profit motives of guides and the humanitarian approach of shelters is essential. However, as most shelter workers are not paid, there is a strong incentive to make a few easy bucks, especially when the coyotes want to find migrants and the migrants are also looking for a trust-worthy guide. As researchers, we were often privy to who is involved with human smuggling in ways the official shelter workers were not. As anonymous research-ers, we made it a point not to report unless we saw dangerous activity take place.

Shelters are a complex research environment, with layers of motives, desires, and agendas. Despite the sometimes harsh treatment or unethical behavior, it is important to note the difficulty of this work, as thousands of people come each year. The constant flood of people, the challenges of maintenance, the stress that comes from threats, all take a toll. As academics accustomed to deliver-ing sophisticated critiques, we must stop and ask ourselves what would the consequences be if these shelters were to close? It would cause intense harm, put people out on the street and in even more danger than they already are. Therefore, we must be careful when attempting to critique these spaces, as our rebukes could have detrimental impacts on the provision of day-to-day services along the border. It was always imperative that we did not interfere with the operations of the shelter. We tried to balance our research needs with the needs of the shelters.

We would attempt to conduct at least one interview before helping to serve dinner if possible. We made sure to keep track of the sleeping, showering, and eating schedules so as not to hamper access to these much-needed services. We would help out in shelters cooking, cleaning, serving food, and doing intake interviews as a way to give back. We would generally give donations to the shelters because we found that incentivizing the interviewees created prob-lems, as we were able to interview only a small number of people each time. However, we did give out phone cards at some sites so that people could call home. Through our long-term engagement in shelters we were able to establish a level of comfort in these spaces that, even though many of the people arrived and disappeared within a day, increased people's confidence that we were well established and had benign intentions for our interviews. I have no doubt that this contributes to our high response rate.

Some scholars have criticized research in shelters as pressuring people to tell "the most fucked up stories."[1] Certainly, the concentration of people having recently experienced the dangers of the desert, mistreatment by authorities, and the depression of being deported to Mexico makes for a large amount of one-upmanship, war stories, and competition of who has heard of the worst instances of violence. This is particularly exacerbated in any group interview session, making us wary of the potential for any focus-group research. However, we dealt with this by never including anything that was not a firsthand account or anything that occurred before their most recent crossing attempt. By isolating our inquiry to the most recent crossing attempt, we made each migration history comparable. Some migrants have crossed dozens of times, while others we interviewed may have crossed only once. Therefore, often, the most sensational stories do not enter into our research.

Moreover, none of this research relies on stories that were told secondhand, and we did not rely on the stories of shelter workers and owners. Because of their years of experience working with migrants, shelter workers have a highly developed perspective, albeit one that often has an agenda—namely, generating interest and concern for their life's work.

Moreover, by adhering to a strict protocol that will dictate whether to record a story or not and random selection rather than asking for volunteers, it greatly reduces the possibility of a stilted view of migration. Further, this attitude of the "inauthenticity" of shelters negates the very real stories, experiences, and traumas that occur. We frequently found individuals who had never talked about their stories and those who said they will never tell their family about what they went through. Grown men would frequently break down crying during interviews. The trauma and despair present among deportees is not an inflated or invented phenomenon. We were able to conduct one-on-one interviews in the shelters, allowing for a greater level of intimacy, which we feel ultimately improved the quality of the research.

The systematic approach also generated a level of respect. By the time we were finished surveying, people knew the time and the level of care needed to go chronologically through every type of abuse, problem, or situation that could arise during their journeys. While survey research can come across as stilted and boring for interviewees, it does communicate the true purpose of research quite clearly. We would encourage more researchers to engage with these shelters, keeping in mind that shelters are often inundated by journalists and researchers who parachute in and do not share the results of their work. These are important, complex spaces where migratory experiences are concentrated.

NOTE

1.   J. De León, *The Land of Open Graves: Living and Dying on the Migrant Trail* (Berkeley: University of California Press, 2015), 314.

CONTRIBUTORS

Jeremy Slack is an assistant professor of geography in the Department of Sociology and Anthropology at the University of Texas, El Paso. He received his PhD in geography from the University of Arizona in 2015. Slack is a coprincipal investigator of the Migrant Border Crossing Study. His research focuses on deportation and the problems forced removal creates for individuals and their families, the connections to place that are severed, and how it has intersected with drug-related violence on the border. His research interests include state theory, illegal and illicit activity, the U.S.-Mexico border, drug trafficking, violence, participatory/activist-oriented research methodology, and public scholarship.

Daniel E. Martínez is an assistant professor of sociology at the University of Arizona. He received his PhD in sociology from the University of Arizona in 2013. Martínez is a coprincipal investigator of the Migrant Border Crossing Study, which is a binational research project focusing on unauthorized migrants' border crossing, apprehension, and repatriation experiences. His research and teaching interests include criminology, juvenile delinquency, race and ethnicity, and unauthorized immigration. Martínez also does extensive research on migrant deaths along the U.S.-Mexico border.

Scott Whiteford is the director of the Mexican Initiative for SBS and emeritus professor of the Center for Latin American Studies at the University of

Arizona. He served as the director of Latin American studies and professor of anthropology at Michigan State University and director of the Center for Latin American Studies at the University of Arizona. His research interests include international migration, violence, power, human rights, research methods, and political ecology of water. He has carried out research in eight Latin American countries and the United States. While at Michigan State University, he was awarded prestigious teaching and research awards. He has won collaborative grants from the National Science Foundation, the National Endowment for the Humanities, the U.S. Department of Education, the William and Flora Hewlett Foundation, the Ford Foundation, CEPAL, and the Fulbright Commission. In collaboration with colleagues, he has written and edited fourteen books, published in Spanish and English, based on long-term research.

Howard Campbell is a professor of cultural anthropology and chairman of the Department of Sociology and Anthropology at the University of Texas at El Paso. He is the author or editor of six academic volumes, including *Drug War Zone: Frontline Dispatches from the Streets of El Paso and Juárez*.

Josiah Heyman (PhD, CUNY 1988) is professor of anthropology, endowed professor of border trade issues, and director of the University of Texas at El Paso's Center for Inter-American and Border Studies. He is the author or editor of four books and over 120 scholarly articles, chapters, and essays. A central theme in that work is U.S.-border policies, officers, power contexts, and human rights. His latest coedited book is *The U.S.-Mexico Transborder Region: Cultural Dynamics and Historical Interactions* (University of Arizona Press, 2017).

Alison Elizabeth Lee is an associate professor of anthropology at the Universidad de las Américas Puebla in Puebla, Mexico. Her recent research focuses on the political economic context of return migration to Mexico, the gendered process of economic and social reinsertion during and after the Great Recession, and the quotidian experiences of "illegality" for Mexicans on both sides of the border.

Ricardo Martínez-Schuldt is a doctoral candidate in the department of sociology at the University of North Carolina, Chapel Hill. His research focuses on how sending states, through consulate offices, facilitate the integration of migrants as well as how local contexts affect the needs of immigrant populations and enable or constrain consular efficacy. In addition, he conducts research on neighborhood and city-level correlates of crime with an emphasis on the immigration-crime nexus.

Emily Peiffer is an attorney who completed a JD/MA dual-degree program in law and Latin American studies at the University of Arizona in 2013. Born and raised in Canada, she worked on the Migrant Border Crossing Study with a U.S. student visa and required plenty of paperwork to cross the border frequently for the project. She resolved her own immigration status and is now the managing attorney of the largest plaintiffs' personal injury firm in Tucson.

Prescott L. Vandervoet works in the fresh produce import and marketing industry in Nogales, Arizona. He is the chairman-elect of the Fresh Produce Association of the Americas, an industry advocacy organization for cross border trade of fresh fruits and vegetables. Before that he was involved in a variety of research projects related to immigration issues as well as natural resource uses along the Arizona-Mexico border region. His interests in these issues continue, and he is the past board president of Friends of the Santa Cruz River, a southern Arizona nonprofit focused on environmental and community health along the binational Santa Cruz River.

Matthew Ward is an assistant professor in the Department of Anthropology and Sociology at the University of Southern Mississippi. He received his PhD in sociology from the University of Arizona in 2013. His research interests include social movements, immigration/border issues, contemporary racial/ethnic disparities, and the legacies of racial/ethnic violence and minority social control in the United States. His recent projects have focused on the foundations of social conflict and social movement mobilization surrounding Latino immigration to the United States.

INDEX